Rick Steves' ®
SNAPSHOT

Scotland

CONTENTS

INTRODUCTION

This Snapshot guide, excerpted from the latest edition of my guide-book *Rick Steves' Great Britain*, introduces you to rugged, feisty, colorful Scotland. The home of kilts, bagpipes, whisky, golf, lochs, and shortbread lives up to its clichéd image—but there's so much more. This book includes a mix of big cities, small towns, and the countryside. Explore the Scottish capital of Edinburgh—with its attractions-studded Royal Mile and stirring hilltop castle—and grittier but quickly gentrifying Glasgow. Golfers and students make a pilgrimage to St. Andrews, with its world-famous links, sandy beaches, and colorful university life. To commune with the traditional Scottish soul, head for the desolate Highlands, with the evocative "Weeping Glen" of Glencoe, handy home-base city of Inverness, historic site of "Bonnie" Prince Charlie's disastrous Battle of Culloden, and mysterious Loch Ness. And hardy souls can set sail for some of Scotland's rugged islands: Iona and Mull (from Oban), or the super-scenic Isle of Skye.

To help you have the best trip possible, I've included the following topics in this book:

• **Planning Your Time,** with advice on how to make the most of your limited time

• **Orientation,** including tourist information (abbreviated as TI), tips on public transportation, local tour options, and helpful hints

• **Sights** with ratings:

▲▲▲—Don't miss

▲▲—Try hard to see

▲—Worthwhile if you can make it

No rating—Worth knowing about

• **Sleeping** and **Eating,** with good-value recommendations in every price range

- **Connections,** with tips on trains, buses, and driving

Practicalities, near the end of this book, has information on money, phoning, hotel reservations, transportation, and more.

To travel smartly, read this little book in its entirety before you go. It's my hope that this guide will make your trip more meaningful and rewarding. Traveling like a temporary local, you'll get the absolute most out of every mile, minute, and pound.

Happy travels!

Rick Steves

SCOTLAND

SCOTLAND

The country of Scotland makes up about a third of Britain's geographical area (30,400 square miles), but has less than a tenth of its population (just over five million). This sparsely populated chunk of land stretches to Norwegian latitudes. Its Shetland Islands, at about 60°N (similar to Anchorage, Alaska), are the northernmost point in Britain.

The southern part of Scotland, called the Lowlands, is relatively flat and urbanized. The northern area—the Highlands—

features a wild, severely undulating terrain, punctuated by lochs (lakes) and fringed by sea lochs (inlets) and islands. The Highland Boundary Fault that divides Scotland geologically also divides it culturally. Historically, there was a big difference between grizzled, kilt-wearing Highlanders in the northern wilderness, and the more refined Lowlanders in the southern flatlands and cities. The Highlanders spoke and acted like "true Scots," while the Lowlanders often seemed more "British" than Scottish.

Although this division has faded over time, some Scots still cling to it today—city slickers down south think that Highlanders are crude and unrefined, and those who live at higher latitudes grumble about the soft, pampered urbanites in the Lowlands.

The Lowlands are dominated by a pair of rival cities: Edinburgh, the old royal capital, teems with Scottish history and is the country's best tourist attraction. Glasgow, once a gloomy industrial city, is becoming a hip, laid-back city of today, known for its modern architecture. The medieval university town and golf mecca of St. Andrews, the whisky village of Pitlochry, and the historic city of Stirling round out the Lowlands' top sights.

The Highlands provide your best look at traditional Scotland. The sights are subtle, but the warm culture and friendly people are engaging. There are a lot of miles, but they're scenic, the roads are

Scotland

••• FERRY ROUTES (NOT ALL SHOWN)

ATLANTIC OCEAN

ORKNEY
STROMNESS
KIRKWALL

50 MILES
30 KM

THURSO
JOHN O'GROATS

LEWIS
ULLAPOOL

NORTH UIST
KYLE OF LOCHALSH
MORAY FIRTH
CULLODEN
INVERNESS

SOUTH UIST
PORTREE
SKYE
HIGHLANDS
CALEDONIAN CANAL
LOCH NESS
ABERDEEN

RUM
BEN NEVIS
NORTH SEA

MALLAIG
FT. WILLIAM
PITLOCHRY

COLL
GLENCOE
DUNDEE

TIREE
PERTH

MULL
OBAN
LOCH LOMOND
ST. ANDREWS
EAST NEUK

IONA
STIRLING
FIRTH OF FORTH

JURA
BANNOCKBURN

ISLAY
GLASGOW
EDINBURGH

CAMPBELTOWN
TROON
BERWICK-UPON-TWEED

ARRAN
AYR
LOWLANDS

NORTHERN IRELAND
CAIRNRYAN
STRANRAER
ENGLAND
CARLISLE

LARNE
HADRIAN'S WALL
NEW-CASTLE

BELFAST

DCH
TO DUBLIN
IRISH SEA
TO LAKE DISTRICT
TO YORK & LONDON

good, and the traffic is light. Generally, the Highlands are hungry
for the tourist dollar, and everything overtly Scottish is exploited to
the kilt. You'll need more than a quick visit to get away from that.
But if two days is all you have, you can get a feel for the area with
a quick drive to Oban, through Glencoe, then up the Caledonian
Canal to Inverness. With more time, the islands of Iona and Mull
(an easy day trip from Oban), the Isle of Skye, and countless brooding countryside castles will flesh out your Highlands experience.

The Highlands are more rocky and harsh than other parts
of the British Isles. It's no wonder that most of the scenes around
Hogwarts in the Harry Potter movies were filmed in this moody,
sometimes spooky landscape. Though Scotland's "hills" are

technically too short to be called "mountains," they do a convincing imitation. Scotland has 284 hills over 3,000 feet. A list of these was compiled in 1891 by Sir Hugh Munro, and to this day the Scots still call their high hills "Munros." According to the Scottish Mountaineering Club,

more than 4,300 intrepid hikers can brag that they've climbed all of the Munros.

In this northern climate, cold and drizzly weather isn't uncommon—even in midsummer. The blazing sun can quickly be covered over by black clouds and howling wind. Scots warn visitors to prepare for "four seasons in one day." Because the Scots feel personally responsible for bad weather, they tend to be overly optimistic about forecasts. Take any Scottish promise of "sun by the afternoon" with a grain of salt—and bring your raincoat.

In the summer, the Highlands swarm with tourists...and midges. These tiny biting insects—like "no-see-ums" in some parts of North America—are bloodthirsty and determined. Depending on the weather, they can be an annoyance from late May through September. Hot sun or a stiff breeze blows the tiny buggers away, but they thrive in damp, shady areas. Locals suggest blowing or brushing them off, rather than swatting them—since killing them only seems to attract more (likely because of the smell of fresh blood). Scots say, "If you kill one midge, a million will come to his funeral." Even if you don't usually travel with bug spray, consider bringing or buying some for a summer visit—or your most vivid

memory of your Scottish vacation might be itchy arms and legs.

Keep an eye out for another Scottish animal: shaggy Highland cattle, with their hair falling in their eyes. Dubbed "hairy coos," these adorable beasts will melt your heart. With a heavy coat to keep them insulated, hairy coos graze on sparse vegetation that other animals ignore. And of course, there are a lot of sheep around.

The major theme of Scottish history is the drive for independence, especially from England. (Scotland's rabble-rousing national motto is *Nemo me impune lacessit*—"No one provokes me with impunity.") Like Wales, Scotland is a country of ragtag Celts sharing an island with wealthy and powerful Anglo-Saxons. Scotland's Celtic culture is a result of its remoteness—the invading Romans were never able to conquer this rough-and-tumble people, and even built Hadrian's Wall to lock off this distant corner of their empire. The Anglo-Saxons, and their descendants the English, fared little better than the Romans did. Even King Edward I—who so successfully dominated Wales—was unable to hold on to Scotland for long, largely thanks to the relentlessly rebellious William Wallace (a.k.a. "Braveheart").

Failing to conquer Scotland by the blade, England eventually absorbed it politically. In 1603, England's Queen Elizabeth I died without an heir, so Scotland's King James VI took the throne, becoming King James I of England. It took another century or so of battles, both military and diplomatic, but the Act of Union in 1707 definitively (and controversially) unified the Kingdom of Great Britain. In 1745, Bonnie Prince Charlie attempted to reclaim the Scottish throne on behalf of the deposed Stuarts, but his army was slaughtered at the Battle of Culloden (described in the Inverness and the Northern Highlands chapter). This cemented English rule over Scotland, and is seen by many Scots as the last gasp of the traditional Highlands clan system.

Scotland has been joined—however unwillingly—to England ever since, and the Scots have often felt oppressed by their English countrymen. During the Highland Clearances in the 18th and 19th centuries, landowners (mostly English) decided that vast tracks of land were more profitable as grazing land for sheep, than as farmland for people. Many Highlanders were forced to abandon their traditional homes and lifestyles and seek employment elsewhere. Large numbers ended up in North America, especially parts of eastern Canada, such as Prince Edward Island and Nova Scotia (literally, "New Scotland").

Today, Americans and Canadians of Scottish descent enjoy coming "home" to Scotland. If you're Scottish, your surname will tell you which clan your ancestors likely belonged to. The prefix "Mac" (or "Mc") means "son of"—so "MacDonald" means the same thing as "Donaldson." Tourist shops everywhere are happy

to help you track down your clan's tartan, or distinctive plaid pattern—many clans have several.

Is Scotland really a country? It's not a sovereign state, but it is a "nation" in that it has its own traditions, ethnic identity, languages (Gaelic and Scots, described below), and football league. To some

Scottish Words

Scotch may be the peaty drink the bartender serves you, but the nationality of the bartender is **Scots** or **Scottish.** Here are some other Scottish words that may come in handy during your time here:

aye	yes
auld	old
ben	mountain
blether	talk
bonnie	beautiful
brae	slope, hill
burn	creek or stream
cairn	pile of stones
close	an alley leading to a courtyard or square
craig	rock, cliff
firth	estuary
innis	island
inver	mouth of a river
ken	to know
kirk	church
kyle	strait
loch	lake
nae	no (as in "nae bother"—you're welcome)
neeps	turnips
ree	king, royal ("righ" in Gaelic)
tattie	potato
wee	small
wynd	tight, winding lane connecting major streets

A sharp intake of breath (like a little gasp), sometimes while saying "aye," means "yes."

extent, it even has its own government: Over the past several years, Scotland has enjoyed its greatest measure of political autonomy in centuries—a trend called "devolution." In 1998, the Scottish parliament opened its doors in Edinburgh for the first time in almost 300 years. Though the Scottish parliament's powers are limited (most major decisions are still made in London), the Scots are enjoying the refreshing breeze of increased independence. Today, some politicians are poised to ask the EU to recognize Scotland as a separate country.

Scotland even has its own currency. While Scots use the same coins as England, Scotland also prints its own bills (with Scottish rather than English people and landmarks). Just to confuse tourists, three different banks print Scottish pound notes, each with a different design. In the Lowlands (around Edinburgh and Glasgow), you'll receive both Scottish and English pounds from ATMs and in change. But in the Highlands, you'll almost never see English pounds. Though most merchants in England accept Scottish pound notes, a few might balk—especially at the rare one-pound note, which their cash registers don't have a slot for. (They are, however, legally required to accept your Scottish currency.)

The Scottish flag—a diagonal, X-shaped white cross on a blue field—represents the cross of Scotland's patron saint, the Apostle Andrew (who was crucified on an X-shaped cross). You may not realize it, but you see the Scottish flag every time you look at the Union Jack: England's flag (the red St. George's cross on a white field) superimposed on Scotland's (a blue field with a white diagonal cross). The diagonal red cross (St. Patrick's cross) over Scotland's white one represents Northern Ireland. (Wales gets no love on the Union Jack.)

Scots are known for their inimitable burr, but they are also proud of their old Celtic language, Scottish Gaelic (pronounced "gallic"; Ireland's closely related Celtic language is spelled the same but pronounced "gaylic"). Gaelic thrives only in the remotest corners of Scotland. In major towns and cities, virtually nobody speaks Gaelic every day, but the language is kept on life-support by a Scottish population keen to remember their heritage. New Gaelic schools are opening all the time, and Scotland recently passed a law to replace road signs with new ones listing both English and Gaelic spellings (e.g., Edinburgh/Dùn Èideann).

Scotland has another language of its own, called Scots (a.k.a. "Lowland Scots," to distinguish it from Gaelic). Aye, you're likely already a wee bit familiar with a few Scots words, ye lads and lassies. As you travel, you're sure to pick up a bit more (see sidebar) and enjoy the lovely musical lilt as well. Many linguists argue that Scots is technically an ancient dialect of English, rather than a distinct language. These linguists have clearly never heard a Scot read aloud the poetry of Robert Burns, who wrote in unfiltered (and often unintelligible) Scots. (Opening line of "To a Louse": *Ha! Whaur ye gaun, ye crowlin ferlie?*) Fortunately, you're unlikely to meet anyone quite that hard to understand; most Scots speak Scottish-accented standard English, peppered with their favorite Scots phrases. If you have a hard time understanding someone, ask them to translate—you may take home some new words as souvenirs.

Scottish cuisine is down-to-earth, often with an emphasis on local produce. Both seafood and "land food" (beef and chicken) are common. One Scottish mainstay—eaten more by tourists than by Scots these days—is the famous haggis, a rich assortment of oats and sheep organs stuffed into a chunk of sheep intestine, liberally seasoned and boiled. Usually served with "neeps and tatties" (turnips and potatoes), it's tastier than it sounds and worth trying... once.

The "Scottish Breakfast" is similar to the English version, but they add a potato scone (like a flavorless, soggy potato pancake) and occasionally haggis (which is hard enough to get down at dinnertime).

Breakfast, lunch, or dinner, the Scots love their whisky—and touring one of the country's many distilleries is a sightseeing treat. The Scots are fiercely competitive with the Irish when it comes to this peaty spirit. Scottish "whisky" is distilled twice, whereas Irish "whiskey" adds a third distillation (and an extra *e*). Grain here is roasted over peat fires, giving it a smokier flavor than its Irish cousin. Also note that what we call "scotch"—short for "scotch whisky"—is just "whisky" here. I've listed several of the most convenient and interesting distilleries to visit, but if you're a whisky connoisseur, make a point of tracking down and touring your favorite.

Another unique Scottish flavor to sample is the soft drink called Irn-Bru (pronounced "Iron Brew"). This bright-orange beverage tastes not like orange soda, but like bubblegum with a slightly bitter aftertaste. (The diet version is even more bitter.) While Irn-Bru's appeal eludes non-Scots, it's hugely popular here, even outselling Coke. Be cautious sipping it—as the label understates, "If spilt, this product may stain."

Whether toasting with beer, whisky, or Irn-Bru, enjoy meeting the Scottish people. Many travelers fall in love with the irrepressible spirit and beautiful landscape of this faraway corner of Britain.

EDINBURGH

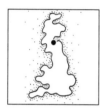

Edinburgh is the historical and cultural capital of Scotland. Once a medieval powerhouse sitting on a lava flow, it grew into Europe's first great grid-planned modern city. The colorful hometown of Robert Louis Stevenson, Sir Walter Scott, and Robert Burns, Edinburgh is Scotland's showpiece and one of Europe's most entertaining cities. Historic, monumental, fun, and well-organized, it's a tourist's delight—especially in August, when the Edinburgh Festival takes over the town.

Promenade down the Royal Mile through Old Town. Historic buildings pack the Royal Mile between the grand castle (on the top) and the Palace of Holyroodhouse (on the bottom). Medieval skyscrapers stand shoulder to shoulder, hiding peaceful courtyards connected to High Street by narrow lanes or even tunnels. This colorful jumble is the tourist's Edinburgh.

Edinburgh (ED'n-burah) was once the most crowded city in Europe—famed for its skyscrapers and filth. The rich and poor lived atop one another. In the Age of Enlightenment, a magnificent Georgian city (today's New Town) was laid out to the north, giving Edinburgh's upper class a respectable place to promenade. Georgian Edinburgh—like the city of Bath—shines with broad boulevards, straight streets, square squares, circular circuses, and elegant mansions decked out in colonnades, pediments, and sphinxes in the proud Neoclassical style of 200 years ago.

While the Georgian city celebrated the union of Scotland and England (with streets and squares named after English kings and emblems), "devolution" is the latest trend. For the past several centuries, Scotland was ruled from London, and Parliament had not met in Edinburgh since 1707. But in a 1998 election, the Scots

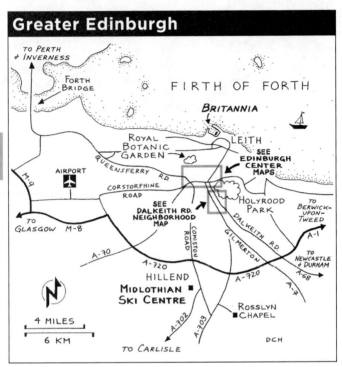

Greater Edinburgh

voted to gain more autonomy and bring their Parliament home. In 1999, Edinburgh resumed its position as home to the Scottish parliament (although London still calls the strategic shots). A strikingly modern Parliament building, which opened in 2004, is one more jewel in Edinburgh's crown. Today, you'll notice many references to the "nation" of Scotland.

Planning Your Time

While the major sights can be seen in a day, on a three-week tour of Britain, I'd give Edinburgh two days and three nights.

Day 1: Tour the castle (open from 9:30). Then consider catching one of the city bus tours for a one-hour loop (departing from a block below the castle at The Hub/Tolbooth Church; you could munch a sandwich from the top deck if you're into multitasking). Back at the castle, catch the 14:15 Mercat Tours walk (1.5 hours, leaves from Mercat Cross on the Royal Mile). Spend the remainder of your day enjoying the Royal Mile's shops and museums, or touring the Palace of Holyroodhouse (at the bottom of the Mile).

Day 2: Visit the Museum of Scotland. After lunch, stroll through the Princes Street Gardens and the National Gallery of Scotland. Then tour the good ship *Britannia*.

Evenings: Options include various "haunted Edinburgh" walks, literary pub crawls, or live music in pubs. Sadly, traditional folk shows are just about extinct, surviving only in excruciatingly schmaltzy variety shows put on for tour-bus groups. Perhaps the most authentic evening out is just settling down in a pub to sample the whisky and local beers while meeting the natives...and attempting to understand them through their thick Scottish accents.

Orientation to Edinburgh

(area code: 0131)

The center of Edinburgh, a drained lake bed, holds the Princes Street Gardens park and Waverley Bridge, where you'll find the TI, Princes Mall, the train station, the bus info office (starting point for most city bus tours), the National Gallery, and a covered dance-and-music pavilion. Weather blows in and out—bring your sweater and be prepared for rain. Locals say the bad weather is one of the disadvantages of living so close to England.

You might notice the city is pretty dug up. It's all in preparation for the city's new tram system, which is scheduled to begin running in 2012.

Tourist Information

The crowded TI is as central as can be atop the Princes Mall and train station (Mon–Sat 9:00–17:00, Sun 10:00–17:00, July–Aug daily until 19:00, tel. 0845-225-5121, www.edinburgh.org). The staff is knowledgeable and eager to help, but much of their information—including their assessment of museums and even which car-rental companies "exist"—is skewed by tourism payola. The TI at the airport is more helpful.

At either TI, pick up a free map or buy the excellent £4.50 *Collins Discovering Edinburgh* map (which comes with opinionated commentary and locates almost every major shop and sight). If you're interested in late-night music, ask for the free monthly entertainment *Gig Guide.* (The best monthly entertainment listing, *The List,* sells for a few pounds at newsstands.) The free *Essential Guide to Edinburgh,* while not truly essential, lists additional sights and services (when it's in stock). The TIs also sell the mediocre Edinburgh Pass, which provides unlimited travel on Lothian buses (includes the airport) and entry to dozens of B-list sights (£26.50/1 day, £39/2 days, £51.50/3 days, doesn't include Edinburgh Castle, www.edinburgh.org/pass).

Book your room direct, using my listings (the TIs charge you a £4 booking fee, and also take a 10 percent cut, which means that B&Bs end up charging more for rooms booked this way).

Browse the racks—tucked away in the hallway at the back of

the central TI—for brochures on the various Scottish folk shows, walking tours, regional bus tours, and other touristic temptations. Computers with Internet access are beyond the brochure racks (£1/30 minutes).

Arrival in Edinburgh

By Train: Arriving by train at Waverley Station puts you in the city center and below the TI. Taxis queue almost trackside; the ramp they come and go on leads to Waverley Bridge. If there's a long line for taxis, I hike up the ramp and hail one on the street. From the station, *Way Out-1-Princes Street* signs lead up to the TI and the city bus stop (for bus directions from here to my recommended B&Bs, see below). For picnic supplies, a **Marks & Spencer Simply Food** is near platform 2.

By Bus: Both Scottish Citylink and National Express buses use the bus station (with luggage lockers) in the New Town, two blocks north of the train station on St. Andrew Square.

By Plane: Edinburgh's slingshot of an airport is located 10 miles northwest of the center. Airport flight info: tel. 0870-040-0007, www.edinburghairport.com.

Taxis between the airport and the city center are pricey (£20–25, 20 minutes to downtown or to Dalkeith Road B&Bs). Fortunately, the airport is well-connected to central Edinburgh by the convenient, frequent, cheap Lothian **Airlink bus #100** (£3.50, £6 round-trip, 6/hour, 30 minutes, buses run all day and 2/hour through the night, tel. 0131/555-6363, www.flybybus.com). The bus drops you at the center of Waverley Bridge. From here, to reach my recommended B&Bs near Dalkeith Road, you can either take a taxi (about £7), or hop on a bus (during tram construction, you may have to walk over to North Bridge, on the other side of the train station, to catch the bus). Ride bus #14, #30, #33, or #48, and get off at the first or second stop after the bus makes a right turn onto Dalkeith Road (£1.20, have coins ready—drivers don't make change, buses leave frequently, confirm specific directions with your B&B).

If you're headed *to* the airport, you can take the same Airlink bus described above. To reach the Airlink bus stop from the Dalkeith Road B&Bs, ride the bus to the end of North Bridge and hop out just after the bus turns left at the grand Balmoral Hotel; exit the bus to your right and walk a short distance down Princes Street to the next bridge, Waverley, where you'll find the Airlink bus stop. (Rather than taking a £25 taxi all the way to the airport, you can save money by taking a £7 taxi to this stop, then hopping the bus to the airport.)

By Car: If you're arriving from the north, rather than drive through downtown Edinburgh to the recommended B&Bs, circle the city on the A720 City Bypass road. Approaching Edinburgh on M9, take M8 (direction: Glasgow) and quickly get onto A720 City Bypass (direction: Edinburgh South). After four miles, you'll hit a roundabout. Ignore signs directing you into *Edinburgh North* and stay on A720 for 10 more miles to the next and last round-about, named *Sheriffhall*. Exit the roundabout on the first left (A7 Edinburgh). From here it's four miles to the B&B neighborhood. After a while, A7 becomes Dalkeith Road. If you see a huge build-ing with a swimming pool (or a pool-shaped construction zone, if you're here before its renovation is complete), you've gone a couple of blocks too far.

If you're driving in on A68 from the south, take the A7 Edinburgh exit off the roundabout and follow the directions above.

Helpful Hints

Sunday Activities: Many Royal Mile sights close on Sunday (except during August and the Edinburgh Festival), but other major sights are open. Sunday is a good day to catch a guided walking tour along the Royal Mile or a city bus tour (buses go faster in light traffic). Arthur's Seat is lively on weekends.

Festivals: August is a crowded, popular month to visit Edinburgh because of the multiple festivals hosted here, including the official Edinburgh Festival (Aug 12–Sept 4 in 2011). Book ahead if you'll be visiting during this month, and expect to pay significantly more for your accommodations.

Internet Access: Get online at the central TI (£1/30 minutes, see "Tourist Information," earlier); the recommended and atmospheric **Elephant House Café** (Mon–Fri 8:00–23:00, 4 stations, 24 George IV Bridge, off top of Royal Mile); or **E-Corner Internet Café and Call Shop,** a funky little place just off the Royal Mile, next to the Smart City Hostel (£1/30 minutes, Mon–Fri 9:00–21:30, Sat–Sun 10:00–21:30, in win-ter daily 10:00–21:00, packed with fast terminals and digital services, 54 Blackfriars Street, tel. 0131/558-7858).

Baggage Storage: At the train station, you'll find pricey, high-security luggage storage near platform 2 (£6/24 hours, daily 7:00–23:00). It's cheaper to use the lockers at the bus station on St. Andrew Square, just a five-minute walk from the train sta-tion (£3–5 depending on size—even smallest locker is plenty big, coins only, station open daily 6:00–24:00).

Laundry: Ace Cleaning Centre launderette is located near the recommended B&Bs (Mon–Fri 8:00–20:00, Sat 9:00–17:00, Sun 10:00–16:00, self-service or drop-off; along the bus route to the city center at 13 South Clerk Street, opposite Queens

Edinburgh at a Glance

▲▲▲**Edinburgh Castle** Iconic 11th-century hilltop fort and royal residence complete with crown jewels, Romanesque chapel, memorial, and fine military museum. **Hours:** Daily April–Oct 9:30–18:00, Nov–March 9:30–17:00. See page 21.

▲▲▲**Royal Mile** Historic road—good for walking—stretching from the castle down to the palace, lined with museums, pubs, and shops. **Hours:** Always open, but best during business hours, with walking tours daily. See page 28.

▲▲▲**National Museum of Scotland** Intriguing, well-displayed artifacts from prehistoric times to the 20th century. **Hours:** Daily 10:00–17:00. See page 41.

▲▲**Gladstone's Land** Sixteenth-century Royal Mile merchant's residence. **Hours:** Daily July–Aug 10:00–18:30, April–June and Sept–Oct 10:00–17:00, closed Nov–March. See page 31.

▲▲**St. Giles' Cathedral** Preaching grounds of Calvinist John Knox, with spectacular organ, Neo-Gothic chapel, and distinctive crown spire. **Hours:** May–Sept Mon–Fri 9:00–19:00, Sat 9:00–17:00, Sun 13:00–17:00; Oct–April Mon–Sat 9:00–17:00, Sun 13:00–17:00. See page 33.

▲▲**Scottish Parliament Building** New headquarters for the recently returned Parliament. **Hours:** Mon–Fri 10:00–17:30, until 16:30 Oct–March, Sat 11:00–17:30 year-round, closed Sun. See page 39.

▲▲**Georgian New Town** Elegant 1776 subdivision spiced with trendy shops, bars, and eateries. **Hours:** Always open. See page 44.

▲▲**Georgian House** Intimate peek at upper-crust life in the late 1700s. **Hours:** Daily July–Aug 10:00–18:30, April–June and Sept–Oct 10:00–17:00, March 11:00–16:00, Nov 11:00–15:00, closed Dec–Feb. See page 45.

▲▲**National Gallery of Scotland** Choice sampling of European masters and Scotland's finest. **Hours:** Daily 10:00–17:00, Thu until 19:00. See page 45.

▲▲*Britannia* The royal yacht with a history of distinguished passengers, a 15-minute trip out of town. **Hours:** Daily July–Sept

9:30–16:30, April–June and Oct 10:00–16:00, Nov–March 10:00–15:30 (these are last entry times). See page 48.

▲**Writers' Museum at Lady Stair's House** Tribute to Scottish literary triumvirate: Robert Burns, Sir Walter Scott, and Robert Louis Stevenson. **Hours:** Mon–Sat 10:00–17:00, closed Sun except during Festival 12:00–17:00. See page 32.

▲**Mary King's Close** Underground street and houses last occupied in the 17th century, viewable by guided tour. **Hours:** April–Oct daily 10:00–21:00; Nov–March Sun–Thu 10:00–17:00, Fri–Sat 10:00–21:00. See page 37.

▲**Museum of Childhood** Five stories of historic fun. **Hours:** Mon–Sat 10:00–17:00, Sun 12:00–17:00. See page 38.

▲**John Knox House** Reputed 16th-century digs of the great reformer. **Hours:** Mon–Sat 10:00–18:00, closed Sun except in July–Aug 12:00–18:00. See page 38.

▲**Cadenhead's Whisky Shop** Sample whisky straight from the distilleries. **Hours:** Mon–Sat 10:30–17:30, closed Sun except possibly in Aug 12:30–17:30. See page 38.

▲**People's Story** Proletarian life from the 18th to 20th centuries. **Hours:** Mon–Sat 10:00–17:00, closed Sun except during Festival 12:00–17:00. See page 39.

▲**Museum of Edinburgh** Historic mementos, from the original National Covenant inscribed on animal skin to early golf balls. **Hours:** Mon–Sat 10:00–17:00, closed Sun except during Festival 12:00–17:00. See page 39.

▲**Palace of Holyroodhouse** The Queen's splendid home away from home, with lavish rooms, 12th-century abbey, and gallery with rotating exhibits. **Hours:** Daily April–Oct 9:30–18:00, Nov–March 9:30–16:30, closed during royal visits. See page 40.

▲**Sir Walter Scott Monument** Climbable tribute to the famed novelist. **Hours:** April–Sept daily 10:00–19:00; Oct–March Mon–Sat 9:00–16:00, Sun 10:00–16:00. See page 46.

Hall; tel. 0131/667-0549). For a small extra fee, they collect and drop off laundry at the neighborhood B&Bs.

Bike Rental: The laid-back crew at **Cycle Scotland** offers bike tours and happily recommends good bike routes (£15/3 hours, £20/day, £25/24 hours, daily 10:00–18:00, just off Royal Mile at 29 Blackfriars Street, tel. 0131/556-5560, www.cycle scotland.co.uk).

Car Rental: All of these places have offices both in the town center and at the airport: **Avis** (5 West Park Place, tel. 0844-544-6059, airport tel. 0844-544-6004), **Europcar** (24 East London Street, tel. 0131/557-3456, airport tel. 0131/333-2588), **Hertz** (10 Picardy Place, tel. 0870-846-0013, airport tel. 0870-846-0009), and **Budget** (will meet you at train station and take you to their office at 1 Murrayburn Road, tel. 0131/455-7314, airport tel. 0844-544-4605). Some downtown offices are closed on Sunday, but the airport locations tend to be open daily—call ahead to confirm. If you're going to rent a car, pick it up on your way out of Edinburgh—you won't need it in town.

Blue Badge Local Guides: The following guides charge similar prices and offer half-day and full-day tours. **Ken Hanley** wears his kilt as if pants didn't exist, knows all the stories, and loves sharing his passion for Edinburgh and Scotland (£90/half-day, £120/day, extra charge if he uses his car—which fits up to 6, tel. 0131/666-1944, mobile 0771-034-2044, www.small -world-tours.co.uk, k.hanley@blueyonder.co.uk). Other good guides include **Jean Blair** (£130/day, £310/day with car, tel. 0150/682-5930, mobile 0798-957-0287, www.travelthrough scotland.com, jean@travelthroughscotland.com), **Sergio La Spina** (an Argentinean who adopted Edinburgh as his home-town more than 20 years ago, £130/day, tel. 0131/664-1731, mobile 0797-330-6579, sergiolaspina@aol.com), and **Anne Doig** (£120/day, mobile 0777-590-1792, annedoig2@hotmail .com).

Getting Around Edinburgh

Many of Edinburgh's sights are within walking distance of one another, but buses come in handy. Two companies handle the city routes: Lothian (which dominates) and First. Lothian sells a day pass valid only on their buses (£3, buy from driver). Buses run from about 6:00 to 23:00 (£1.20/ride, buy tickets on bus, Lothian Buses transit office at Old Town end of Waverley Bridge has schedules and route maps, tel. 0131/555-6363, www.lothianbuses.com). Tell the driver where you're going, have change handy (buses require exact change—you lose any extra you put in), take your ticket as you board, and ping the bell as you near your stop. Double-deckers come with fine views upstairs.

The 1,300 **taxis** cruising Edinburgh's streets are easy to flag down (a ride between downtown and the B&B neighborhood costs about £7). They can turn on a dime, so hail them in either direction.

Tours in Edinburgh

Royal Mile Walking Tours—**Edinburgh Tour Guides** offers your best basic historical walk (without all the ghosts and goblins). The staff of committed guides heads out as long as they have at least two people. Their Royal Mile tour is a gentle two-hour downhill stroll from the castle to the palace (£12; daily at 9:30, 14:00, and 19:00; meet outside Gladstone's Land, near the top of the Royal Mile, call to confirm and reserve, tel. 0131/443-3200, mobile 0789/994-8585, www.edinburghtour guides.com).

Mercat Tours offers 1.5-hour guided walks of the Mile, which are more entertaining than intellectual (£9, daily at 14:15, leaves from Mercat Cross on the Royal Mile, tel. 0131/225-5445, www .mercattours.com). The guides, who enjoy making a short story long, ignore the big sights and take you behind the scenes with piles of barely historical gossip, bully-pulpit Scottish pride, and fun but forgettable trivia. These tours can move quickly, scaling the steep hills and steps of Edinburgh—wear good shoes. They also offer several ghost tours, as well as one focused on 18th-century underground vaults on the southern slope of the Royal Mile.

The **Voluntary Guides Association** offers free two-hour walks, but only during the Edinburgh Festival. You don't need a reservation, but it's a good idea to call the TI or drop by there to double-check details, such as departure point and time (daily at about 10:00 and 14:00, generally depart from Cannonball House at Castle Esplanade, www.edinburghfestivalguides.org).

The Real Mary King's Close runs Auld Town walking tours by a guide in the character of a 17th-century local (£7, £2 discount with recommended underground tour of Mary King's Close, 1 hour; generally runs daily at 11:30, 13:00, and 15:00; leaves from Mary King's Close, across from St. Giles' Church; tel. 0845-070-6244, www.realmarykingsclose.com).

Evening **ghost walks** and **pub tours** are described later, under "Nightlife in Edinburgh" on page 51.

Edinburgh Bus Tours—Four different one-hour hop-on, hop-off bus tours circle the town center, stopping at the major sights. You can hop on and off at any stop all day with one ticket (pick-ups about every 10–15 minutes). All tours are narrated. Two of the tours have live guides: **Mac Tours' City Tour** (focuses on

EDINBURGH

Edinburgh

🧭 VIEW

¼ MILE

400 METERS

WATER OF LEITH

MORAY PLACE

QUEEN

QUEEN ST. GARDENS

GEORGIAN HOUSE

HILL

NEW

ST. ANDREW'S

CHAR-LOTTE SQ.

GEORGE

ST.

ST. AND-REW SQ.

SEE DETAIL MAP

ROSE

CASTLE

FREDE-RICK

❷

HANOVER

ST.

DAVID

TOWN

SCOTT MON.

SHANDWICK PLACE

PRINCES STREET

❻

PRINCES ST. GARDENS

THE MOUND

NATIONAL GALLERY

WAVERLEY BRIDGE

TO HAYMARKET STN., A-8, AIRPORT & GLASGOW

LOTHIAN

EDINBURGH CASTLE →

ESPLANADE

RO

MORRISON

BREAD

GRASS-MARKET

GEORGE IV BRIDGE

ST. GILES'

COW-

FOUNTAIN-BRIDGE

OLD

TOWN

❶ Edinburgh City Centre Holiday Inn Express
❷ Travelodge Rose Street
❸ Travelodge Waterloo Place
❹ Edinburgh Central Youth Hostel
❺ Bus to Dalkeith Rd. B&Bs
❻ Half-Price Hut (Fringe Tickets)

LAURISTON PL.

NATIONAL MUSEUM OF SCOTLAND

Old Town, most comprehensive, live Mon–Fri with "vintage buses") and **Edinburgh Tour** (focuses on the wider city, more panoramic, always live). Avoid the **City Sightseeing Tours,** which have a recorded narration (better for non-English speakers). The tours all have virtually the same route, cost, and frequency, except the **Majestic Tour,** whose regular route is longer and includes a stop at the *Britannia* and the Royal Botanic Garden (£12/tour, £15 for all four tours, tick-

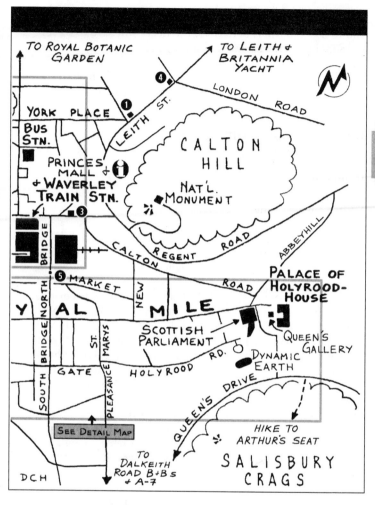

TO ROYAL BOTANIC GARDEN

TO LEITH & BRITANNIA YACHT

LONDON ROAD

YORK PLACE

BUS STN.

LEITH ST.

❶

❹

CALTON HILL

NAT'L. MONUMENT

PRINCES MALL & WAVERLEY TRAIN STN.

ℹ️

❸

REGENT ROAD

CALTON

ABBEYHILL

❺ MARKET

NEW ST.

ROAD

PALACE OF HOLYROOD-HOUSE

Y AL MILE

SCOTTISH PARLIAMENT

QUEEN'S GALLERY

SOUTH BRIDGE

NORTH BRIDGE

ST. MARYS

PLEASANCE

GATE

HOLYROOD RD.

DYNAMIC EARTH

QUEEN'S DRIVE

SEE DETAIL MAP

TO DALKEITH ROAD B&Bs & A-7

HIKE TO ARTHUR'S SEAT

SALISBURY CRAGS

DCH

ets give small discounts on most sights along the route, valid 24 hours, buy on bus, tel. 0131/220-0770, www.edinburghtour.com). Buses run daily year-round; April–Oct in peak season, they leave Waverley Bridge every day between around 9:30 and 19:00 (hours shrink off-season). On sunny days they go topless (the buses), but come with increased traffic noise and exhaust fumes. All of these companies are actually run by Lothian Buses (which has to splinter its offerings this way because of local antimonopoly laws).

Busy sightseers might want to get the **Royal Edinburgh Ticket** (£40), which covers two days of unlimited travel on Lothian city buses—including all four tour buses, as well as admission to Edinburgh Castle (£14), the Palace of Holyroodhouse (£10.25), and the *Britannia* (£10.50). If you plan to visit all these sights and to use a tour bus both days, the ticket will save you a few pounds (and, in the summer, help you bypass any lines). You can buy these tickets online, from the TI, or from the staff at the tour-bus pick-up point on Waverley Bridge. If your main interest is seeing the Britannia, you'll save money by taking a regular bus instead.

Day Trips from Edinburgh

Many companies run a variety of day trips to regional sights. Study the brochures at the TI's rack.

Highlands Tours—By far the most popular tour is the all-day Highlands trip. The standard Highlands tour gives those with limited time a chance to experience the wonders of Scotland's wild and legend-soaked Highlands in a single long day (about £35–45, roughly 8:30–20:30). You'll generally see the vast and brutal Rannoch Moor; Glencoe, still evocative with memories of the clan massacre; views of Britain's highest mountain, Ben Nevis; Fort Augustus on Loch Ness (some tours have a 1.5-hour stop here with an optional £9 boat ride); and a 45-minute tea or pub break in the fine town of Pitlochry. You learn about the Loch Ness monster, and a bit about Edinburgh to boot as you drive in and out. Various competing companies run these tours (each offering a slightly different combination of sights), including **Timberbush Highland Tours** (£37, 7- to 36-seat air-con buses, reliable, depart from entrance to Edinburgh Castle, tel. 0131/226-6066, www.timberbushtours.com); **Gray Line** (£39, tel. 0131/555-5558, www.graylinescotland.com); **Rabbie's Trail Burners** (£39-45, maximum 16 per tour, guaranteed departures, depart from their office at 207 High Street, tel. 0131/226-3133, www.rabbies.com); and **Heart of Scotland Tours** (£38, £3 Rick Steves discount on all their tours—mention when booking, departures daily at 8:00, leaves from opposite Travelodge on Waterloo Place near Waverley Station, tel. 01828/627-799, www.heartofscotlandtours.co.uk, run by Nick Roche). As Heart of Scotland is a small company, they may need to cancel if the requisite six people don't sign up. Be sure to leave a contact number so you can be notified. A final decision is made by 18:00 the night before.

    Haggis Adventures runs cheap and youthful tours on 16- to 39-seat buses with a very Scottish driver/guide. Their day trips (£28–42) include a distillery visit and the northern Highlands, or Loch Lomond and the southern Highlands. Their overnight trips are designed for young backpackers, but they welcome travelers of any age who want a quick look at the countryside and are up for hosteling (2- to 10-day trips, office hours: Mon–Sat 9:00–18:00 in summer, until 17:00 in winter; Sun 9:00–12:00, often closed Sun

Edinburgh Castle

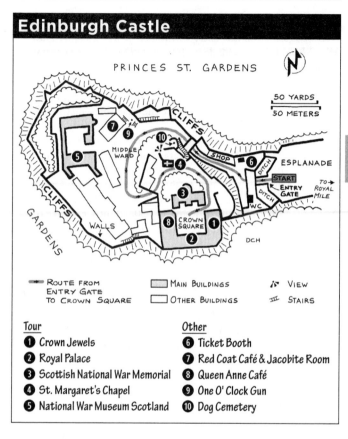

PRINCES ST. GARDENS

| 50 YARDS |
| 50 METERS |

CLIFFS

MIDDLE WARD

SHOP

ESPLANADE

DITCH

START

ENTRY GATE

TO → ROYAL MILE

WC

CLIFFS

GARDENS

WALLS

CROWN SQUARE

D.C.H

EDINBURGH

- ➡️ ROUTE FROM ENTRY GATE TO CROWN SQUARE
- ▢ MAIN BUILDINGS
- ▢ OTHER BUILDINGS
- ⚲ VIEW
- ⊞ STAIRS

Tour
❶ Crown Jewels
❷ Royal Palace
❸ Scottish National War Memorial
❹ St. Margaret's Chapel
❺ National War Museum Scotland

Other
❻ Ticket Booth
❼ Red Coat Café & Jacobite Room
❽ Queen Anne Café
❾ One O' Clock Gun
❿ Dog Cemetery

in winter; 60 High Street, at Blackfriars Street, tel. 0131/557-9393, www.haggisadventures.com).

Sights in Edinburgh

▲▲▲Edinburgh Castle

The fortified birthplace of the city 1,300 years ago, this imposing symbol of Edinburgh sits proudly on a rock high above you.

While the castle has been both a fort and a royal residence since the 11th century, most of the buildings today are from its more recent use as a military garrison. This fascinating and multifaceted sight deserves several hours of your time.

Cost and Hours: £14, daily April–Oct 9:30–18:00, Nov–March 9:30–17:00, last entry 45 minutes before closing, National War Museum Scotland closes 15 minutes before rest of castle, tel. 0131/225-9846, www.edinburghcastle.gov.uk.

Avoiding Lines: The least crowded time is usually between 10:00 and 11:00. To avoid ticket lines (worst in August), book online and pick up your ticket at the machines just inside the entrance.

Tours: Twenty-minute guided introductory tours are free with admission (2–4/hour, depart from entry gate, see clock for next departure; fewer tours off-season). The excellent audioguide provides a good supplement to the live guided tour, offering four hours of quick-dial digital descriptions of the sights, including the National War Museum Scotland (£3.50, slightly cheaper if purchased with entry ticket, pay at the ticket booth and pick it up at the entry gate).

Services: The clean WC at the entry routinely wins "British Loo of the Year" awards. For lunch, you have two choices. **The Red Coat Café and Jacobite Room**—located within Edinburgh Castle—is a big, bright, efficient cafeteria with great views (£6 quick, healthy meals). Punctuate the two parts of your castle visit (the castle itself and the impressive National War Museum Scotland) with a smart break here. The **Queen Anne Café,** in a building at the top of the hill, right across from the crown jewels, serves sit-down meals in its small, tight space (last orders 30 minutes before castle complex closes).

Getting There: You can walk to the castle, catch a bus (which drops you off a short uphill walk away), or take a taxi (taxis let you off right at the bottom of the esplanade, in front of the gate).

❍ Self-Guided Tour: Start at the entry gate, where you can pick up your audioguide and enjoy the droll 20-minute introductory tour with a live guide. (It'd be a shame to miss this included and charmingly entertaining intro tour.)

The castle has five essential stops: the crown jewels, Royal Palace, Scottish National War Memorial, St. Margaret's Chapel (with a city view), and the excellent National War Museum Scotland. The first four are at the highest and most secure point—on or near the castle square, where your introductory guided tour ends (and the sights described below begin). The separate National War Museum Scotland is worth a serious look—allow at least a half-hour (50 yards below the cafeteria and big shop).

William Wallace
(c. 1270–1305)

In 1286, Scotland's king died without an heir, plunging the prosperous country into a generation of chaos. As Scottish nobles bickered over naming a successor, the English King Edward I—nicknamed "Longshanks" because of his height—invaded and assumed power (1296). He placed a figurehead on the throne, forced Scottish nobles to sign a pledge of allegiance to England (the "Ragman's Roll"), moved the British parliament north to York, and carried off the highly symbolic 336-pound Stone of Scone to London, where it would remain for the next seven centuries.

A year later, the Scots rose up against Edward, led by William Wallace (nicknamed "Braveheart"). A mix of history and legend portrays Wallace as the son of a poor-but-knightly family that refused to sign the Ragman's Roll. Exceptionally tall and strong, he learned Latin and French from two uncles, who were priests. In his teenage years, his father and older brother were killed by the English. Later, he killed an English sheriff to avenge the death of his wife, Marion. Wallace's rage inspired his fellow Scots to revolt.

In the summer of 1297, Wallace and his guerrillas scored a series of stunning victories over the English. On September 11, a large, well-equipped English army of 10,000 soldiers and 300 horsemen began crossing Stirling Bridge. Half of the army had made it across when Wallace's men attacked. In the chaos, the bridge collapsed, splitting the English ranks in two, and the ragtag Scots drove the confused English into the river. The Battle of Stirling Bridge was a rout, and Wallace was knighted and appointed Guardian of Scotland.

All through the winter, King Edward's men chased Wallace, continually frustrated by the Scots' hit-and-run tactics. Finally, at the Battle of Falkirk (1298), they drew Wallace's men out onto the open battlefield. The English with their horses and archers easily destroyed the spear-carrying Scots. Wallace resigned in disgrace and went on the lam, while his successors negotiated truces with the English, finally surrendering unconditionally in 1304. Wallace alone held out.

In 1305, the English tracked him down and took him to London, where he was convicted of treason and mocked with a crown of oak leaves as the "King of Scotland." On August 23, they stripped him naked and dragged him to the execution site. There he was strangled to near death, castrated, and dismembered. His head was stuck on a stick atop London Bridge, while his body parts were sent on tour around the realm to spook would-be rebels. But Wallace's martyrdom only served to inspire his countrymen, and the torch of independence was picked up by Robert the Bruce.

① Crown Jewels: There are two ways to get to the jewels. You can go in directly from the top palace courtyard, Crown Square, but there's often a line. To avoid the line, head to the left as you're facing the building and find the entrance near the WCs. This route takes you through the "Honors of Scotland" exhibition—an interesting, if Disney-esque, series of displays (which often moves at a very slow shuffle) telling the story of the crown jewels and how they survived the harrowing centuries.

Scotland's **crown jewels,** though not as impressive as England's, are older and treasured by the locals. Though Oliver Cromwell destroyed England's jewels, the Scots managed to hide theirs. Longtime symbols of Scottish nationalism, they were made in Edinburgh—in 1540 for a 1543 coronation—out of Scottish diamonds, gems, and gold...some say the personal gold of King Robert the Bruce. They were last used to crown Charles II in 1651. When the Act of Union was forced upon the Scots in 1707—dissolving Scotland's parliament into England's to create the United Kingdom—part of the deal was that the Scots could keep their jewels locked up in Edinburgh. The jewels remained hidden for more than 100 years. In 1818, Sir Walter Scott and a royal commission rediscovered them intact. In 1999, for the first time in nearly three centuries, the crown of Scotland was brought from the castle for the opening of the Scottish parliament (see photos on the wall where the "Honors of Scotland" exhibit meets the crown jewels room; a smiling Queen Elizabeth II presides over the historic occasion).

The **Stone of Scone** (a.k.a. the "Stone of Destiny") sits plain and strong next to the jewels. This big gray chunk of rock is the coronation stone of Scotland's ancient kings (ninth century). Swiped by the English, it sat under the coronation chair at Westminster Abbey from 1296 until 1996. Queen Elizabeth finally agreed to let the stone go home, on one condition: that it be returned to Westminster Abbey in London for all future coronations. With major fanfare, Scotland's treasured Stone of Scone returned to Edinburgh on Saint Andrew's Day, November 30, 1996. Talk to the guard for more details.

② The Royal Palace: Scottish royalty lived here only when safety or protocol required it (they preferred the Palace of Holyroodhouse at the bottom of the Royal Mile). The Royal Palace, facing the castle square under the flagpole, has two historic yet unimpressive rooms (through door marked "1566") and the Great Hall (separate entrance from opposite side of square; see below). Enter the **Mary, Queen of Scots room,** where in 1566 the queen gave birth to James VI of Scotland, who later became King James I of England. The Presence Chamber leads into **Laich Hall** (Lower Hall), the dining room of the royal family.

The **Great Hall** was the castle's ceremonial meeting place in

British, Scottish, and English

Scotland and England have been tied together for 300 years, since the Act of Union in 1707. For a century and a half afterward, Scottish nationalists rioted for independence in Edinburgh's streets and led rebellions in the Highlands. In this controversial union, history is clearly seen through two very different filters.

If you tour a British-oriented sight, such as the National War Museum Scotland, you'll find things told in a "happy union" way, which ignores the long history of Scottish resistance—from the ancient Picts through the time of Robert the Bruce. The official line: In 1706–1707, it was clear to England and some of Scotland (especially landowners from the Lowlands) that it was in their mutual interest to dissolve the Scottish government and fold it into Britain, to be ruled from London.

But talk to a cabbie or your B&B host, and you may get a different spin. In a clever move by England to deflate the military power of its little sister, Scottish Highlanders were often sent to fight and die for Britain in disproportionately higher numbers than their English counterparts. Poignant propaganda posters in the National War Museum Scotland show a happy lad with the message, "Hey, look! Willie's off to Singapore with the Queen's Own Highlanders."

Scottish independence is still a hot-button issue today. In 2007, the Scottish National Party (SNP) won a major election, and now has the largest majority in the fledgling Scottish parliament. Alex Salmond, SNP leader and the First Minister of Scotland, is widely expected to push for Scotland to be recognized as an independent nation within the EU. (English leaders are obviously not in favor of breaking up the "united kingdom," though there's a like-minded independence movement in Wales, as well.)

The deep-seated rift shows itself in sports, too. While the English may refer to a British team in international competition as "English," the Scots are careful to call it "British." If a Scottish athlete does well, the English call him "British." If he screws up...he's a clumsy Scot.

the 16th and 17th centuries. In later times, it was a barracks and a hospital. Although most of what you see is Victorian, two medieval elements survive: the fine hammer-beam roof and the big iron-barred peephole (above fireplace on right). This allowed the king to spy on his subjects while they partied.

❸ **The Scottish National War Memorial:** This commemorates the 149,000 Scottish soldiers lost in World War I, the 58,000 who died in World War II, and the nearly 800 (and counting) lost in British battles since. This is a somber spot (put away your

Robert the Bruce
(1274–1329)

William Wallace's story paints the Scottish fight for independence in black-and-white terms—the oppressive English versus the plucky Scots. But Scotland had to overcome its own divisiveness, and no one was more divided than Robert the Bruce. As Earl of Carrick, he was born with blood ties to England and a long-standing family claim to the Scottish throne.

When England's King Edward I ("Longshanks") conquered Scotland in 1296, the Bruce family welcomed it, hoping Edward would defeat their rivals and put Bruce's father on the throne. They dutifully signed the "Ragman's Roll" of allegiance...and then Edward chose someone else as king.

Twentysomething Robert the Bruce (the "the" comes from his original family name of "de Bruce") then joined William Wallace's revolt against the English. Legend has it that it was he who knighted Wallace after the victory at Stirling Bridge. When Wallace fell from favor, Bruce became co-Guardian of Scotland (caretaker ruler in the absence of a king) and continued fighting the English. But when Edward's armies again got the upper hand in 1302, Robert—along with Scotland's other nobles—diplomatically surrendered and again pledged loyalty.

In 1306, Robert the Bruce murdered his chief rival and boldly claimed to be King of Scotland. Few nobles supported him. Edward crushed the revolt and kidnapped Bruce's wife, the Church excommunicated him, and Bruce went into hiding on a distant North Sea island. He was now the king of nothing. Legend says he gained inspiration by watching a spider patiently build its web.

The following year, Bruce returned to Scotland and weaved alliances with both nobles and the Church, slowly gaining acceptance as Scotland's king by a populace chafing under English rule. On June 24, 1314, he decisively defeated the English (now led by Edward's weak son, Edward II) at the Battle of Bannockburn. After a generation of turmoil (1286–1314), England was finally driven from Scotland, and the country was united under Robert I, King of Scotland.

As king, Robert the Bruce's priority was to stabilize the monarchy and establish clear lines of succession. His descendants would rule Scotland for the next 400 years, and even today, Bruce blood runs through the veins of Queen Elizabeth II, Prince Charles, and princes William and Harry.

camera, phone, etc.). Paid for by public donations, each bay is dedicated to a particular Scottish regiment. The main shrine, featuring a green Italian-marble memorial that contains the original WWI rolls of honor, sits—almost as if it were sacred—on an exposed chunk of the castle rock. Above you, the archangel Michael is busy slaying a dragon. The bronze frieze accurately shows the attire of various wings of Scotland's military. The stained glass starts with Cain and Abel on the left, and finishes with a celebration of peace on the right. To appreciate how important this place is, consider that Scottish soldiers died at twice the rate of other British soldiers in World War I.

❹ St. Margaret's Chapel: The oldest building in Edinburgh is dedicated to Queen Margaret, who died here in 1093 and was sainted in 1250. Built in 1130 in the Romanesque style of the Norman invaders, it's wonderfully simple, with classic Norman zigzags decorating the round arch that separates the tiny nave from the sacristy. It was used as a powder magazine for 400 years; very little survives. You'll see a facsimile of St. Margaret's 11th-century gospel book and small windows featuring St. Margaret, St. Columba (who brought Christianity to Scotland via Iona), and William Wallace (the brave-hearted defender of Scotland). The place is popular for weddings—and, as it seats only 20, it's particularly popular with brides' fathers.

Mons Meg, in front of the church, is a huge and once-upon-a-time frightening 15th-century siege cannon that fired 330-pound stones nearly two miles. It was a gift from the Belgians, who shared a common enemy with the Scots—England—and were eager to arm Scotland.

Belly up to the banister (outside the chapel, below the cannon) to enjoy the grand view. Beneath you are the guns—which fire the one o'clock salute—and a sweet little line of doggie tombstones, marking the soldiers' pet cemetery. Beyond stretches the Georgian New Town (read the informative plaque).

Crowds gather for the 13:00 gun blast, a tradition that gives ships in the bay something to set their navigational devices by. (The frugal Scots don't fire it at high noon, as that would cost 11 extra rounds a day.)

❺ The National War Museum Scotland: This museum is a pleasant surprise, thoughtfully covering four centuries of Scottish military history. Instead of the usual musty, dusty displays of endless armor, this museum has an interesting mix of short films, uniforms, weapons, medals, mementos, and eloquent excerpts from soldiers' letters. Just when you thought your castle visit was about over, you'll likely find yourself lingering at this stop, which rivals any military museum you'll see in Europe (closes 15 minutes before rest of castle complex).

Here you'll learn the story of how the fierce and courageous Scottish warrior changed from being a symbol of resistance against Britain to being a champion of that same empire. Along the way, these military men received many decorations for valor and did more than their share of dying in battle. But even when fighting for—rather than against—England, Scottish regiments still promoted their romantic, kilted-warrior image.

Queen Victoria fueled this ideal throughout the 19th century. (She was infatuated with the Scottish Highlands and the culture's untamed, rustic mystique.) Highland soldiers, especially officers, went to great personal expense to sport all their elaborate regalia, and the kilted men fought best to the tune of their beloved bagpipes. For centuries the stirring drone of bagpipes accompanied Highland soldiers into battle—inspiring them, raising their spirits, and announcing to the enemy that they were about to meet a fierce and mighty foe.

This museum shows the human side of war, and the cleverness of government-sponsored ad campaigns that kept the lads enlisting. Two centuries of recruiting posters make the same pitch that still works today: a hefty signing bonus, steady pay, and job security with the promise of a manly and adventurous life—all spiked with a mix of pride and patriotism.

Leaving the Castle: As you exit, turn around and look back at the gate. There stand King Robert the Bruce (on the left, 1274–1329) and Sir William Wallace (Braveheart—on the right, 1270–1305). Wallace—now well-known to Americans, thanks to Mel Gibson—fought long and hard against English domination before being executed in London. Bruce beat the English at Bannockburn in 1314. Bruce and Wallace still defend the spirit of Scotland. The Latin inscription above the gate between them reads, more or less, "What you do to us...we will do to you."

▲▲▲Royal Mile

The Royal Mile is one of Europe's most interesting historic walks. Consisting of a series of four different streets—Castlehill, Lawnmarket, High Street, and Canongate (each with its own set of street numbers)—the Royal Mile is actually 200 yards longer than a mile. And every inch is packed with shops, cafés, and lanes leading to tiny squares.

Start at the castle at the top and amble down to the palace. These sights are listed in walking order. Entertaining guided walks bring the legends and lore of the

Royal Mile alive (described earlier, under "Tours in Edinburgh").

As you walk, remember that originally there were two settlements here, divided by a wall: Edinburgh lined the ridge from the castle at the top. The lower end, Canongate, was outside the wall until 1856. By poking down the many side alleys, you'll find a few surviving rough edges of an Old Town well on its way to becoming a touristic mall. Be glad you're here now; in a few years it'll be all tartans and shortbread, with tourists slaloming through the postcard racks on bagpipe skateboards.

Royal Mile Terminology: A "close" is a tiny alley between two buildings (originally with a door that closed it at night). A close usually leads to a "court," or courtyard. A "land" is a tenement block of apartments. A "pend" is an arched gateway. A "wynd" is a narrow, winding lane. And "gate" is from an old Scandinavian word for street.

Castle Esplanade—At the top of the Royal Mile, the big parking lot leading up to the castle was created as a military parade ground in 1816. It's often cluttered with bleachers for the Military Tattoo—a spectacular massing of the bands, filling the square nightly for most of August. At the bottom, on the left (where the square hits the road), a plaque above the tiny witches' fountain memorializes 300 women who were accused of witchcraft and burned here. Scotland burned more witches per capita than any other country—17,000 between 1479 and 1722. The plaque shows two witches: one good and one bad.

Walking downhill, you'll pass a touristy "Weaving Mill and Exhibition" that was once the Old Town's reservoir (you'll see the wellheads it served all along this walk). At Ramsey Lane, the street just before the Camera Obscura, turn left and walk one block. At the corner, enjoy a commanding **Edinburgh view:** Nelson's column stands atop Calton Hill with a Greek temple folly from 1822 (they ran out of money to finish this memorial to the British victory over France in the Napoleonic era). The big clock tower marks the Balmoral Hotel—built as a terminal hotel above Waverley Station in 1903. The lacy Neo-Gothic Sir Walter Scott Memorial is to the left. Below, two Neoclassical buildings—the National Gallery and Royal Scottish Academy—stand on The Mound.

Now head back out to the Mile.

Camera Obscura—A big deal when it was built in 1853, this observatory topped with a mirror reflected images onto a disc before the wide eyes of people who had never seen a photograph or a captured image. Today, you can climb 100 steps for an entertaining 20-minute demonstration (3/hour). At the top, enjoy the best view anywhere of the Royal Mile. Then work your way down through five floors of illusions, holograms, and early photos. This is a big hit with kids, but sadly overpriced (£9.25, daily July–Aug

EDINBURGH

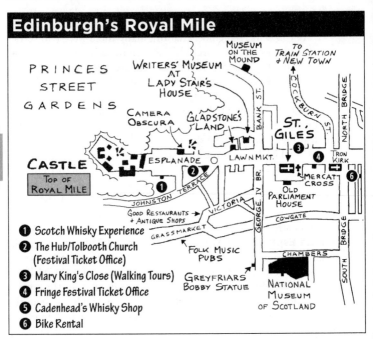

Edinburgh's Royal Mile

PRINCES
STREET
GARDENS

WRITERS' MUSEUM AT LADY STAIR'S HOUSE

MUSEUM ON THE MOUND

TO TRAIN STATION + NEW TOWN

COCKBURN ST.

NORTH BRIDGE

CAMERA OBSCURA

GLADSTONE'S LAND

BANK ST.

ST. GILES

CASTLE

ESPLANADE

LAWN MKT.

❸

TRON KIRK

TOP OF ROYAL MILE

❶

❷

MERCAT CROSS

❹

❻

JOHNSTON TERRACE

VICTORIA

GEORGE IV BR.

OLD PARLIAMENT HOUSE

GOOD RESTAURANTS → + ANTIQUE SHOPS

COWGATE

SOUTH BRIDGE

GRASSMARKET

CHAMBERS

❶ Scotch Whisky Experience

❷ The Hub/Tolbooth Church (Festival Ticket Office)

❸ Mary King's Close (Walking Tours)

❹ Fringe Festival Ticket Office

❺ Cadenhead's Whisky Shop

❻ Bike Rental

FOLK MUSIC PUBS

GREYFRIARS BOBBY STATUE

NATIONAL MUSEUM OF SCOTLAND

9:30–19:30, April–June and Sept–Oct 9:30–18:00, Nov–March 10:00–17:00, last demonstration one hour before closing, tel. 0131/226-3709, www.camera-obscura.co.uk).

Scotch Whisky Experience (a.k.a. "Malt Disney")—This gimmicky ambush is designed only to distill £11.50 out of your pocket. You kick things off with a little whisky-barrel train-car ride that goes to great lengths to make whisky production seem thrilling (things get pretty psychedelic when you hit the yeast stage). A presentation on whisky in Scotland includes sampling a wee dram, and the chance to stand amid the world's largest Scotch whisky collection (almost 3,500 bottles). At the end, you'll find yourself in the bar, which is worth a quick look for its wall of unusually shaped whisky bottles. If you're visiting Oban, Pitlochry, or the Isle of Skye, you'll find cheaper, less hokey distillery tours there. People do seem to enjoy this place, but that might have something to do with the sample (daily 10:00–18:30, last tour at 17:00, tel. 0131/220-0441, www.scotchwhiskyexperience.co.uk). Serious connoisseurs of the Scottish firewater will want to pop into Cadenhead's Whisky Shop at the bottom of the Royal Mile.

The Hub (Tolbooth Church)—This Neo-Gothic church (1844), with the tallest spire in the city, is now The Hub, Edinburgh's Festival Ticket and Information Centre. It also houses a handy café (£5–8 lunches).

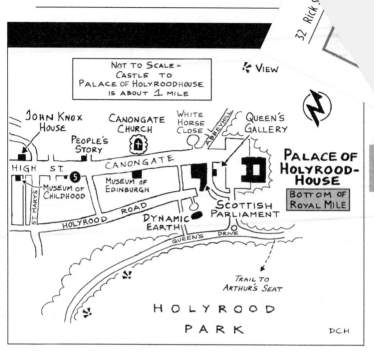

NOT TO SCALE –
CASTLE TO
PALACE OF HOLYROODHOUSE
IS ABOUT 1 MILE

⚡ VIEW

JOHN KNOX
HOUSE

CANONGATE
CHURCH

WHITE
HORSE
CLOSE

ABBEYHILL

QUEEN'S
GALLERY

PEOPLE'S
STORY

CANONGATE

HIGH ST.   5

MUSEUM OF
CHILDHOOD

MUSEUM OF
EDINBURGH

ST. MARYS

HOLYROOD   ROAD

DYNAMIC
EARTH

SCOTTISH
PARLIAMENT

QUEEN'S   DRIVE

PALACE OF
HOLYROOD-
HOUSE

BOTTOM OF
ROYAL MILE

TRAIL TO
ARTHUR'S SEAT

H O L Y R O O D

P A R K

DCH

EDINBURGH

▲▲**Gladstone's Land**—This is a typical 16th- to 17th-century merchant's house. "Land" means tenement, and these multistory buildings—in which merchants ran their shops on the ground floor and lived upstairs—were typical of the time. (For an interesting comparison of life in the Old Town versus the New Town, also visit the Georgian House—described later.) Gladstone's Land comes complete with an almost-lived-in, furnished interior and guides in each room who love to talk. Keep this place in mind as you stroll the rest of the Mile, imagining other houses as if they still looked like this on the inside (£5.50, daily July–Aug 10:00–18:30, April–June and

Sept–Oct 10:00–17:00, last entry 30 minutes before closing, closed Nov–March, no photos allowed, tel. 0844-493-2100, www.nts.org.uk/Property/25).

For a good Royal Mile photo, climb the curved stairway outside the museum to the left of the entrance (or to the right as you're leaving). Notice the snoozing pig outside the front door. Just like every house has a vacuum cleaner today, in the good old days

EDINBURGH

Scotland's Literary Greats: Burns, Stevenson, and Scott

Edinburgh was home to Scotland's three greatest literary figures: Robert Burns, Robert Louis Stevenson, and Sir Walter Scott.

Robert Burns (1759–1796) was Scotland's bard. An ardent supporter of the French Revolution, this poor farmer was tuned into the social inequities of the late 1700s. Even though Robby, as he's lovingly called even today, dared to speak up for the common man and attack social rank, he was a favorite of Edinburgh's high society, who'd gather in fine homes to hear the national poet recite his works.

One hundred years later, **Robert Louis Stevenson** (1850–1894) also stirred the Scottish soul with his pen. An avid traveler who always packed his notepad, Stevenson created settings that are vivid and filled with wonder. Traveling through Scotland, Europe, and around the world, he distilled his adventures into Romantic classics, including *Kidnapped* and *Treasure Island* (as well as *The Strange Case of Dr. Jekyll and Mr. Hyde*). Stevenson, who spent his last years in the South Pacific, wrote, "Youth is the time to travel—both in mind and in body—to try the manners of different nations." He said, "I travel not to go anywhere...but to simply go." Travel was his inspiration and his success.

Sir Walter Scott (1771–1832) wrote the *Waverley* novels, including *Ivanhoe* and *Rob Roy*. He's considered the father of the Romantic historical novel. Through his writing, he generated a worldwide interest in Scotland, and re-awakened his fellow countrymen's pride in their inheritance. An avid patriot, he wrote, "Every Scottish man has a pedigree. It is a national prerogative, as unalienable as his pride and his poverty." Scott is so revered in Edinburgh that his towering Neo-Gothic monument dominates the city center. With his favorite hound by his side, Sir Walter Scott overlooks the city that he inspired, and that inspired him.

The best way to learn about and experience these literary greats is to visit the Writers' Museum at Lady Stair's House (see below) and to take Edinburgh's Literary Pub Tour.

a snorting rubbish collector was a standard feature of any well-equipped house.

▲**Writers' Museum at Lady Stair's House**—This aristocrat's house, built in 1622, is filled with well-described manuscripts and knickknacks of Scotland's three greatest literary figures: Robert Burns, Sir Walter Scott, and Robert Louis Stevenson. Edinburgh's high society would gather in homes like this in the 1780s to hear the great poet Robby Burns read his work. Burns' work is meant to be read aloud rather than to oneself. In the Burns room, you can hear his poetry—worth a few minutes for anyone, and essential for fans (free, Mon–Sat 10:00–17:00, closed Sun except during Festival 12:00–17:00, no photos, tel. 0131/529-4901).

Wander around the courtyard here. Edinburgh was a wonder in the 17th and 18th centuries. Tourists came here to see its skyscrapers, which towered 10 stories and higher. No city in Europe was as densely populated—or polluted—as "Auld Reekie."

Deacon Brodie's Tavern—Read the "Doctor Jekyll and Mister Hyde" story of this pub's notorious namesake on the wall facing Bank Street. Then, to see his spooky split personality, check out both sides of the hanging signpost.

Deacon Brodie's Tavern lies at the intersection of the Royal Mile and George IV Bridge. At this point, you may want to consider several detours. If you head down the street to your right, you'll reach some recommended eateries (The Elephant House and The Outsider), as well as the excellent National Museum of Scotland, the famous Greyfriars Bobby statue, and the photogenic Victoria Street, which leads to the fun pub-lined Grassmarket square (all described later in this chapter). To your left, down Bank Street, is the Museum on the Mound (free exhibit on banking history, described later). All are a five-minute walk from here.

Heart of Midlothian—Near the street in front of the cathedral, a heart-shaped outline in the brickwork marks the spot of a gallows and the entrance to a prison (now long gone). Traditionally, locals stand on the rim of the heart and spit into it. Hitting the middle brings good luck. Go ahead...do as the locals do.

Across the street is a seated green statue of hometown boy **David Hume** (1711–1776)—one of the most influential thinkers not only of the Scottish Enlightenment, but in all of Western philosophy. (Fun fact: Born David *Home*, he changed the spelling of his name after getting tired of hearing the English say it without the correct Scottish pronunciation.)

Look around to understand Royal Mile plumbing. About 65 feet uphill is a **wellhead** (the square stone with a pyramid cap). This was the neighborhood well, served by the reservoir up at the castle before buildings had plumbing. Imagine long lines of people in need of water standing here, until buildings were finally retrofitted with water pipes—the ones you see running outside of buildings.

▲▲**St. Giles' Cathedral**—This is Scotland's most important church. Its ornate spire—the Scottish crown steeple from 1495—

is a proud part of Edinburgh's skyline. As the church functions as a kind of Westminster Abbey of Scotland, the interior is fascinating.

Cost and Hours: Free but donations encouraged, £2 to take photos; May–Sept Mon–Fri 9:00–19:00, Sat 9:00–17:00, Sun 13:00–17:00; Oct–April Mon–Sat 9:00–17:00, Sun 13:00–17:00; tel. 0131/225-9442, www.stgilescathedral.org.uk.

Concerts: St. Giles' busy concert schedule includes organ recitals and visiting choirs (frequent free events at 12:15, £8–10 concerts often Wed at 20:00 and Sun at 18:00, buy tickets at door or in gift shop, see schedule or ask for *Music at St. Giles'* pamphlet in gift shop).

◯ **Self-Guided Tour:** Today's facade is 19th-century Neo-Gothic, but most of what you'll see inside is from the 14th and 15th centuries. You'll also find cathedral guides trolling around, hoping you'll engage them in conversation. You'll be glad you did.

Just inside the entrance, turn around to see the modern stained-glass **Robert Burns window,** which celebrates Scotland's favorite poet. It was made in 1985 by the Icelandic artist Leifur Breidfjord. The green of the lower level symbolizes the natural world—God's creation. The middle zone with the circle shows the brotherhood of man—Burns was a great internationalist. The top is a rosy red sunburst of creativity, reminding Scots of Burns' famous line, "My love is like a red, red rose"—part of a song near and dear to every Scottish heart.

To the right of the Burns window is a fine **Pre-Raphaelite window.** Like most in the church, it's a memorial to an important patron (in this case, John Marshall). From here stretches a great swath of war memorials.

As you walk along the north wall, find **John Knox's statue.** (There's no set location; they move him around like a six-foot-tall bronze chess piece.) Look into his eyes for 10 seconds from 10 inches away, and think of the Reformation struggles of the 16th century. Knox, the great Reformer and founder of austere Scottish Presbyterianism, first preached here in 1559. His insistence that every person should be able to read the word of God gave Scotland an educational system 300 years ahead of the rest of Europe. Thanks partly to Knox, it was Scottish minds that led the way in math, science, medicine, and engineering. Voltaire called Scotland "the intellectual capital of Europe."

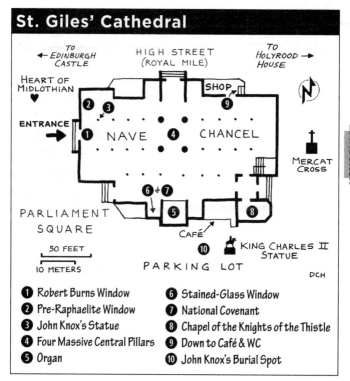

St. Giles' Cathedral

TO ← EDINBURGH CASTLE

HIGH STREET (ROYAL MILE)

TO HOLYROOD → HOUSE

HEART OF MIDLOTHIAN ♥

SHOP

ENTRANCE →

NAVE ❹ CHANCEL

N

MERCAT CROSS

PARLIAMENT SQUARE

CAFÉ

50 FEET

10 METERS

PARKING LOT

KING CHARLES II STATUE

DCH

EDINBURGH

❶ Robert Burns Window
❷ Pre-Raphaelite Window
❸ John Knox's Statue
❹ Four Massive Central Pillars
❺ Organ
❻ Stained-Glass Window
❼ National Covenant
❽ Chapel of the Knights of the Thistle
❾ Down to Café & WC
❿ John Knox's Burial Spot

Knox preached Calvinism. Consider that the Dutch and the Scots both embraced this creed of hard work, frugality, and strict ethics. This helps explain why Scots are so different from the English (and why the Dutch and the Scots—both famous for their thriftiness and industriousness—are so much alike).

The oldest parts of the cathedral—the **four massive central pillars**—date from 1120. After the English burned the cathedral, in 1385, it was rebuilt bigger and better than ever, and in 1495 its famous crown spire was completed. During the Reformation—when Knox preached here (1559–1572)—the place was simplified and whitewashed. Before this, when the emphasis was on holy services provided by priests, there were lots of little niches. With the new focus on sermons rather than rituals, the grand pulpit took center stage. Knox even had the church's fancy medieval glass windows replaced with clear glass, but 19th-century Victorians took them out and installed the brilliantly colored ones you see today.

Cross over to the **organ** (1992, Austrian-built, one of Europe's finest) and take in its sheer might. For a peek into the realm of the organist, duck around back to look through the glass panel.

Immediately to the right of the organ (as you're facing it) is a tiny chapel for silence and prayer. The dramatic **stained-glass window** above (c. 1570) shows the commotion that surrounded Knox when he preached. Bearded, fiery-eyed Knox had a huge impact on this community. Notice how there were no pews back then. The church was so packed, people even looked through clear windows from across the street. With his hand on the holy book, Knox seems to conduct divine electricity to the Scottish faithful.

Between this window and the organ is a copy of the **National Covenant.** It was signed in blood in 1638 by Scottish heroes who refused to compromise their religion for the king's. Most who signed were martyred (their monument is nearby in Grassmarket).

Head toward the east (back) end of the church, and turn right to see the Neo-Gothic **Chapel of the Knights of the Thistle** and its intricate wood carving. Built in two years (1910–1911), entirely with Scottish materials and labor, it is the private chapel of the Knights of the Thistle, the only Scottish chivalric order. It's used about once a year to inaugurate new members. Scotland recognizes its leading citizens by bestowing upon them a membership. The Queen presides over the ritual from her fancy stall, marked by her Scottish coat of arms—a heraldic zoo of symbolism. Are there bagpipes in heaven? Find the tooting angel at a ceiling joint to the left of the altar.

Downstairs is an inviting, recommended café, along with handy public toilets.

Just outside, behind the church, is the **burial spot of John Knox**—with appropriate austerity, he's under the parking lot, at spot 23. The statue among the cars shows King Charles II riding to a toga party back in 1685.

• Near parking spot 15, enter the...

Old Parliament House—The building now holds the civil law courts, so you'll need to go through security first; stay to the left to allow lawyers to get waved through quickly. Step in to see the grand hall, with its fine 1639 hammer-beam ceiling and stained glass. This space housed the Scottish parliament until the Act of Union in 1707. Find the big stained-glass depiction of the initiation of the first Scottish High Court in 1532. Just under it, you'll find a history exhibition explaining the Scottish parliament. The building now holds the civil law courts and is busy with wigged and robed lawyers hard at work in the old library (peek through the door) or pacing the hall deep in discussion. Look for the "Box

Corridor," a hallway filled with haphazard mailboxes for attorneys (the white dot indicates which lawyers have email). The friendly doorman is helpful (free, public welcome Mon–Fri 9:00–16:30, closed Sat–Sun, no photos, enter behind St. Giles' Cathedral; open-to-the-public trials are just across the street at the High Court—doorman has day's docket). The cleverly named Writz Café, in the basement, is literally their supreme court's restaurant (cheap, Mon–Fri 9:00–14:00, closed Sat–Sun).

▲**Mary King's Close**—For an unusual peek at Edinburgh's gritty, crowded past, join a costumed guide on a trip through a recently excavated underground street and buildings on the northern slope of the Royal Mile. Tours cover the standard goofy, crowd-pleasing ghost stories, but also provide authentic and interesting historical insight into a part of town entombed by later construction. It's best to book ahead—even though tours leave every 20 minutes, groups are small and the sight is popular (£11; April–Oct daily 10:00–21:00; Nov–March Sun–Thu 10:00–17:00, Fri–Sat 10:00–21:00; these are last tour times, no kids under 5, across from St. Giles' at 2 Warriston's Close, tel. 0845-070-6244, www.realmarykingsclose.com). The same company also runs Auld Town walking tours (see "Tours in Edinburgh," earlier).

Mercat Cross—This chunky pedestal, on the downhill side of St. Giles', holds a slender column topped with a white unicorn. Royal proclamations have been read at this market cross since the 14th century. In 1952 a town crier heralded the news that Britain had a new queen—three days (traditionally the time it took for a horse to speed here from London) after the actual event. Today, Mercat Cross is the meeting point of various walking tours—both historic and ghostly.

• *A few doors downhill is the...*

Police Information Center—This center provides a pleasant police presence (say that three times) and a little local law-and-order history to boot (free, daily May–Aug 10:00–21:30, April and Sept–Oct until 19:30, Nov–March until 18:00). Ask the officer on duty about the grave-robber William Burke's skin and creative poetic justice, Edinburgh-style. Seriously—drop in and discuss whatever law-and-order issue piques your curiosity.

Along this stretch of the Royal Mile, which is traffic-free most of the day (notice the bollards that raise and lower for permitted traffic), you'll see the Fringe Festival office (at #180), street musicians, and another wellhead (with horse "sippies," dating from 1675).

Cockburn Street—This street was cut through High Street's dense wall of medieval skyscrapers in the 1860s to give easy access to the Georgian New Town and the train station. Notice how the sliced buildings were thoughtfully capped with facades in a faux-16th-century Scottish baronial style. In the Middle Ages, only tiny lanes (like the Fleshmarket Lane just uphill from Cockburn Street) interrupted the long line of Royal Mile buildings.

• *Continue downhill 100 yards to the...*

▲**Museum of Childhood**—This five-story playground of historical toys and games is rich in nostalgia and history (free, Mon–Sat 10:00–17:00, Sun 12:00–17:00, last entry 30 minutes before closing). Just downhill is a fragrant fudge shop offering delicious free samples.

▲**John Knox House**—Intriguing for Reformation buffs, this fine 16th-century house offers a well-explained look at the life of the great reformer. Although most contend he never actually lived here, preservationists called it "Knox's house" to save it from the wrecking ball in 1850. On the top floor, there's a fun cape, hat, and feather pen photo op (£4, Mon–Sat 10:00–18:00, closed Sun except in July–Aug 12:00–18:00, 43 High Street, tel. 0131/556-9579).

The World's End—For centuries, a wall halfway down the Royal Mile marked the end of Edinburgh and the beginning of Canongate, a community associated with Holyrood Abbey. Today, where the Mile hits St. Mary's and Jeffrey Streets, High Street becomes Canongate. Just below the John Knox House (at #43), notice the hanging sign showing the old gate. At the intersection, find the brass bricks that trace the gate (demolished in 1764). The cornerside Tass Pub is a great venue for live traditional music—pop in and see what's on tonight. Look down St. Mary's Street about 200 yards to see a surviving bit of that old wall.

• *Entering Canongate, you leave what was Edinburgh and head for...*

▲**Cadenhead's Whisky Shop**—The shop is not a tourist sight. Founded in 1842, this firm prides itself on bottling good malt whisky from casks straight from the best distilleries, without all the compromises that come with profitable mass production (coloring with sugar to fit the expected look, watering down to lessen the alcohol tax, and so on). Those drinking from Cadenhead-bottled whiskies will enjoy the pure product as the distilleries owners themselves do, not as the sorry public does.

If you want to learn about whisky—and perhaps pick up a bottle—chat up Mark and Alan, who love to talk. To buy whisky here, ask for a sample first. Sip once. Consider the flavor. Add a little water and sip again. Buy a small bottle of your favorite (£12 for about 7 ounces) and enjoy it in your hotel room night after night. Unlike wine, it has a long shelf life after it's opened. If you want to savor it post-trip, keep in mind that customs laws prohibit you from shipping whisky home, so you'll have to pack it in your checked luggage. Fortunately, the bottles are extremely durable—just ask Mark or Alan to demonstrate (Mon–Sat 10:30–17:30, closed Sun except possibly in Aug 12:30–17:30, 172 Canongate, tel. 0131/556-5864, www.wmcadenhead.com).

▲**People's Story**—This interesting exhibition traces the conditions of the working class through the 18th, 19th, and 20th centuries (free, Mon–Sat 10:00–17:00, last entry 15 minutes before closing, closed Sun except during Festival 12:00–17:00, tel. 0131/529-4057). Curiously, while this museum is dedicated to the proletariat, immediately around the back (embedded in the wall of the museum) is the tomb of Adam Smith—the author of *Wealth of Nations* and the father of modern free-market capitalism (1723–1790).

▲**Museum of Edinburgh**—Another old house full of old stuff, this one is worth a look for its early Edinburgh history and handy ground-floor WC. Don't miss the original copy of the National Covenant (written in 1638 on an animal skin), sketches of pre-Georgian Edinburgh (which show a lake, later filled in to become Princes Street Gardens when the New Town was built), and early golf balls. A favorite Scottish say-it-aloud joke: "Balls," said the queen. "If I had two, I'd be king." The king laughed—he had to (free, same hours as People's Story—listed above, tel. 0131/529-4143).

White Horse Close—Step into this 17th-century courtyard (bottom of Canongate, on the left, a block before the Palace of Holyroodhouse). It was from here that the Edinburgh stagecoach left for London. Eight days later, the horse-drawn carriage would pull into its destination: Scotland Yard.

• *Across the street is the...*

▲▲**Scottish Parliament Building**—Scotland's parliament originated in 1293 and was dissolved by England in 1707. In 1998 it was decided that "there shall be a Scottish parliament guided by justice, wisdom, integrity, and compassion," and in 1999 it was formally reopened by Queen Elizabeth. Except for matters of

defense, foreign policy, and taxation, Scotland now enjoys home rule. The current government, run by the Scottish Nationalist Party (or at least until the elections in May 2011), is pushing for more independence.

In 2004 the Parliament moved into its striking new home. Although its cost ($800 million) and perceived extravagance made it controversial from the start, an in-person visit wins most people over. The eco-friendly building, by the Catalan architect Enric Miralles, mixes wild angles, lots of light, bold windows, oak, and local stone into a startling complex that would, as he envisioned, "arise from the sloping base of Arthur's Seat and arrive into the city as if almost surging out of the rock."

Since it celebrates Scottish democracy, the architecture is not a statement of authority. There are no statues of old heroes. There's not even a grand entry. You feel like you're entering an office park. The building is people-oriented. Signs are written in both English and Gaelic (the Scots' Celtic tongue). Anyone is welcome to attend the committee meetings (viewable by live video hookups throughout the nation's libraries).

For a peek at the building and a lesson in how the Scottish parliament works, drop in, pass through security, and find the visitors' desk. You're welcome into the public parts of the building, including the impressive "Debating Chambers." Worthwhile

hour-long tours by proud locals are offered (free, call or check online for times and details). Or you can call or sign up online to witness the Scottish parliament's hugely popular debates—best on Thursdays 12:00–12:30, when the First Minister is on the hot seat and has to field questions from members across all parties (other debate slots usually Wed 14:00–18:00, Thu 9:00–11:40 & 14:00–18:00, tel. 0131/348-5200).

Cost and Hours: Free, Mon–Fri 10:00–17:30, until 16:00 Oct–March, Tue–Thu 9:00–18:30 when Parliament in session, Sat 11:00–17:30 year-round, last entry 30 minutes before closing, closed Sun, www.scottish.parliament.uk. Generally Parliament is in recess for a week in February, from early July to early September, two weeks in October, and around Chrismas—dates are posted on their website.

▲**Palace of Holyroodhouse**—Since the 14th century, this palace has marked the end of the Royal Mile. An abbey—part of a 12th-century Augustinian monastery—originally stood in its place. It was named for a piece of the cross brought here as a relic by Queen (and later Saint) Margaret. Because Scotland's royalty preferred living at Holyroodhouse to the blustery castle on the rock, the palace evolved over time.

Consider touring the interior. The building, rich in history and decor, is filled with elegantly furnished rooms and a few darker, older rooms with glass cases of historic bits and Scottish pieces that locals find fascinating.

Bring the palace to life with the included one-hour **audio-**

guide. You'll learn which of the kings featured portraits lining the Great Gallery are real and which what touches were added to the bedchambers to f ... King Charles II, and why the exiled Comte d'Artois took refuge in the palace. You'll also hear a goofy reenactment of the moment when conspirators—dispatched by Mary, Queen of Scots' jealous second husband—stormed into the queen's chambers and stabbed her male secretary. Royal diehards can pick up a palace guidebook for £4.50.

Cost and Hours: £10.25 includes a quality audioguide, £14.30 combo-ticket includes Queen's Gallery—listed below, tickets sold in Queen's Gallery, daily April–Oct 9:30–18:00, Nov–March 9:30–16:30, last entry one hour before closing, tel. 0131/556-5100, www.royalcollection.org.uk. It's still a working palace, so it's closed when the Queen or other VIPs are in residence.

Nearby: After exiting, you're free to stroll through the ruined abbey (destroyed by those dastardly English during the time of Mary, Queen of Scots, in the 16th century) and the queen's gardens (closed in winter). Hikers: Note that the wonderful trail up Arthur's Seat starts just across the street from the gardens.

Queen's Gallery—This small museum features rotating exhibits of artwork from the royal collection. For more than five centuries, the royal family has amassed a wealth of art treasures. While the Queen keeps most in her many private palaces, she shares an impressive load of it here, with exhibits changing about every six months. Though the gallery occupies just a few rooms, it can be

exquisite. The entry fee includes an excellent audioguide, written and read by the curator (£5.50, £14.30 combo-ticket includes Palace of Holyroodhouse, daily April–Oct 9:30–18:00, Nov–March until 16:30, café, last entry one hour before closing, on the palace grounds, to the right of the palace entrance, www. royalcollection.org.uk). Buses #35 and #36 stop outside, and can save you a walk to or from Princes Street/North Bridge.

Sights Just Off the Royal Mile

▲▲▲**National Museum of Scotland**—This huge museum has amassed more historic artifacts than every other place I've seen in Scotland combined. It's all wonderfully displayed with fine descriptions offering a best-anywhere hike through the history of Scotland. Start in the basement and work your way through the story: prehistoric, Roman, Viking, the "birth of Scotland,"

Edinburgh's witch-burning craze, clan massacres, all the way to life in the 20th century. Free audioguides offer a pleasant description of various rooms and exhibits, and even provide mood music for your wanderings.

The **Kingdom of the Scots** exhibit, on the first three floors, shows evidence of a vibrant young nation. While largely cut off from Europe by hostilities with England, Scotland connected with the Continent through trade, the Church, and their monarch, Mary, Queen of Scots. Throughout Scotland's long, underdog struggle with England, its people found inspiration from romantic (and almost legendary) Scottish leaders, including Mary. Educated and raised in France during the Renaissance, Mary brought refinement to the Scottish throne. After she was imprisoned and then executed by the English, her countrymen rallied each other by invoking her memory. Pendants and coins with her portrait stoked the irrepressible Scottish spirit. Near the replica of Mary's tomb are tiny cameos, pieces of jewelry, and coins with her image.

The industry exhibit explains how (eventually) the Scots were tamed, and the union with England brought stability and investment to Scotland. Powered by the Scottish work ethic and the new opportunities that came from the Industrial Revolution, the country came into relative prosperity. Education and medicine thrived. Cast iron and foundries were huge, and this became one of the most industrialized places in Europe. With the dawn of the modern age came leisure time, the concept of "healthful sports," and golf—a Scottish invention. The first golf balls, which date from about 1820, were leather stuffed with feathers.

Cost and Hours: Free, daily 10:00–17:00; free 1-hour "Highlights" tours daily at 11:30 and 13:30, themed tours at 14:30—confirm tour schedule at info desk; 2 long blocks south of Royal Mile from St. Giles' Cathedral, Chambers Street, off George IV Bridge, tel. 0131/247-4422, www.nms.ac.uk.

Restaurant: On the museum's top floor, the upscale **Tower restaurant** serves surprisingly good food (£15 two-course lunch special, £16 afternoon tea 15:00–16:30, £15 early-dinner special 17:00–18:30, and fancy £18–25 meals, open daily 12:00–23:00—later than the museum itself, tel. 0131/225-3003).

Nearby: The **Royal Museum,** next door, fills a fine iron-and-glass Industrial Age building (built to house the museum in 1851) with all the natural sciences as it "presents the world to Scotland." It's great for school kids, but of no special interest to foreign visitors (closed until 2011).

Greyfriars Bobby—This famous statue of Edinburgh's favorite dog is across the street from the National Museum of Scotland. Every business nearby, it seems, is named for this terrier, who stood by his master's grave for 14 years and was immortalized in a 1960s Disney flick.

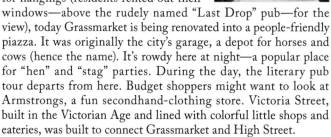

Grassmarket—Once Edinburgh's site for hangings (residents rented out their windows—above the rudely named "Last Drop" pub—for the view), today Grassmarket is being renovated into a people-friendly piazza. It was originally the city's garage, a depot for horses and cows (hence the name). It's rowdy here at night—a popular place for "hen" and "stag" parties. During the day, the literary pub tour departs from here. Budget shoppers might want to look at Armstrongs, a fun secondhand-clothing store. Victoria Street, built in the Victorian Age and lined with colorful little shops and eateries, was built to connect Grassmarket and High Street.

Hiding in the blur of traffic is a monument to the "Covenanters." These strict 17th-century Scottish Protestants were killed for refusing to accept the king's Episcopalian prayer book. To this day, Scots celebrate their emphatically democratic church government. Rather than big-shot bishops (as in the Anglican or Roman Catholic churches), they have a low-key "moderator" who's elected each year.

Museum on the Mound—Located in the basement of the grand Bank of Scotland building (easily spotted from a distance), this exhibit tells the story of the bank, which was founded in 1695 (making it only a year younger than the Bank of England). Featuring displays on cash production, safe technology, and bank robberies, this museum struggles mightily, with some success, to make banking interesting (the case holding £1 million is cool). It's worth popping in if you have some time or find the subject appealing. But no matter how well the information is presented, it's still about... yawn...banking (free, Tue–Fri 10:00–17:00, Sat–Sun 13:00–17:00, closed Mon, down Bank Street from the Royal Mile—follow the street around to the left and enter through the gate, tel. 0131/243-5464, www.museumonthemound.com).

Dynamic Earth—Located about a five-minute walk from the Palace of Holyroodhouse, this immense exhibit tells the story of our planet, filling several underground floors under a white vast Gore-Tex tent. It's pitched, appropriately, at the base of the Salisbury Crags. The exhibit is designed for younger kids and does the same thing an American science exhibit would do—but with a charming Scottish accent. Standing in a time tunnel, you

watch the years rewind from Churchill to dinosaurs to the Big Bang. After viewing several short films on stars, tectonic plates, ice caps, and world-wide weather (in a new "4D" exhibit), you're free to wander past salty pools, a re-created rain forest, and various TV screens (£10.50; daily 10:00–17:30, Nov–March closed Mon–Tue; last ticket sold 2 hours before closing, on Holyrood Road, between the palace and mountain, tel. 0131/550-7800, www.dynamicearth.co.uk). Dynamic Earth is a stop on the hop-on, hop-off bus route.

Bonnie Wee Sights in the New Town

▲▲**Georgian New Town**—Cross Waverley Bridge and walk through the Georgian New Town. According to the 1776 plan, the New Town was three streets (Princes, George, and Queen) flanked by two squares (St. Andrew and Charlotte), woven together by alleys (Thistle and Rose). George Street—20 feet wider than the others (so a four-horse carriage could make a U-turn)—was the main drag. And, while Princes Street has gone down-market, George Street still maintains its old grace. The entire elegantly planned New Town— laid out when George III was king—celebrated the hard-to-sell notion that Scotland was an integral part of the United Kingdom. The streets and squares are named after the British royalty (Hanover was the royal family surname). Even Thistle and Rose Streets (the national flowers of Scotland and England, respectively) are emblems of the two happily paired nations. Mostly pedestrianized Rose Street is famous for its rowdy pubs; where it hits St. Andrew Square, the street is flanked by the venerable Jenners department store and a Sainsbury's supermarket. Sprinkled with popular restaurants and bars, the stately New Town is turning trendy.

Princes Street—Edinburgh's main drag will likely be torn up for tram construction during your visit. If it's patched up, it'll be busy with buses and taxis (and trams, if running). Jenners department store is an institution. Notice how statues of women support the building—just as real women support the business. The arrival of new fashions here was such a big deal that they'd announce it by flying flags on the Nelson Monument. Step inside. The cen-

EDINBURGH

tral space—filled with a towering tree at Christmas—is classic Industrial Age architecture. The Queen's coat of arms high on the wall indicates she shops here.

St. Andrew Square—This green space bookends the Georgian New Town opposite Charlotte Square. In the early 19th century, there were no shops around here—just fine residences; this was a private garden for the fancy people living here. Now open to the public, the square is a popular lunch hangout for workers. The Melville Monument honors a powermonger Member of Parliament who, for four decades (around 1800), was nicknamed the "uncrowned king of Scotland."

St. Andrew's and St. George's Church—Designed as part of the New Town in the 1780s, the church is a product of the Scottish Enlightenment. It has an elliptical plan (the first in Britain) so that all can focus on the pulpit. A fine leaflet tells the story of the church, and a handy cafeteria downstairs serves cheap and cheery lunches.

▲▲Georgian House—This refurbished Georgian house, set on Edinburgh's finest Georgian square, is a trip back to 1796. It recounts the era when a newly gentrified and well-educated Edinburgh was nicknamed the "Athens of the North." A volunteer guide in each of the five rooms shares stories and trivia—from the kitchen in the basement to the fully stocked medicine cabinet in the bedroom. Start your visit in the basement and view the interesting 16-minute video, which shows the life of one family who owned this property and touches on the architecture of the Georgian period. A walk down George Street after your visit here can be fun for the imagination.

Cost and Hours: £5.50, daily July–Aug 10:00–18:30, April–June and Sept–Oct 10:00–17:00, March 11:00–16:00, Nov 11:00–15:00, last entry 30 minutes before closing, closed Dec–Feb, 7 Charlotte Square, tel. 0131/226-3318, www.nts.org.uk/Property/56.

▲▲National Gallery of Scotland—The elegant Neoclassical building has a delightfully small but impressive collection of European masterpieces, from Raphael, Titian, and Peter Paul Rubens to Thomas Gainsborough, Claude Monet, and Vincent van Gogh. A highlight (along with guards in plaid trousers) is Canova's exquisite *Three Graces,* and it offers the best look you'll get at Scottish paintings (in the basement). Check out one of Scotland's best-known paintings, *The Skating Minister,* by Sir Henry Raeburn. There's no audioguide,

but each painting is well-described.

Cost and Hours: Free, daily 10:00–17:00, Thu until 19:00, no photos, tel. 0131/624-6200, recorded info 0131/624-6336, www. nationalgalleries.org.

Related Sights: The skippable **Royal Scottish Academy,** next door, hosts temporary art exhibits and is connected to the National Gallery at the garden level (underneath the gallery) by the Weston Link building (same hours as the gallery, fine café and restaurant).

Two other museums are associated with the National Gallery, but are outside the downtown core: the Scottish National Portrait Gallery (closed until November 2011) and the Scottish National Gallery of Modern Art.

The Mound—The National Gallery sits upon what's known as "The Mound." When the lake was drained and the Georgian New Town was built, rubble from the excavations was piled into The Mound (c. 1770) to allay Old Town merchant concerns about being disconnected from the future heart of the city. The two fine Neoclassical buildings here (which house museums) date from the 1840s. From The Mound you can enjoy fine views of "Auld Reekie" (medieval Edinburgh), with its 14-story "skyscrapers."

Princes Street Gardens—The grassy park, a former lakebed, separates Edinburgh's New and Old Towns and offers a wonderful escape from the bustle of the city. Once the private domain of wealthy locals, it was opened to the public around 1870—not as a democratic gesture, but because it was thought that allowing the public into the park would increase sales for the Princes Street department stores. Join the office workers for a picnic lunch break, or see the oldest floral clock in the world. In summer you can also watch Scottish country dancing in the park (£3.50, May–July Mon and sometimes Tue 19:30–21:30, at Ross Bandstand, tel. 0131/228-8616, www.princesstreetgardensdancing.org.uk).

The big lake, Nor' Loch, was drained around 1800 as part of the Georgian expansion of Edinburgh. Before that, the lake was the town's sewer, water reservoir, and handy place for drowning witches. Much was written about the town's infamous stink (a.k.a. the "flowers of Edinburgh"). The town's nickname, "Auld Reekie," referred to both the smoke of its industry and the stench of its squalor.

Although the loch is now long gone, memories of the countless women drowned as witches remain. With their thumbs tied to their ankles, they'd be lashed to dunking stools. Those who survived the ordeal were considered "aided by the devil" and burned as witches. If they died, they were innocent and given a good Christian burial. Until 1720, Edinburgh was Europe's witch-burning mecca—any perceived "sign," including a small birthmark, could condemn you.

▲**Sir Walter Scott Monument**—Built in 1840, this elaborate Neo-Gothic monument honors the great author, one of Edinburgh's many illustrious sons. When Scott died in 1832, it was said that "Scotland never owed so much to one man." To all of Western literature, he's considered the father of the Romantic historical novel. The 200-foot monument shelters a marble statue of Scott and his favorite pet, Maida, a deerhound who was one of 30 canines this dog-lover owned during his lifetime. They're surrounded by busts of 16 great Scottish poets and 64 characters from his books. Climbing the tight, stony spiral staircase of 287 steps earns you a peek at a tiny museum midway, a fine city view at the top, and intimate encounters going up and down.

Cost and Hours: £3; April–Sept daily 10:00–19:00, Oct–March Mon–Sat 9:00–16:00, Sun 10:00–16:00; last entry one hour before closing, tel. 0131/529-4068.

Activities

▲▲Arthur's Seat Hike—A 45-minute hike up the 822-foot remains of an extinct volcano (surrounded by a fine park overlooking Edinburgh) starts from the Palace of Holyroodhouse. You can run up like they did in *Chariots of Fire,* or just stroll—at the summit you'll be rewarded with commanding views of the town and surroundings. On May Day, be on the summit at dawn and wash your face in the morning dew to commemorate the Celtic holiday of Beltaine, the celebration of spring. (Morning dew is supposedly very good for your complexion.)

From the parking lot below the Palace of Holyroodhouse, there are two trailheads. Take the wide path on the left (easier grade, through the abbey ruins and "Hunter's Bog"). After making the summit, you can return along the other path (to the right, with the steps), which skirts the base of the cliffs.

Those staying at my recommended B&Bs can enjoy a pre-breakfast or late-evening hike starting from the other side (in June, the sun comes up early, and it stays light until nearly midnight). From the Commonwealth Pool, take Holyrood Park Road, turn right on Queen's Drive, and continue to a small parking lot. From here it's a 20-minute hike.

If you have a car, you can drive up most of the way from behind (follow the one-way street from palace, park safely and for free by the little lake, and hike up).

Brush Skiing—If you like skiing, but not all that pesky snow, head a little south of town to Hillend, where the Midlothian

Snowsports Centre has a hill with a chairlift, two slopes, a jump slope, and rentable skis, boots, and poles. It feels like snow-skiing on a slushy day, even though you're schussing over what seems like a million toothbrushes. Beware: Doctors are used to treating an ailment called "Hillend Thumb"—thumbs dislocated when people fall here and get tangled in the brush. Locals say that skiing here is "like falling on a carrot grater" (£9.50/first hour, then £4/hour, includes gear, beginners must take a lesson, generally Mon–Tue 18:30–21:00, Wed–Fri 13:00–21:00, Sat–Sun 10:00–19:00—but call to confirm before showing up, probably closes if it snows, Lothian bus #4 from Princes Street—garden side, tel. 0131/445-4433, www.midlothian.gov.uk).

More Hikes—You can hike along the river (called Water of Leith) through Edinburgh. Locals favor the stretch between Roseburn and Dean Village, but the 1.5-mile walk from Dean Village to the Royal Botanic Garden is also good. For more information on these and other hikes, ask at the TI for the free *Walks In and Around Edinburgh* one-page flier (if it's unavailable, consider their £2 guide to walks).

Prestonfield Golf Club—At the foot of Arthur's Seat, just a mile and a half from town, the Prestonfield Golf Club has golfers feeling like they're in a country estate (£32–38/person plus £10 for clubs, dress code enforced, 6 Priestfield Road North, tel. 0131/667-9665, www.prestonfieldgolf.com).

Shopping—The streets to browse are Princes Street (the elegant old Jenners department store is nearby on Rose Street, at St. Andrew Square), Victoria Street (antiques galore), Nicolson Street (south of the Royal Mile, line of interesting secondhand stores), and the Royal Mile (touristy but competitively priced). Shops are usually open from 10:00 to 18:00 (later on Thu).

Near Edinburgh

▲▲*Britannia*—This much-revered vessel, which transported Britain's royal family for more than 40 years and 900 voyages before being retired in 1997, is permanently moored at the Ocean Terminal Shopping Mall in Edinburgh's port of Leith. It's open to the public and worth the 15-minute bus or taxi ride from the center. Explore the museum, filled with engrossing royal-family-afloat history. Then, armed with your included audioguide, you're welcome aboard.

This was the last in a line of royal yachts that stretches back to 1660. With all its royal functions, the ship required a crew of more than 200. The captain's bridge feels like it's been preserved from the day it was launched in 1953. Queen Elizabeth II, who enjoyed the ship for 40 years, said, "This is the only place I can truly relax." The Sunny Lounge, just off the back Veranda Deck, was the queen's favorite, with teak from Burma (now Myanmar, in Southeast Asia) and the same phone system she was used to in Buckingham Palace.

The back deck was the favorite place for outdoor entertainment. Ronald Reagan, Boris Yeltsin, Bill Clinton, and Nelson Mandela all sipped champagne here with the Queen. When she wasn't entertaining, the Queen liked it quiet. The crew wore sneakers, communicated in hand signals, and (at least near the Queen's quarters) had to be finished with all their work by 8:00 in the morning.

The state dining room, decorated with gifts given by the ship's many noteworthy guests, enabled the Queen to entertain a good-size crowd. The silver pantry was just down the hall. The drawing room, while rather simple, was perfect for casual relaxing among royals. Princess Diana played the piano, which is bolted to the deck. Royal family photos evoke the fine times the Windsors enjoyed on the *Britannia*. Visitors can also see the crew's quarters and engine room.

Cost and Hours: £10.50, daily July–Sept 9:30–16:30, April–June and Oct 10:00–16:00, Nov–March 10:00–15:30, these are last entry times, tea room, tel. 0131/555-5566, www.royalyacht britannia.co.uk.

Getting There: From central Edinburgh, catch Lothian bus #1, #11, #22, #34, or #35 at Waverley Bridge to Ocean Terminal. If you're doing a city bus tour, consider the Majestic Tour, which includes transportation to the *Britannia*.

Rosslyn Chapel—Founded in 1446 by the Knights Templar, this church became famous for its role in the final scenes of *The Da Vinci Code* (£7.50, Mon–Sat 9:30–18:00, until 17:00 Oct–March, Sun 12:00–16:45 year-round, last entry 30 minutes before closing, no photos, located in Roslin Village, www.rosslynchapel.org.uk). To get to the chapel by bus, ride Lothian bus #15 from the station at St. Andrew Square (1–2/hour). By car, take A701 to Penicuik/Peebles, and follow signs for *Roslin;* once you're in the village, you'll see signs for the chapel.

Royal Botanic Garden—Britain's second-oldest botanical garden (after Oxford) was established in 1670 for medicinal herbs, and this 70-acre refuge is now one of Europe's best (gardens free, greenhouse admission-£4, daily April–Sept 10:00–19:00, March and Oct 10:00–18:00, Nov–Feb 10:00–16:00, 1-hour tours April–Sept daily at 10:00 and 14:00 for £3, café, a mile north of the city center at Inverleith Row; take Lothian bus #8, #23, or #27; Majestic Tour stops here, tel. 0131/552-7171, www .rbge.org.uk).

Experiences in Edinburgh

Edinburgh Festival

One of Europe's great cultural events, Edinburgh's annual festival turns the city into a carnival of the arts. There are enough music, dance, drama, and multicultural events to make even the most jaded traveler giddy with excitement. Every day is jammed with formal and spontaneous fun. A riot of festivals—official, fringe, book, and jazz and blues—rages simultaneously for about three weeks each August, with the Military Tattoo starting a week earlier (the best overall website is www.edinburghfestivals .co.uk). Many city sights run on extended hours, and those along the Royal Mile that are normally closed on Sunday are open in the afternoon. It's a glorious time to be in Edinburgh—if you have (and can afford) a room.

The official **Edinburgh International Festival** (Aug 12–Sept 4 in 2011) is the original, more formal, and most likely to get booked up. Major events sell out well in advance. The ticket office is at **The Hub,** located in the former Tolbooth Church, near the top of the Royal Mile (tickets-£8–64, booking from late March, office open Mon–Sat 10:00–17:00 or longer, in Aug 9:00–19:30 plus Sun 10:00–19:30, tel. 0131/473-2000, www.hubtickets.co.uk or www.eif.co.uk). Call and order your ticket through The Hub with your credit-card number. Pick up your ticket at the office on the day of the show or at the venue before showtime. Several publications—including the festival's official schedule, the *Edinburgh Festivals Guide Daily, The List,* the *Fringe Program,* and the *Daily Diary*—list and evaluate festival events.

The less-formal **Fringe Festival,** featuring "on the edge" comedy and theater, is huge—with 2,000 shows—and desperate for an audience (Aug 5–28 in 2011, ticket/info office just below St. Giles' Cathedral on the Royal Mile, 180 High Street, tel. 0131/226-0026, bookings tel. 0131/226-0000, can book online from mid-June on, www.edfringe.com). Tickets may be available at the door, and half-price tickets for some events are sold on the day of the show at the Half-Price Hut, located at the Mound, by the National Gallery (daily 10:00-21:00).

The **Military Tattoo** is a massing of bands, drums, and bagpipes, with groups from all over the former British Empire. Displaying military finesse with a stirring lone-piper finale, this grand spectacle fills the Castle Esplanade nightly except Sunday, normally from a week before the festival starts until a week before it finishes (Aug 5–27 in 2011, Mon–Fri at 21:00, Sat at 19:30 and 22:30, £15–50, booking starts in Dec, Fri–Sat shows sell out first, all seats generally sold out many months ahead, some scattered same-day tickets may be available; office open Mon–Fri 10:00–

16:30, closed Sat–Sun, during Tattoo open until show time and Sat 10:00–22:30, closed Sun; 32 Market Street, behind Waverley Station, tel. 0131/225-1188, www.edinburgh-tattoo.co.uk). The last day is broadcast as a big national television special.

The **Festival of Politics,** adding yet another dimension to Edinburgh's festival action, is held in August in the new Scottish Parliament building. It's a busy four days of discussions and lectures on environmentalism, globalization, terrorism, gender, and other issues (www.festivalofpolitics.org.uk).

Other summer festivals cover jazz and blues (early August, tel. 0131/467-5200, www.edinburghjazzfestival.co.uk), film (mid-June, tel. 0131/228-4051, www.edfilmfest.org.uk), and books (mid-late August, tel. 0131/718-5666, www.edbookfest.co.uk).

If you do manage to hit Edinburgh during a festival, book a room far in advance and extend your stay by a day or two. Once you know your dates, reserve tickets to any show you really want to see.

Nightlife in Edinburgh

▲▲**Literary Pub Tour**—This two-hour walk is interesting even if you think Sir Walter Scott was an Arctic explorer. You'll follow the witty dialogue of two actors as they debate whether the great literature of Scotland was high art or the creative re-creation of fun-loving louts fueled by a love of whisky. You'll wander from the Grassmarket, over the Old Town to the New Town, with stops in three pubs as your guides share their takes on Scotland's literary greats. The tour meets at The Beehive pub on Grassmarket (£10, book online and save £1, May–Sept nightly at 19:30, March–April and Oct Thu–Sun, Nov–Feb Fri only, call 0800-169-7410 to confirm, www.edinburghliterarypubtour.co.uk).

▲**Ghost Walks**—These walks are an entertaining and cheap night out (offered nightly, most around 19:00 and 21:00, easy socializing for solo travelers). The theatrical and creatively staged **Witchery Tours,** the most established outfit, offers two different walks: "Ghosts and Gore" (1.5 hours, May–early Sept only) and "Murder and Mystery" (1.25 hours, year-round). The former is better-suited for kids than the latter (either tour £7.50, includes book of stories, leave from top of Royal Mile, outside the Witchery Restaurant, near Castle Esplanade, reservations required, tel. 0131/225-6745, www.witcherytours.com).

Auld Reekie Tours offers a scary array of walks daily and nightly (£8–12, 50–75 minutes, leaves from front steps of the Tron Kirk building on Cockburn Street, tel. 0131/557-4700, pick up brochure or visit www.auldreekietours.com). Auld Reekie is into the paranormal, witch covens, and pagan temples, taking groups into

Sampling Whisky

While pub-hopping tourists generally think in terms of beer, many pubs are just as enthusiastic about serving whisky. If you are unfamiliar with whisky (what Americans call "Scotch"), it's a great conversation-starter. Many pubs (including Leslie's, described on next page) have lists of dozens of whiskies available. Lists include descriptions of their personalities (peaty, heavy iodine finish, and so on), which are much easier to discern than most wine flavors. A glass generally costs around £2.50. Let a local teach you how to drink it "neat," then add a little water. Learn how to swish it around and let your gums taste it, too. Keep experimenting until you discover "the nurse's knickers."

the "haunted vaults" under the old bridges "where it was so dark, so crowded, and so squalid that the people there knew each other not by how they looked, but by how they sounded, felt, and smelt." If you want more, there's plenty of it (complete with screaming Gothic "jumpers").

Scottish Folk Evenings—These £35–40 dinner shows, generally for tour groups intent on photographing old cultural clichés, are held in the huge halls of expensive hotels. (Prices are bloated to include 20 percent commissions.) Your "traditional" meal is followed by a full slate of swirling kilts, blaring bagpipes, and Scottish folk dancing with an "old-time music hall" emcee. If you like Lawrence Welk, you're in for a treat. But for most travelers, these are painfully cheesy variety shows. You can sometimes see the show without dinner for about two-thirds the price. The TI has fliers on all the latest venues.

Prestonfield House offers its kitschy Scottish folk evening—a plaid fantasy of smiling performers accompanied by electric keyboards—with or without dinner Sunday to Friday. For £40 you get the show with two drinks and a wad of haggis; £53 buys you the same, plus a four-course meal and wine (be there at 18:45, dinner at 19:00, show runs 20:00–22:00, May–Oct only). It's in the stables of "the handsomest house in Edinburgh," which is now home to the recommended Rhubarb Restaurant (Priestfield Road, a 10-minute walk from Dalkeith Road B&Bs, tel. 0131/225-7800, www.scottishshow.co.uk).

Theater—Even outside of festival time, Edinburgh i□
for lively and affordable theater. Pick up *The List* fo□
rundown of what's on (sold at newsstands for a few pounds).

▲**Live Music in Pubs**—Edinburgh used to be a good place for
traditional folk music, but in the last few years, pub owners—out
of economic necessity—are catering to college-age customers more
interested in beer-drinking. Pubs that were regular venues for folk
music have gone pop. Rather than list places likely to change their
format in a few months, I'll simply recommend the monthly *Gig
Guide* (free at TI, accommodations, and various pubs, www.gig
guide.co.uk). This simple little sheet lists 8 or 10 places each night
that have live music. Listings are divided by genre (pop, rock,
world, and folk).

Pubs in the Old Town: The **Grassmarket** neighborhood
(below the castle) bustles with live music and rowdy people spilling
out of the pubs and into what was (once upon a time) a busy market square. It's fun to just wander through this area late at night
and check out the scene at pubs such as Finnegans Wake, Biddy
Mulligan, and White Hart Inn. Thanks to the music and crowds,
you'll know where to go...and where not to. Have a beer and follow
your ear.

Pubs on the Royal Mile: Several bars here feature live folk
music every night. **Tass Pub** is a great and accessible little place
with a love of folk and traditional music and free performances
nearly every night from 21:00 (runs 18:00–21:00 on Sun, no music
on Tue). Drop by during your sightseeing—as you walk the lower
part of the Royal Mile—and ask what's on tonight (across from
World's End, #1 High Street, tel. 0131/556-6338). **Whistlebinkies**
is famous for live music (rock, pop, blues, South Bridge, tel.
0131/557-5114).

Pubs in the New Town: All the beer-drinkers seem to head for
the pedestrianized Rose Street, famous for having the most pubs
per square inch anywhere in Scotland—and plenty of live music.

Pubs near Dalkeith Road B&Bs: The first three listed below
are classic pubs (without a lot of noisy machines and rowdy twen-
tysomethings). Located near the Dalkeith Road B&B neighborhood, they cluster within 100 yards of each other around the
intersection of Duncan Street and Causewayside.

Leslie's Pub, sitting between a working-class and an upper-
class neighborhood, has two sides. Originally, the gang would go
in on the right to gather around the great hardwood bar, glittering
with a century of *Cheers* ambience. Meanwhile, the more delicate
folks would slip in on the left, with its discreet doors, plush snugs
(cozy private booths), and ornate ordering windows. Since 1896,
this Victorian classic has been appreciated for both its "real ales"
and its huge selection of fine whiskies (listed on a six-page menu).

Dive into the whisky mosh pit on the right, and let them show you how whisky can become "a very good friend." (Leslie's is a block downhill from the next two pubs, at 49 Ratcliffe Terrace.)

The Old Bell Inn, with a nostalgic sports-bar vibe, serves only drinks after 19:00.

Swanny's Pub is not quite as welcoming and plays music videos, but it's a quintessential hangout for the working-class boys of the neighborhood, with some fun characters to get to know.

A few blocks away, you'll find **Bierex,** a much younger and noisier scene. It's a favorite among young people for its cheap drinks (132 Causewayside).

Sleeping in Edinburgh

The advent of big, inexpensive hotels has made life more of a struggle for B&Bs, which are tending to go plush to compete. Still, book ahead, especially in August, when the annual festival fills Edinburgh. Conventions, rugby matches, school holidays, and weekends can make finding a room tough at almost any time of year. For the best prices, book direct rather than through the TI, which charges a higher room fee and levies a £4 booking fee. "Standard" rooms, with toilets and showers a tissue-toss away, are cheaper than "en suite" rooms (with a private bathroom). At B&Bs, you can usually save some money by paying cash; although most B&Bs take credit cards, many add the card service fee to your bill (about three percent of the price).

B&Bs off Dalkeith Road

South of town near the Royal Commonwealth Pool, these B&Bs—just off Dalkeith Road—are nearly all top-end, sporting three or four stars. While pricey, they come with uniformly friendly hosts and great cooked breakfasts, and are a good value for people with enough money. At these not-quite-interchangeable places, character is provided by the personality quirks of the hosts.

Most listings are on quiet streets and within a two-minute walk of a bus stop. Though you won't find phones in the rooms, most have Wi-Fi and several offer Internet access. Most can provide triples or even quads for families.

The quality of all these B&Bs is more than adequate. Prices listed are for most of peak season; if there's a range, prices slide up with summer demand. *During the festival in August prices are higher; B&Bs also do not accept bookings for one-night stays during this time.* Conversely, in winter, when there's no demand, prices get really soft (less than what's listed here). These prices are for cash; expect a 3–5 percent fee for using your credit card.

Near the B&Bs, you'll find plenty of great eateries (see "Eating

Sleep Code

(£1 = about $1.60, country code: 44, area code: 0131)
S = Single, **D** = Double/Twin, **T** = Triple, **Q** = Quad, **b** = bathroom,
s = shower only. You can assume credit cards are accepted
unless otherwise noted.

To help you sort easily through these listings, I've divided
the rooms into three categories based on the price for a
standard double room with bath (during high season):

$$$ Higher Priced—Most rooms £80 or more.
$$ Moderately Priced—Most rooms between £60-80.
$ Lower Priced—Most rooms £60 or less.

Prices can change without notice; verify the hotel's
current rates online or by email. For other updates, see www
.ricksteves.com/update.

in Edinburgh," later) and several good, classic pubs (see "Nightlife
in Edinburgh," earlier). A few places have their own private parking spots; others offer access to easy, free street parking, though the
neighborhood may convert to metered parking (ask about it when
booking—better yet, don't rent a car for your time in Edinburgh).

If you bring in take-out food, your host would probably prefer
you eat it in the breakfast area rather than muck up your room—
ask. The nearest launderette is Ace Cleaning Centre (which picks
up and drops off).

Getting There: This comfortable, safe neighborhood is a
10-minute bus ride from the Royal Mile. From the train station,
the nearest place to catch the bus (at least while tram construction
is underway), is around the corner on North Bridge (exit the station onto Princes Street, turn right, cross the street, and walk up
the bridge). If you're here after the Princes Street construction is
finished, use the bus stop in front of the H&M store (£1.20, use
exact change; catch Lothian bus #14, #30, #33, or #48, or First
bus #86). Tell the driver your destination is Dalkeith Road; about
10 minutes into the ride, after following South Clerk Street for
a while, the bus makes a left turn, then a right—depending on
where you're staying, you'll get off at the first or second stop after
the turn. Ping the bell and hop out. These buses also stop at the
corner of North Bridge and High Street on the Royal Mile. Buses
run from 6:00 (9:00 on Sun) to 23:00. Taxi fare between the train
station or Royal Mile and the B&Bs is about £7. Taxis are easy to
hail on Dalkeith Road if it isn't raining.

$$$ Hotel Ceilidh-Donia rents 17 soothing, contemporary
rooms with a pleasant back deck, a quiet bar, a free DVD lend-

EDINBURGH

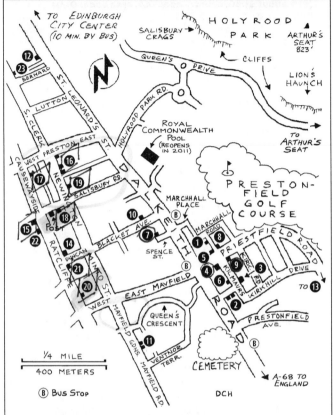

Edinburgh's Dalkeith Road Neighborhood

1 Hotel Ceilidh-Donia

2 AmarAqua Guest House & Aonach Mor B&B

3 Airdenair Guest House

4 Dunedin Guest House

5 Ard-Na-Said B&B

6 Kenvie Guest House

7 Gil Dun Guest House

8 Dorstan Hotel

9 Priestville Guest House

10 Belford Guest House

11 23 Mayfield Guest House & Glenalmond House

12 Blonde Restaurant

13 To Rhubarb Restaurant & Prestonfield House

14 The New Bell & The Old Bell Inn

15 Bierex Pub

16 Reverie Bar, Metropole Café & Wild Elephant Thai Restaurant

17 Hewat's Restaurant & Hanedan Turkish Restaurant

18 Hellers Kitchen

19 Il Positano Ristorante

20 Leslie's Pub

21 Swanny's Pub

22 Tesco Express Supermarket

23 Launderette

ing library, and a guest-only restaurant (Sb-£50–60, Db-£70–100, more in Aug and for special events, less off-season, includes breakfast, restaurant open 18:00–20:00 Mon–Thu only, free Internet access and Wi-Fi for guests, 14–16 Marchhall Crescent, tel. 0131/667-2743, www.hotelceilidh-donia.co.uk, reservations @hotelceilidh-donia.co.uk, Max and Annette).

$$$ AmarAgua Guest House is an inviting Victorian home away from home, with five welcoming rooms and a Japanese garden. It's given a little extra sparkle by its energetic proprietors and former entertainers, Dawn-Ann and Tony Costa (Db-£74-98 in June–Sept, Db-£64–88 in April–May and Oct, less in winter, more for fancy four-poster rooms, 2-night minimum, free Internet access and Wi-Fi, 10 Kilmaurs Terrace, tel. 0131/667-6775, www .amaragua.co.uk, reservations@amaragua.co.uk).

$$ Airdenair Guest House, offering views and a friendly welcome, has five attractive rooms on the second floor with a lofty above-it-all feeling. Homemade scones are a staple here, and Jill's dad regularly makes batches of "tablet"—a Scottish delicacy that's sweet as can be (Sb-£40, Db-£70–80, Tb-£85–95, less off-season, free Wi-Fi, 29 Kilmaurs Road, tel. 0131/668-2336, www.airdenair .com, jill@airdenair.com, Jill and Doug McLennan).

$$ Dunedin Guest House (dun-EE-din) is a fine value: bright, plush, and elegantly Scottish, with seven nice, airy rooms and a spacious breakfast room (S with private b on hall-£45–55, Db-£75, family rooms for up to five, less off-season, free Wi-Fi, 8 Priestfield Road, tel. 0131/668-1949, www.dunedinguesthouse .co.uk, reservations@dunedinguesthouse.co.uk, David and Irene Wright).

$$ Ard-Na-Said B&B is an elegant 1875 Victorian house with a comfy lounge. It offers thoughtful touches and luxurious modern bathrooms in seven bright and spacious rooms—including one ground-floor room with a pleasant patio (Sb-£35–50, Db-£60–80, huge four-poster Db-£70–100, Tb-£90–120, prices depend on size of room as well as season, family room, free Internet access and Wi-Fi, DVD players, free parking, 5 Priestfield Road, tel. 0131/667-8754, www.ardnasaid.co.uk, jim@ardnasaid.co.uk, Jim and Olive Lyons).

$$ Aonach Mor B&B's plush rooms have views of either nearby Arthur's Seat or walled gardens (Db-£65–85, more in July–Aug, less Nov–March, online specials, free Wi-Fi, 14 Kilmaurs Terrace, tel. 0131/667-8694, www.aonachmor.com, info@aonach mor.com, Chris and Lee).

$$ Kenvie Guest House, expertly run by Dorothy Vidler, comes with six pleasant rooms (one small twin-£56, D-£58–64, Db-£66–74, these prices with cash and this book through 2011—must claim when you reserve, family deals, free Internet access and Wi-Fi, 16 Kilmaurs Road, tel. 0131/668-1964, www.kenvie.co.uk, dorothy @kenvie.co.uk).

$$ Gil Dun Guest House, with eight rooms on a quiet cul-de-sac just off Dalkeith Road, is comfortable, pleasant, and managed with care by Gerry McDonald and Bill (Sb-£35–40, Db-£70–80, or £120 in Aug, great bathrooms, family deals, free Wi-Fi, pleasant garden, 9 Spence Street, tel. 0131/667-1368, www .gildun.co.uk, gildun.edin@btinternet.com).

$$ Dorstan Hotel is a little bigger than my other listings in this area, but it's still friendly and relaxed. Several of its 14 thought-fully decorated rooms are on the ground floor (S-£30–50, Sb-£35–55, Ds-£40–60, Db-£50–70, Tb-£60–100, family rooms and suites available, free Wi-Fi, lounge, parking lot, 7 Priestfield Road, tel. 0131/667-6721, www.dorstan-hotel.demon.co.uk, reservations @dorstan-hotel.demon.co.uk, Richard and Maki Stott).

$$ Priestville Guest House is homey, with a dramatic sky-light above the stairs, a sunny breakfast room, and cozy charm—not fancy, but more than workable, and great for families. The six rooms have Wi-Fi, VCRs, and a free video library (D-£50–64, Db-£56–72, Tb-£100, Q-£120, discount for 2 or more nights, free Internet access and Wi-Fi, family rooms, 10 Priestfield Road, tel. 0131/667-2435, www.priestville.com, bookings@priestville.com, Trina and Colin Warwick and their "rescue dog" Torrie).

$ The Belford Guest House is a tidy, homey place offering three basic rooms with renovated bathrooms and a warm welcome. The two en-suite rooms are twins; the lone double has its own bath-room outside the room (Sb-£45, Db-£60, family room, cheaper for longer stays, cash only, free parking, 13 Blacket Avenue—no sign out front, tel. 0131/667-2422, www.belfordguesthouse.com, tom @belfordguesthouse.com, Tom Borthwick).

Guest Houses on Mayfield Gardens

These two very-well-run B&Bs are set back from a busy four-lane highway. They come with a little street noise, but are bigger buildings with more spacious rooms, finer public lounges, and nice comforts (such as iPod-compatible bedside radios).

$$ At 23 Mayfield Guest House, Ross and Kathleen (and Grandma Mary) rent nine thoughtfully appointed rooms in an outstanding house. Every detail has been chosen with care, from the historically accurate paint colors to the "James Bond bath-rooms." Being travelers themselves, they know the value of little extras, offering a wide breakfast selection and a comfy lounge with cold soft drinks at an "honesty bar" (Sb-£55-65, Db-£65–80, bigger Db-£70–100, 4-poster Db-£80–110, family room for up to

4, free Internet access and Wi-Fi, swap library, free parking, 23 Mayfield Gardens, tel. 0131/667-5806, www.23mayfield.co.uk, info@23mayfield.co.uk).

$$ Glenalmond House, run by Jimmy and Fiona Mackie, has 10 beautiful rooms with fancy modern bathrooms (Db-£70–80, bigger 4-poster Db up to £95, Tb-£75–105, Qb-£80–120, 5 percent Rick Steves discount if you book direct and pay cash, less off-season, discount for longer stays, free Internet access and Wi-Fi, free parking, 25 Mayfield Gardens, tel. 0131/668-2392, www.glenalmondhouse.com, enquiries@glenalmondhouse.com).

Big, Modern Hotels

The first listing's a splurge. The next four are cheaper than most of the city's other chain hotels, and offer more comfort than character. In each case I'd skip the institutional breakfast and eat out. You'll generally pay £10 a day to park near these hotels.

$$$ Macdonald Holyrood Hotel, my only fancy listing, is an opulent four-star splurge, with 156 rooms up the street from the new Parliament building. With its classy marble-and-wood decor, fitness center, and pool, it's hard to leave. On a gray winter day in Edinburgh, this could be worth it. Prices can vary wildly (Db-£110–170, breakfast extra, check for specials online, near bottom of Royal Mile, across from Dynamic Earth, 81 Holyrood Road, tel. 0131/550-4500, www.macdonaldhotels.co.uk).

$$$ Jurys Inn offers a more enjoyable feeling than the Ibis and Travelodge (listed next). A cookie-cutter place with 186 dependably comfortable and bright rooms, it is capably run and well-located a short walk from the station (Sb/Db/Tb-£99, less on weekdays, can be much cheaper off-season and for online bookings, 2 kids sleep free, breakfast-£10, some views, Wi-Fi, laundry service, pub/restaurant, on quiet street just off Royal Mile and just above the train station, 43 Jeffrey Street, tel. 0131/200-3300, www .jurysinns.com).

$$$ Ibis Hotel, at the middle of the Royal Mile, is well-run and perfectly located. It has 99 soulless but clean and comfy rooms drenched in prefab American "charm." Room rates vary widely— book online to get their best offers (Db in June–Sept-£80–100, more during Festival, less off-season, breakfast-£7 extra, pay Internet access and Wi-Fi, 6 Hunter Square, tel. 0131/240-7000, fax 0131/240-7007, www.ibishotels.com, h2039@accor.com).

$$$ Edinburgh City Centre Holiday Inn Express rents 160 rooms with stark modern efficiency in a fine location, a five-minute walk from the train station. You can add up to two adults for £10 each, so two couples or a family can find a great deal here (Db-£95–135 depending on day, generally most expensive on Fri–Sat,

EDINBURGH

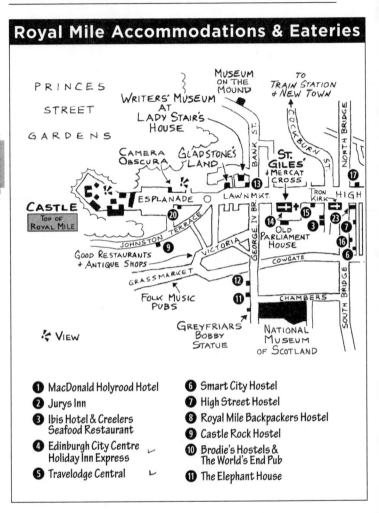

Royal Mile Accommodations & Eateries

- ❶ MacDonald Holyrood Hotel
- ❷ Jurys Inn
- ❸ Ibis Hotel & Creelers Seafood Restaurant
- ❹ Edinburgh City Centre Holiday Inn Express
- ❺ Travelodge Central
- ❻ Smart City Hostel
- ❼ High Street Hostel
- ❽ Royal Mile Backpackers Hostel
- ❾ Castle Rock Hostel
- ❿ Brodie's Hostels & The World's End Pub
- ⓫ The Elephant House

much more during Festival, cheaper off-season, for best rates book online, includes breakfast, free Wi-Fi, just down Leith Street from the station at 16 Picardy Place, tel. 0131/558-2300, www.hiexpress .co.uk). There's another location just off the Royal Mile (Db-£95– 135, 300 Cowgate, tel. 0131/524-8400).

$$ Travelodge Central has 193 well-located, no-nonsense rooms, all decorated in dark blue. All rooms are the same and suitable for two adults with two kids, or three adults. While sleepable, it has a cheap feel with a quickly revolving staff (Sb/ Db/Tb-£60–70, weekend Db-£70–85, Aug Db-£150, cheaper off-season and when booked online in advance, breakfast-£8 extra, 33 St. Mary's Street, a block off Royal Mile, tel. 0871-984-8484,

NOT TO SCALE — CASTLE TO PALACE OF HOLYROODHOUSE IS ABOUT 1 MILE

JOHN KNOX HOUSE

CANONGATE CHURCH

WHITE HORSE CLOSE

ABBEYHILL

QUEEN'S GALLERY

PEOPLE'S STORY

CANONGATE

PALACE OF HOLYROOD-HOUSE

BOTTOM OF ROYAL MILE

MUSEUM OF CHILDHOOD

MUSEUM OF EDINBURGH

STREET

ST MARY'S

HOLYROOD RD.

SCOTTISH PARLIAMENT

DYNAMIC EARTH

QUEEN'S DRIVE

TRAIL TO ARTHUR'S SEAT

HOLYROOD PARK

DCH

⑫ The Outsider Restaurant
⑬ Deacon Brodie's Tavern
⑭ St. Giles' Cathedral Café
⑮ Always Sunday Food Co.
⑯ Piemaker Café
⑰ Dubh Prais Scottish Rest.

⑱ Wedgwood Restaurant
⑲ David Bann Restaurant
⑳ The Witchery by the Castle
㉑ Clarinda's Tea Room
㉒ Tass Pub
㉓ Whistlebinkies Pub

www.travelodge.co.uk). They have two other locations in the New Town: at 37–43 Rose Street and at 3 Waterloo Place, on the east end of Princes Street.

Hostels

Edinburgh has two five-star hostels with dorm beds for about £20, slick modern efficiency, and careful management. They offer the best cheap beds in town. These places welcome families—travelers of any age feel comfortable here. Anyone on a tight budget wanting a twin room should think of these as simple hotels. The alternative is one of Edinburgh's scruffy bohemian hostels, each of which offers a youthful, mellow ambience and beds for around £15.

$ Edinburgh Central Youth Hostel rents 300 beds in rooms with one to eight beds (all with private bathrooms and lockers). Guests can eat cheap in the cafeteria or cook for the cost of groceries in the members' kitchen. Prices include sheets; towel rental costs extra (£16–28/person in 4- to 8-bed rooms, Sb-£34–49, Db-£51–95, Tb-£67–115, Qb-£89–145, depends on season, nonmembers pay £1 extra per night, single-sex dorms, £6 cooked breakfast, £4.25 continental breakfast, open 24/7, pay Internet access and Wi-Fi, laundry facilities, 10-minute walk to Waverley Station, Lothian bus #22 from station, 9 Haddington Place off Leith Walk, tel. 0131/524-2090. www.syha.org.uk).

$ Smart City Hostel is a godsend for backpackers and anyone looking for simple, efficient rooms in the old center for cheap. You'll pay £13–28 (depends on season) for a bed in an austere, industrial-strength 4- to 12-bed dorm—each with its own private bathroom. But it can get crazy with raucous weekend stag and hen parties. The Smart City Café in the basement has an inviting lounge with cheap meals. Half of the rooms function as a university dorm during the school year, becoming available just in time for the tourists (620 beds, Db-£50–125, bunky Qb-£70–150, includes linens and towels, £5 cooked breakfast, some female-only rooms, lockers, kitchen, lots of modern and efficient extras, free Wi-Fi, coin-op laundry, 50 Blackfriars Street, tel. 0131/524-1989, www.smartcityhostels.com, info@smartcityhostels.com).

Cheap and Scruffy Bohemian Hostels in the Center: These first three sister hostels—popular crash pads for young, hip backpackers—are beautifully located in the noisy center (£13.50–18 depending on time of year, twin D-£40–55, www.scotlandstop hostels.com): **High Street Hostel** (130 beds, 8 Blackfriars Street, just off High Street/Royal Mile, tel. 0131/557-3984); **Royal Mile Backpackers** (40 beds, dorms only—no private rooms, 105 High Street, tel. 0131/557-6120); and **Castle Rock Hostel** (200 beds, just below the castle and above the pubs, 15 Johnston Terrace, tel. 0131/225-9666). **Brodie's Hostels,** somewhere between spartan and dumpy in the middle of the Royal Mile, rents 130 cheap beds in 4- to 16-bed dorms (£10–13 beds, D-£39, Db-£45, includes linens, lockers, kitchen, Internet access-£1/20 minutes, laundry, 93 High Street, tel. 0131/556-2223, www.brodieshostels.co.uk).

Eating in Edinburgh

Reservations for restaurants are essential in August and on weekends, and a good idea anytime. All restaurants in Scotland are smoke-free.

Along the Royal Mile

Historic pubs and doily cafés with reasonable, unremarkable meals abound. Though the eateries along this most-crowded stretch of the city are invariably touristy, the scene is fun and competition makes a well-chosen place a good value. Here are some handy, affordable options for a good bite to eat (listed in downhill order). Sprinkled in this list are some places a block or two off the main drag offering better values—and correspondingly filled with more locals than tourists.

The first two restaurants are in a cluster of pleasant eateries happily removed from the Royal Mile melee. Consider stopping at one of these on your way to the National Museum of Scotland, which is a half-block away.

The Elephant House, two blocks out of the touristy zone with an unmarked front door, is a comfy neighborhood coffee shop

where relaxed patrons browse newspapers in the stay-awhile back room, listen to soft rock, enjoy the castle and cemetery vistas, and sip coffee or munch a light meal. During the day you'll pick up food at the counter and grab your own seat; after 18:00, the café switches to table service. It's easy to imagine J. K. Rowling annoying waiters with her baby pram while spending long afternoons here writing the first Harry Potter book (£7 plates, "gourmet" pizza, great desserts, daily 8:00–23:00, 4 computers with cheap and fast Internet access, vegetarian options, 2 blocks south of Royal Mile near National Museum of Scotland at 21 George IV Bridge, tel. 0131/220-5355).

The Outsider, also without a hint of Royal Mile tourism, is a sleek spot serving creative and trendy cuisine (good fish and grilled meats and vegetables) in a minimalist, stylish, hardwood, candlelit castle-view setting. It's noisy with enthusiasm, and the service is crisp and youthful. As you'll be competing with yuppies, reserve for dinner (£6 lunch plates, £11–14 entrées, always a vegetarian course, good wines by the glass, daily 12:00–23:00, 30 yards up from Elephant House at 15 George IV Bridge, tel. 0131/226-3131).

Deacon Brodie's Tavern, at a dead-center location on the Royal Mile, is a sloppy pub on the ground floor with a sloppy restaurant upstairs serving basic £9 pub meals. While painfully touristy, it comes with a fun history (daily 10:00–22:00, hearty salads, kids' menu, kids welcome upstairs—but they're not allowed to enter after 20:00, tel. 0131/220-0317).

St. Giles' Cathedral Café, hiding under the landmark church, is *the* place for paupers to munch prayerfully. Stairs on the back side of the church lead into the basement, where you'll find simple, light lunches from 11:45 and coffee with cakes all day (Mon–Sat 9:00–17:00, Sun 11:00–16:30, open a little later during Festival, tel. 0131/225-5147).

Always Sunday Food Company is a tiny place with a wonderful formula. It's a flexible fantasy of Scottish and Mediterranean hot dishes, fresh salads, smoked salmon, sharp cheese, and homemade desserts. You're invited to mix and match at their user-friendly create-a-lunch buffet line. They use healthy ingredients and are sensitive to diet concerns. Sit inside or people-watch from Royal Mile tables outside (£6 lunches, Mon–Fri 8:00–18:00, Sat–Sun 9:00–18:00, 30 yards below St. Giles' Cathedral at 170 High Street, tel. 0131/622-0667).

Creelers Seafood Restaurant's Tim and Fran James have been fishing and feeding since 1995. This respected eatery creates a kind of rough, honest, unpretentious ambience with fresh seafood you'd expect from this salty part of Scotland (£18–20 entrées, £8–10 lunch and £17–20 early-dinner specials 17:30–18:45, open daily 12:00–14:30 & 17:30–22:00, open all day Sat, reservations smart, 30 yards off the Royal Mile at 3 Hunter Square, tel. 0131/220-4447).

Piemaker is a great place to grab a quick, cheap, and tasty meal, especially if you're in a hurry. Their meat pies and pastries—try the cherry—are "so fresh they'll pinch your bum and call you darlin'" (most everything under £3, Tue–Sat 9:00–24:00, Sun 11:00–18:00, Mon 9:00–19:00, about 100 yards off the Royal Mile at 38 South Bridge, tel. 0131/556-8566).

Dubh Prais Scottish Restaurant is a dressy nine-table place filling a cellar 10 steps and a world away from the High Street bustle. The owner-chef, James McWilliams, proudly serves Scottish "fayre" at its very best (including gourmet haggis). The daily specials are not printed, to guard against "zombie waiters." They like to get to know you a bit by explaining things (£16-19 entrées, £27 dinners, open Tue–Sat 17:00–22:30, closed Sun–Mon, reservations smart, opposite Radisson SAS Hotel at 123b High Street, tel. 0131/557-5732).

Wedgwood Restaurant is romantic, contemporary, chic, and as gourmet as possible with no pretense. Paul Wedgwood cooks while his partner Lisa serves with appetizing charm. The cuisine: creative, modern Scottish with an international twist and a whiff of Asia. The pigeon and haggis starter is scrumptious. Paul and

Lisa believe in making the meal the event of the evening—don't come here to eat and run. I like the ground level with the Royal Mile view, but the busy kitchen ambience in the basement is also fine (£10 two-course lunch, £7–9 starters, £17–24 entrées, fine wine by the glass, Mon–Sat 12:00–15:00 and 18:00–22:00, Sun 12:30–15:00, 267 Canongate on Royal Mile, tel. 0131/558-8737).

The World's End Pub, a colorful old place, dishes up hearty £8–10 meals from a creative menu in a fun, dark, and noisy space (daily 12:00–21:00, 4 High Street, tel. 0131/556-3628).

David Bann, just a three-minute walk off the Royal Mile, is a worthwhile stop for well-heeled vegetarians in need of a break from the morning fry. While vegetarian as can be, there's not a hint of hippie here. It's upscale (there's a cocktail bar), stylish (gorgeously presented dishes), serious about quality (David is busy in the kitchen), and organic—they serve polenta, tartlets, soups, and light meals (£6 starters, £11 entrées, decadent desserts, Mon–Fri 12:00–22:00, Sat–Sun 11:00–22:00, vegan options, 56–58 St. Mary's Street, tel. 0131/556-5888).

The Witchery by the Castle is set in a lushly decorated 16th-century building just below the castle on the Royal Mile, with wood paneling, antique candlesticks, tapestries, and opulent red leather upholstery. The emphasis is on fresh—and pricey—Scottish meats and seafood (£14 two-course, £30 three-course lunch specials 12:00–16:00, specials also good 17:30–18:30 & 22:30–23:30, £20–25 entrées, daily 12:00–16:00 & 17:30–23:30, reservations critical, tel. 0131/225-5613).

Clarinda's Tea Room, near the bottom of the Royal Mile, is charming and girlish—a fine and tasty place to relax after touring the Mile or the Palace of Holyroodhouse. Stop in for a £5 quiche, salad or soup lunch. It's also great for sandwiches and tea and cake anytime (Mon–Sat 8:30–16:45, Sun 9:30–16:45, 69 Canongate, tel. 0131/557-1888).

In the New Town

While most of your sightseeing will be along the Royal Mile, it's important that your Edinburgh experience stretches beyond this happy tourist gauntlet. Just a few minutes away, in the Georgian town, you'll find a bustling world of office workers, students, and pensioners doing their thing. And at midday, that includes eating. Simply hiking over to one of these places will give you a good helping of modern Edinburgh. All these places are within a few minutes' walk of the TI and main Waverley Bridge tour-bus depot.

Le Café St. Honoré, tucked away like a secret in the Georgian New Town, is a pricey but charming place with walls lined by tempting wine bottles. It serves French-Scottish cuisine in tight, Old World, cut-glass elegance to a dressy crowd (dinner specials

EDINBURGH

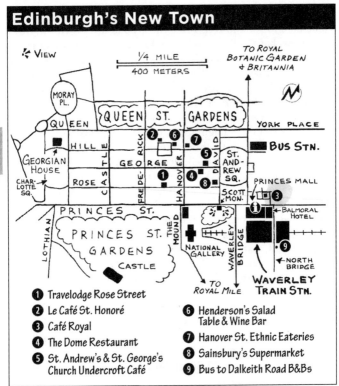

Edinburgh's New Town

① Travelodge Rose Street
② Le Café St. Honoré
③ Café Royal
④ The Dome Restaurant
⑤ St. Andrew's & St. George's Church Undercroft Café
⑥ Henderson's Salad Table & Wine Bar
⑦ Hanover St. Ethnic Eateries
⑧ Sainsbury's Supermarket
⑨ Bus to Dalkeith Road B&Bs

Mon-Sat before 19:00, Sun all night; open Mon–Fri 12:00–14:00 & 17:15–22:00, Sat–Sun 18:00–22:00; reservations smart, down Thistle Street from Hanover Street, 34 Northwest Thistle Street Lane, tel. 0131/226-2211).

Café Royal is a movie producer's dream pub—the perfect *fin de siècle* setting for a coffee, beer, or light meal. (In fact, parts of *Chariots of Fire* were filmed here.) Drop in, if only to admire the 1880 tiles featuring famous inventors (daily 12:00–14:30 & 17:00–22:00, until 21:30 in winter, bar food available during the afternoon, 2 blocks from Princes Mall on 19 West Register Street, tel. 0131/556-1884). There are two eateries here: the noisy pub (£10–20 meals, Mon–Fri 11:00–21:45, Sat–Sun 12:30–22:00) and the dressier restaurant, specializing in oysters, fish, and game (£20 plates, daily 12:00–14:30 & 17:00–22:00, reserve for dinner—it's quite small and understandably popular).

The Dome Restaurant, in what was a fancy bank, serves decent meals around a classy bar and under the elegant 19th-century skylight dome. With soft jazz and chic, white-tablecloth ambience, it feels a world apart (£12–14 plates until 17:00, £12–20 dinners until 21:45, Sun–Wed 10:00–22:00, Thu–Sat 11:00–22:00, modern international cuisine, open for a drink anytime under the dome or in the adjacent Art Deco bar, 14 George Street, tel. 0131/624-8634, reserve for dinner). As you leave, look up to take in the facade of this former bank building—the pediment is filled with figures demonstrating various ways to make money, which they do with all the nobility of classical gods.

The **St. Andrew's and St. George's Church Undercroft Café,** in the basement of a fine old church, is the cheapest place in town for lunch—just £3.50 for sandwich and soup. Your tiny bill helps support the Church of Scotland (Mon–Fri 10:00–14:30, closed Sat–Sun, on George Street, just off St. Andrew Square, tel. 0131/225-3847).

Henderson's Salad Table and Wine Bar has fed a generation of New Town vegetarians hearty cuisine and salads. Even carnivores love this place for its delectable salads and desserts (two-course lunch for £9, Mon–Sat 8:00–22:00, Thu–Sat until 23:00, closed Sun except in July–Aug 10:00–17:00, strictly vegetarian, take-away available, pleasant live music nightly in wine bar—generally guitar or jazz; between Queen and George Streets at 94 Hanover Street, tel. 0131/225-2131). Henderson's two different seating areas use the same self-serve cafeteria line. For the same healthy food with more elegant seating and table service, eat at the attached **Henderson's Bistro** (daily 12:00–20:30, Thu–Sat until 21:30).

Fun Ethnic Eateries on Hanover Street: Hanover Street is lined with Thai, Greek, Turkish, Italian, and other restaurants. Stroll the block to eye your options.

Supermarket: The glorious **Sainsbury's** supermarket, with a tasty assortment of take-away food and specialty coffees, is just one block from the Sir Walter Scott Monument and the lovely picnic-perfect Princes Street Gardens (Mon–Sat 7:00–22:00, Sun 9:00–20:00, on corner of Rose Street on St. Andrew Square, across the street from Jenners, the classy department store).

The Dalkeith Road Area, near Your B&B

All of these places are within a 10-minute walk of my recommended B&Bs. Most are on or near the intersection of Newington Road and East Preston Street. Reserve on weekends and during the Festival. The nearest grocery store is **Tesco Express** (daily 6:00–23:00, 158 Causewayside). For a cozy drink after dinner, visit the recommended pubs in the area (see "Nightlife in Edinburgh," earlier).

Scottish/French Restaurants

Blonde Restaurant, with a modern Scottish and European menu, is less expensive, more crowded than the others, with no set-price dinners. It's a bit out of the way, but a hit with locals and tough to get into—make reservations (about £15–17 for two courses, Tue–Sun 12:00–14:30 & 18:00–22:00, open only for dinner on Mon, good vegetarian options, 75 St. Leonard's Street, tel. 0131/668-2917, Andy).

Rhubarb Restaurant is the hottest thing in Old World elegance. It's in "Edinburgh's most handsome house"—a riot of antiques, velvet, tassels, and fringes. The plush dark rhubarb color theme reminds visitors that this was the place where rhubarb was first grown in Britain. It's a 10-minute walk past the other recommended eateries behind Arthur's Seat, in a huge estate with big, shaggy Highland cattle enjoying their salads al fresco. At night, it's a candlelit wonder. While most spend a wad here (£20–34 plates), take advantage of the two-course lunch for £17, or at least consider the £30 three-course dinner (Sun–Thu 12:00–14:00 & 18:30–23:00, Fri–Sat 12:00–14:00 & 18:00–23:00, afternoon tea served 15:00-18:00, reserve in advance and dress up if you can, in Prestonfield House, Priestfield Road, tel. 0131/225-1333, www.prestonfield.com). For details on the Scottish folk evening offered here, see "Nightlife in Edinburgh," earlier.

The New Bell serves up filling modern Scottish fare, from steak and salmon to haggis, in a Victorian living-room setting above the lovable Old Bell Inn (see below). Along with wonderfully presented meals, you'll enjoy white tablecloths, Oriental carpets on hardwood floors, and a relaxing spaciousness under open beams (£14.50 two-course or £17.50 three-course special until 18:45, £15 plates, open Tue–Sun 17:30–21:30, Fri–Sun also 12:30–14:00, until 22:00 Fri–Sat, closed Mon, always a veggie option, 233 Causewayside, tel. 0131/668-2868).

Scottish Grub and Pubs

The Old Bell Inn, with an old-time sports-bar ambience—fishing, golf, horses—serves simpler £8 pub meals from the same fine kitchen as the fancier New Bell (which is just upstairs, described above). This is a classic snug pub, all dark woods and brass beer taps, littered with evocative knickknacks, and has live folk music Sundays at 20:00. It comes with sidewalk seating and a mixed-age crowd (open daily until 24:00; food served 12:00–14:30 & 17:00–19:00, until 19:30 Mon–Thu, 233 Causewayside, tel. 0131/668-1573).

Bierex, a youthful pub, is the neighborhood favorite for modern dishes (£7–9 plates), camaraderie, and cheap booze. It's a spacious, bright, mahogany-and-leather place popular for its long and varied happy hours (daily until late, food served Mon–Fri 11:00–21:00, Sat–Sun 10:00–21:00, Wi-Fi for customers, 132 Causewayside, tel. 0131/667-2335).

Reverie Bar is just your basic, fun pub with a focus on food rather than drinking and free live music most nights from 21:30 (every other Sun-jazz, Tue-traditional, Thu-blues; £7–9 main dishes, food served daily 12:00–21:00, 3 Newington Road, tel. 0131/667-8870).

Hewat's Restaurant is the neighborhood hit. Sample Scottish cuisine, or their popular steak dishes, in this elegantly whimsical dining space (£10 dinner deals Mon–Thu until 19:30; £14.50 for two courses, £17.50 for three courses until 18:45; open Wed–Sat 12:00–14:00 & 18:00–21:30, Fri–Sat until 22:00, Mon–Tue 18:00–21:30 only, closed Sun, 19–21b Causeway, tel. 0131/466-6660).

Hellers Kitchen is a casual blond-wood space specializing in dishes using local produce and fresh-baked breads and doughs. Check the big chalkboard to see what's on (£5–8 sandwiches, £8–10 pizzas, Mon–Fri 8:30–22:00, Sat 9:00–22:00, Sun 10:00–22:00, next to post office at 15 Salisbury Place, tel. 0130/667-4654).

Metropole Café is a fresh, healthy eatery with a Starbucks ambience, serving light bites for £4 and simple meals for £7 (daily 8:30–22:00, always a good vegetarian entrée, free Wi-Fi, 33 Newington Road, tel. 0131/668-4999).

Ethnic Options

Wild Elephant Thai Restaurant is a small, hardworking eatery that locals consider the best around for Thai (£11–14 entrées, £13 three-course meal available 17:00–19:00, also does take-away, open daily 12:00–14:30 & 17:00–23:00, 21 Newington Road, tel. 0131/662-8822).

Il Positano Ristorante has a spirited Italian ambience, as manager Giuseppe Votta injects a love of life and food into his little restaurant. The moment you step through the door, you know you're in for good, classic Italian cuisine (£7–9 pizzas and pastas, £11–15 plates, daily 12:00–14:00 & 17:00–23:00, 85–87 Newington Road, tel. 0131/662-9977).

Hanedan Turkish Restaurant is generating a huge buzz. This friendly, contemporary 10-table place serves great Turkish grills and vegetarian specials at a fine price (£9 two-course special anytime, £9 entrées, open Tue–Sun 12:00–15:00 & 17:30–24:00, closed Mon, 41 West Preston Street, tel. 0131/667-4242, chef Gürsel Bahar).

Edinburgh Connections

By Train or Bus

From Edinburgh by Train to: Glasgow (4/hour, 50 minutes), **St. Andrews** (train to Leuchars, 1–2/hour, 1–1.25 hours, then 10-minute bus into St. Andrews), **Stirling** (2/hour, 50 minutes),

Pitlochry (6/day direct, 2 hours, more with change in Stirling or Perth), **Inverness** (every 2 hours, 3.5–4 hours, some with change in Stirling or Perth), **Oban** (3/day, 4.25 hours, change in Glasgow), **York** (1–2/hour, 2.5 hours), **London** (1–2/hour, 4.5 hours), **Durham** (at least hourly, 1.75 hours), **Newcastle** (2/hour, 1.5 hours), **Keswick/Lake District** (8/day to Penrith—some via Carlisle, then catch bus to Keswick, fewer on Sun, 3 hours including bus transfer in Penrith), **Birmingham** (at least hourly, 4–5 hours, some with change in York), **Crewe** (every 2 hours, 3 hours), **Bristol** near Bath (hourly, 6–6.5 hours), **Blackpool** (roughly hourly, 3–3.5 hours, transfer in Preston). Train info: tel. 0845-748-4950, www .nationalrail.co.uk.

By Bus to: **Glasgow** (4/hour, 1.25 hours, £3–6.30), **Oban** (7/ day Mon–Sat, 4–5 hours; 1 direct, rest with transfer in Glasgow, Perth, or Tyndrum), **Fort William** (7/day, 4–5 hours, 1 direct, rest with change in Glasgow or Tyndrum), **Portree** on the Isle of Skye (3/day, 7.5–8 hours, transfer in Inverness or Glasgow), **Inverness** (7/day, 3.5–4.5 hours). For bus info, call Scottish Citylink (tel. 0871-266-3333, www.citylink.co.uk) or National Express (tel. 0871-781-8181). You can get info and tickets at the bus desk inside the Princes Mall TI.

Route Tips for Drivers

To Hadrian's Wall: It's 100 miles south from Edinburgh to Hadrian's Wall; to Durham it's another 50 miles. From Edinburgh, Dalkeith Road leads south and eventually becomes A68 (handy Cameron Toll supermarket with cheap gas is on the left as you leave Edinburgh Town, 10 minutes south of Edinburgh; gas and parking behind store). The A68 road takes you to Hadrian's Wall in two hours. You'll pass Jedburgh and its abbey after one hour. (For one last shot of Scotland shopping, there's a coach tour's delight just before Jedburgh, with kilt-makers, woolens, and a sheepskin shop.) Across from Jedburgh's lovely abbey is a free parking lot, a good visitors center, and public toilets (£0.020 to pee). The England/ Scotland border is a fun, quick stop (great view, ice cream, and tea caravan). Just after the turn for Colwell, turn right onto A6079, and roller-coaster four miles down to Low Brunton. Then turn right onto B6318, and stay on it by turning left at Chollerford, following the Roman wall westward.

ST. ANDREWS

For many, St. Andrews is synonymous with golf. But there's more to this charming town than its famous links. Dramatically situated at the edge of a sandy bay, St. Andrews is the home of Scotland's most important university—think of it as the Scottish Cambridge. And centuries ago, the town was the religious capital of the country.

In its long history, St. Andrews has seen two boom periods. First, in the early Middle Ages, the relics of St. Andrew made the town cathedral one of the most important pilgrimage sites in Christendom. The faithful flocked here from all over Europe, leaving the town with a medieval all-roads-lead-to-the-cathedral street plan that survives today. But after the Scottish Reformation, the cathedral rotted away and the town became a forgotten backwater. A new wave of visitors arrived in the mid-19th century, when a visionary mayor named (appropriately enough) Provost Playfair began to promote the town's connection with the newly in-vogue game of golf. Most buildings in town date from this time (similar to Edinburgh's New Town).

Today St. Andrews remains a popular spot for both students and golf devotees (including professional golfers and celebrities such as Scotsman Sean Connery, often seen out on the links). With vast sandy beaches, golfing opportunities for pros and novices alike, playgrounds of ruins, a fun-loving student vibe, and a string of relaxing fishing villages nearby (the East Neuk), St. Andrews is an appealing place to take a vacation from your busy vacation.

Planning Your Time

St. Andrews, hugging the east coast of Scotland, is a bit off the main tourist track. But it's well-connected by train to Edinburgh (via bus from nearby Leuchars), making it a worthwhile day trip from the capital. Better yet, spend a night (or more, if you're a golfer) to enjoy this university town after dark.

If you're not here to golf, this is a good way to spend a day: Follow my self-guided walk, which connects the golf course, the university quad, the castle, and the cathedral. Dip into the Golf Museum, watch the golfers on the Old Course, and play a round at "the Himalayas" putting green. With more time, walk along the West Sands beach or take a spin by car or bus to the nearby East Neuk.

Orientation to St. Andrews

(area code: 01334)

St. Andrews (pop. 14,000), situated at the tip of a peninsula next to a broad bay, retains its old medieval street plan: Three main roads (North Street, Market Street, and South Street) converge at the cathedral, which overlooks the sea at the tip of town. The middle of these streets—Market Street—has the TI and many handy shops and eateries. North of North Street, the seafront street called The Scores connects the cathedral with the golf scene, which huddles along the West Sands beach at the base of the old town. It's an enjoyably compact town: You can stroll across town—from the cathedral to the historic golf course—in about 15 minutes.

Tourist Information

St. Andrews' helpful TI is on Market Street, about two blocks in front of the cathedral (July–Aug Mon–Sat 9:15–19:00, Sun 10:00–17:00; April–June and Sept–mid-Oct Mon–Sat 9:15–17:00, Sun 11:00–16:00; mid-Oct–March Mon–Sat 9:15–17:00, closed Sun; 70 Market Street, tel. 01334/472-021, www.visitfife.com or www.visitscotland.com). Pick up their stack of brochures on the town and region, and ask about other tours (such as ghost walks or witches walks). They also have Internet access (£1/20 minutes) and can find you a room for a £4 fee.

Arrival in St. Andrews

By Train and Bus: The nearest train station is in the village of Leuchars, five miles away. From there, a 10-minute bus ride takes you right into St. Andrews (£2.45, driver gives change for small bills; buses meet most trains, see schedule at bus shelter for next bus to St. Andrews; while waiting, read the historical info under the nearby flagpole). St. Andrews' bus station is near the base of

Market Street. To reach most B&Bs, turn left out of the station, right at the roundabout, and look for Murray Park on the left. To reach the TI, turn right out of the station, then take the next left and head up Market Street. Taxis from Leuchars into St. Andrews cost about £12.

By Car: For a short stay, drivers can simply head into the town center and park anywhere along the street. Easy-to-use meters dispense stickers (£0.85/hour, coins only, 2-hour limit, monitored Mon–Sat 9:00–17:00). For longer stays, you can park for free along certain streets near the center (such as along The Scores), or use one of the long-stay lots near the entrance to town.

Helpful Hints

Golf Events: Every five years, St. Andrews is swamped with about 100,000 visitors when it hosts the British Open (called simply "The Open" around here; the next one is in 2015). The town also fills up every year in early October for the Alfred Dunhill Links Championship. Unless you're a golf pilgrim, avoid the town at these times. If you are a golf pilgrim, expect room rates to skyrocket.

School Term: The University of St. Andrews has two terms: spring semester ("Candlemas"), from mid-February through May; and fall semester ("Martinmas"), from late September until mid-January. St. Andrews feels downright sleepy in summer, when most students leave and golfers take over the town.

Internet Access: You can get online for free at the **public library,** behind the church on South Street (Mon and Fri–Sat 9:30–17:00, Tue–Thu 9:30–19:00, closed Sun, tel. 01334/659-378). The TI also has two pay Internet terminals.

Walking Tour: June Riches offers good walking tours that bring St. Andrews' history to life. There's no set schedule, so call or email ahead to join a tour or arrange for one of your own (roughly £7/1.5 hours, prices vary by tour and group size, tel. 01334/850-638, june.riches@virgin.net).

Self-Guided Walk

Welcome to St. Andrews

This walk links all of St. Andrews' must-see sights and takes you down hidden medieval streets. Allow at least an hour, or more if you detour for the sights along the way.

• *Start at the base of the seaside street called The Scores, by the historical-information signpost near the green caddies' pavilion. (To get here from the bus station, turn left down City Road, then right onto North Street, then immediately left again onto Golf Place.)*

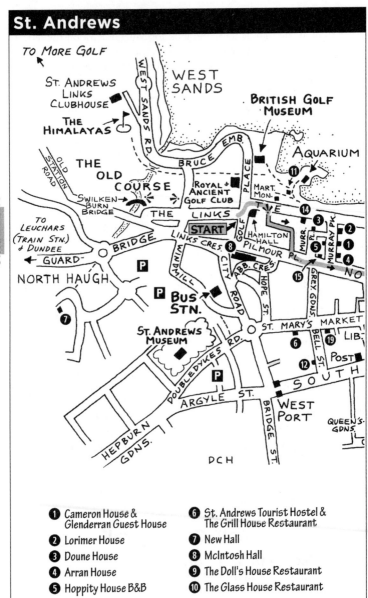

St. Andrews

ST. ANDREWS

TO MORE GOLF

ST. ANDREWS
LINKS
CLUBHOUSE

THE
HIMALAYAS

WEST SANDS RD.

WEST
SANDS

BRITISH GOLF
MUSEUM

AQUARIUM

OLD STATION ROAD

THE
OLD
COURSE

BRUCE EMB.

PLACE

MART.
MON.

⓫

SWILKEN
BURN
BRIDGE

ROYAL &
ANCIENT
GOLF CLUB

TO
LEUCHARS
(TRAIN STN.)
& DUNDEE

OLD STATION ROAD

THE   LINKS

GUARD-

BRIDGE

START

LINKS CRES.

WINDMILL

CITY   ROAD

⓮

GOLF PL.

HAMILTON
HALL

PILMOUR PL.

ⓑ

MURR.
PL.

⓭

MURRAY PK.

②
①
④

NO

NORTH HAUGH

ⓦ

P

P

BUS
STN.

ST. ANDREWS
MUSEUM

P

DOUBLEDYKES RD.

ABB. CRES.

HOPE ST.

⓯

GREY GDNS.

ST. MARY'S   MARKET

⑥

BELL ST.

⓳

LIB.

⓬

POST

SOUTH

ARGYLE   ST.

HEPBURN GDNS.

BRIDGE ST.

WEST
PORT

QUEEN'S
GDNS.

DCH

❶ Cameron House & Glenderran Guest House	❻ St. Andrews Tourist Hostel & The Grill House Restaurant
❷ Lorimer House	❼ New Hall
❸ Doune House	❽ McIntosh Hall
❹ Arran House	❾ The Doll's House Restaurant
❺ Hoppity House B&B	❿ The Glass House Restaurant

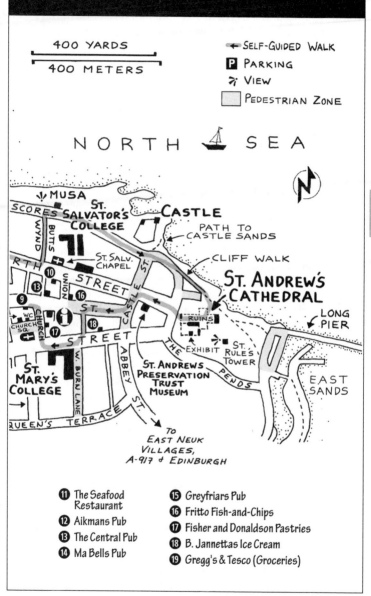

ST. ANDREWS

⑪ The Seafood Restaurant

⑫ Aikmans Pub

⑬ The Central Pub

⑭ Ma Bells Pub

⑮ Greyfriars Pub

⑯ Fritto Fish-and-Chips

⑰ Fisher and Donaldson Pastries

⑱ B. Jannettas Ice Cream

⑲ Gregg's & Tesco (Groceries)

The Old Course

You're standing at the mecca of golf. The 18th hole of the world's first golf course is a few yards away, on your left (for info on playing the course, see "Golfing in St. Andrews," later).

The gray Neoclassical building to the right of the 18th hole is the **Royal and Ancient Golf Club** (or "R&A" for short), which is the world's governing body for golf (like the British version of the PGA). The R&A is closed to the public, and only men can be members (which might seem harmlessly quaint...if it weren't persisting into the 21st century). Women can enter the R&A building only during the Women's British Open on St. Andrew's Day (Nov 30). Anyone can enter the shop nearby, which is a great spot to buy a souvenir for the golf-lover back home. Even if you're not golfing, watch the action for a while. (Serious fans might want to walk around to the low-profile stone bridge across the creek called Swilken Burn, with golf's single most iconic view: back over the 18th hole and the R&A.)

To your right is **Hamilton Hall**, an old hotel long used as a university dormitory and now under renovation to become swanky timeshares. According to town legend, the tall red-sandstone building was built to upstage the R&A by an American upset over being declined membership to the exclusive club. Between Hamilton Hall and the beach is the low-profile **British Golf Museum**.

• *If the weather's decent and you've got the time, take a detour and stroll the **West Sands**, the two-mile-long, broad, sandy beach that stretches below the golf courses. It's a wonderful place for a relaxing and invigorating walk. Or jog the beach, humming the theme to* Chariots of Fire *(this is the beach they run along in the famous opening* scene). *To reach the sands, walk past the R&A and hang a left—just after you've crossed over the creek, you'll find the ramp leading down to the beach.*

*To continue this walk, turn right and start walking up **The Scores**. The street's name may sound golf-inspired, but comes instead from the Norse word for "cliff-top." When you see the obelisk, cross the street.*

Martyrs' Monument

This obelisk commemorates all those who died for their Protestant beliefs during the Scottish Reformation. Walk up to the benches to get a good look at the cliffs on your right. For a time, the sea below was called "Witches' Lake" because of all the women and men pushed off the cliff on suspicion of witchcraft. The Victorian bandstand gazebo recalls the town's genteel heyday as a seaside resort, when the train line ran all the way to town.

Cross back to the other side of the street. Find the covered **alleyway** near Alexander's Restaurant (you may see it next to the

The Scottish Reformation

It's easy to forget that during the 16th-century English Reformation—when King Henry VIII split with the Vatican and formed the Anglican Church (so he could get an officially recognized divorce)—Scotland was still its own independent nation. Like much of northern Europe, Scotland eventually chose a Protestant path, but it was more gradual and grassroots than Henry VIII's top-down, destroy-the-abbeys approach. While the English Reformation resulted in the Church of England (a.k.a. the Anglican Church, called "Episcopal" outside of England), with the monarch at its head, the Scottish Reformation created the Church of Scotland, which had groups of elected leaders (called "presbyteries" in church jargon).

One of the leaders of the Scottish Reformation was John Knox (1514-1572), who learned at the foot of the great Swiss Reformer John Calvin. Returning to Scotland, Knox hopped from pulpit to pulpit, and his feverish sermons incited riots of "born-again" iconoclasts who dismantled or destroyed Catholic churches and abbeys (including St. Andrew's Cathedral). Knox's newly minted Church of Scotland gradually spread from the Lowlands to the Highlands. The southern and eastern part of Scotland, around St. Andrews—just across the North Sea from the Protestant countries of northern Europe—embraced the Church of Scotland long before the more remote and Catholic-oriented part of the country to the north and west. Today about 40 percent of Scots claim affiliation with the Church of Scotland, compared with 20 percent who are Catholic (still mostly in the western Highlands).

blue Gillespie Terrace sign, if it's not obscured by shrubs). Step into the alley and take a quick look back at the magnificent view of the West Sands (in the spring, this archway frames a rainbow nearly every day). Then follow the alley as it winds through the back gardens of the city's stone houses. St. Andrews' street plan typifies that of a medieval pilgrimage town: All main roads lead to the cathedral; only tiny lanes, hidden alleys, and twisting "wynds" such as this one connect the main east-west streets, which converge at the cathedral.

• *The wynd pops you out onto North Street. Make like a pilgrim and head left toward the cathedral. As you walk, listen to the seagulls. Is it just me, or can you detect a Scottish brogue in their squawking?*

Once you've passed the small cinema on your left, you'll see the church tower with the red clock face. Walk past **Butt's Wynd** *(no joke). For some reason, this street sign often goes missing.*

You're standing outside St. Salvator's Chapel, part of...

St. Salvator's College

If you're a student, tread carefully over the cobbles here to avoid stepping on the initials **PH.** They mark the spot where St. Andrews alum and professor Patrick Hamilton—the Scottish Reformation's most famous martyr—was burned at the stake. According to student legend, as he suffered in the flames, Hamilton threatened that any students who stood on this spot would fail their exams. (And you thought you had hard-nosed teachers.)

St. Salvator's Chapel, dating from 1450, is the town's most beautiful medieval church. Try the door—if it's open, you'll be treated to a Gothic gem, with a wooden ceiling, 19th-century stained glass, and (supposedly) the pulpit of reformer John Knox.

• *If the chapel's not open, pass through the archway into the quad of St. Salvator's College—which isn't an institution itself, but rather a group of university buildings. (The archway may be closed off—if so, head to Butt's Wynd and enter at the gate there...which may also be closed. If so, have a peek at the quad through the gate.)*

This grassy square, known to students as **Sally's Quad,** is the heart of St. Andrews University. As most of the university's classrooms, offices, and libraries are spread out across the medieval town, this quad is the one focal point for student gatherings. It's where graduation is held every July, and where the free-for-all food fight of Raisin Monday takes place in November. If you're feeling curious, push a few doors (some seemingly off-limits university buildings, many marked by blue doors, are actually open to the public).

On the outside wall of the chapel are cases holding notices and university information; if you're here in spring, you might see students nervously clustered here, looking to see if they've passed their exams. (Note the other door to the chapel, near the cases, which is worth trying if the one facing North Street is closed.)

Stroll the quad counterclockwise. On the east side, stop to check out the crazy faces on the heads above the second-floor windows. Find the **university's shield** over the door marked *School Six*. The diamonds are from the coat of arms of the bishop who issued the first university charter in 1411; the crescent moon is a shout-out to Pope Benedict XIII, who gave the OK in 1413 to found the university (his given name was Peter de Luna); the lion is from the Scottish coat of arms; and the cross is a stylized version of the Scottish flag (a.k.a. St. Andrew's Cross). On the next building to the left, facing the chapel, is St. Andrew himself (above door of building labeled *Upper & Lower College Halls*).

• *Exit the square at the west end, if the gate's open, and turn right into the wynd (if the gate's closed, backtrack out past Hamilton's initials and hang a right into Butt's Wynd). When the alley ends, you're back at The Scores. Cross the street and head to the right. The turreted stone build-*

ings along here are built in the Neo-Gothic Scots Baronial style, and most are academic departments. Head for the...

Museum of the University of St. Andrews (MUSA)

This free museum is worth a quick stop. The first room has some well-explained medieval paraphernalia, but the highlight is the earliest-known map of the town, made in 1580—back when the town walls led directly to countryside and the cathedral was intact. Notice that the street plan within the town walls has remained the same. The next room has some exhibits on student life; the rest is skippable. For another great view of the West Sands, when you leave the building walk out and around to the back to the small cliff-top patio (free; April–Sept Mon–Sat 10:00–17:00, Sun 12:00–16:00; Oct–March Thu–Sun 10:00–16:00, closed Mon–Wed; 7a The Scores, tel. 01334/461-660, www.st-andrews.ac.uk /musa).

• *Back on The Scores, walk left toward the castle. Along the way you'll pass stately St. Salvator's Hall (on your right, small sign on the wall), the most prestigious of the university residences and former dorm of Prince William. Just past St. Salvator's Hall are the remains of...*

▲St. Andrews' Castle

Overlooking the sea, the castle is basically just an evocative empty shell—another casualty of the Scottish Reformation. Built by a

bishop to entertain visiting diplomats in the late 12th century, the castle was home to the powerful bishops, archbishops, and cardinals of St. Andrews. In 1546, the cardinal burned a Protestant preacher at the stake in front of the castle.

In retribution, Protestant Reformers took the castle and killed the cardinal. In 1547, the French came to attack the castle on behalf of their Catholic ally, Mary, Queen of Scots. During the ensuing siege, a young Protestant refugee named John Knox was captured and sent to France to row on a galley ship. Eventually he traveled to Switzerland and met the Swiss Protestant ringleader, John Calvin. Knox brought Calvin's ideas back home and became Scotland's greatest Reformer.

Today's castle is the ruined post-Reformation version. Your visit starts with a colorful, well-presented exhibit about the history of the castle. Afterward, head outside to explore the ruins. The most interesting parts are underground: the "bottle dungeon," where prisoners were sent never to return (peer down into it in

Student Life in St. Andrews

Although most people associate St. Andrews with golf, it's first and foremost a university town—the home of Scotland's most prestigious university. Founded in 1411, it's the third-oldest in the English-speaking world—only Oxford and Cambridge have been around longer.

The U. of St. A. has about 6,000 undergrads and 1,000 grad students. Though Scots attend for free, others (including students from England) must pay tuition. Some Scots resent the high concentration of upper-class English students (disparagingly dubbed "Yahs" for the snooty way they say "yes"), who treat St. Andrews as a "safety school" if rejected by Cambridge or Oxford. The school has even been called "England's northernmost university" because it has as many English students as Scottish ones. (Adding to the mix, about a quarter of the students come from overseas.) Its most famous recent graduate is Prince William (class of '05). Soon after he started here, the number of female applicants to study art history—his major—skyrocketed. (He later switched to geography.)

As with any venerable university, St. Andrews has its share of quirky customs—as if the university, like the town's street plan, insists on clinging to the Middle Ages. Most students own traditional red woolen academic "gowns" (woolen robes). Today these are only worn for special occasions (such as graduation), but in medieval times, students were required to wear them always—supposedly so they could be easily identified in brothels and pubs. (In a leap of faith, divinity students—apparently beyond temptation—wear black.) The way the robe is worn indicates the student's progress toward graduation: First-year students (called "bejants") wear them normally, on the shoulders; second-years

the Sea Tower); and, around under the main drawbridge, the tight "mine" and even tighter "counter-mine" tunnels (crawling is required to reach it all; go in as far as your claustrophobia allows). This shows how the besieging French army dug a mine to take the castle—but were followed at every turn by the Protestant counterminers.

Just below the castle is a small beach called the Castle Sands, where university students take a traditional and chilly morning dip every May 1. Supposedly, doing this May Day swim is the only way to reverse the curse of having stepped on Patrick Hamilton's initials (explained earlier).

Cost and Hours: £5.20, £7.20 combo-ticket includes cathedral exhibit, daily April–Sept 9:30–17:30, Oct–March 9:30–16:30, last entry 30 minutes before closing, tel. 01334/477-196.

• *Leaving the castle, walk along the cliffside path, downhill toward the sea. Enter the gate to a graveyard. You're standing amid the ruins of...*

("semi-bejants") wear them slightly off the shoulders; third-years ("tertians") wear them off one shoulder (right shoulder for "scientists" and left shoulder for "artists"); and fourth-years ("magistrands") wear them off both shoulders.

There's no better time to see these robes than during the Pier Walk on Sunday afternoons during the university term. After church services (around noon), students clad in their gowns parade out to the end of the lonesome pier beyond the cathedral ruins. The tradition dates so far back that no one's sure how it started (either to commemorate a student who died rescuing victims of a shipwreck, or to bid farewell to a visiting dignitary). Today students participate mostly because it's fun to be a part of the visual spectacle of a long line of red robes flapping in the North Sea wind.

St. Andrews also clings to an antiquated family system, where underclassmen choose an "academic mother and father." In mid-November comes Raisin Monday, named for the raisins traditionally given as treats to one's "parents" (today students usually give wine to their "dad" and lingerie to their "mum"). After receiving their gifts, the upperclassmen dress up their "children" in outrageous costumes and parade them through town. The underclassmen are also obliged to carry around "receipts" for their gifts—often written on unlikely or unwieldy objects (e.g., plastic dinosaurs, microwave ovens, even refrigerators). Any upperclassmen they come across can demand a rendition of the school song (in Latin). The whole scene invariably turns into a free-for-all food fight in St. Salvator's quad (weapons include condiments, shaving cream, and, according to campus rumors, human entrails pilfered by med students).

▲▲St. Andrew's Cathedral

Between the Great Schism and the Reformation (roughly the 14th–16th centuries), St. Andrews was the ecclesiastical capital of Scotland—and this was its showpiece church. Today the site features the remains of the cathedral and cloister (with walls and spires pecked away by centuries of scavengers), a graveyard, and a small exhibit and climbable tower.

Cost and Hours: Cathedral ruins-free; exhibit and tower-£4.20, £7.20 combo-ticket includes castle; daily April–Sept 9:30–17:30, Oct–March 9:30–16:30, last entry 30 minutes before closing, tel. 01334/472-563.

Background: It was the relics of the Apostle Andrew that first put this town on the map and gave it its name. There are numerous legends associated with the relics. According to one of those (likely untrue), in the fourth century, St. Rule was directed in a dream to bring the relics northward from Constantinople. When the ship wrecked offshore from here, it was clear that this was a sacred place. Andrew's bones (an upper arm, a kneecap, some fingers, and a tooth) were kept on this site, and starting in 1160, the cathedral was built and pilgrims began to arrive. Since St. Andrew had a direct connection to Jesus, his relics were believed to possess special properties, making them worthy of pilgrimages on par with St. James' relics in Santiago de Compostela, Spain (of Camino de Santiago fame). St. Andrew became Scotland's patron saint; in fact, the white "X" on the blue Scottish flag evokes the diagonal cross on which St. Andrew was crucified (he chose this type of cross because he felt unworthy to die as Jesus had).

◑ **Self-Guided Tour:** You can stroll around the cathedral **ruins**—the best part of the complex—for free. First walk between

the two tall ends of the church, which used to be the apse (at the sea end) and the main entry (at the town end). Visually trace the gigantic footprint of the former church in the ground, including the bases of columns—like giant sawed-off tree trunks. Plaques identify where elements of the church once stood. Looking at the one wall that's still standing, you can see the architectural changes that were made over the 150 years the cathedral was built—from the rounded, Romanesque windows at the front to

the more highly decorated, pointed Gothic arches near the back. Mentally rebuild the church, and try to imagine it in its former majesty, when it played host to pilgrims from all over Europe. The church wasn't destroyed all at once, like all those ruined abbeys in England (demolished in a huff by Henry VIII when he broke with the pope). Instead, because the Scottish Reformation was more gradual, this church was slowly picked apart over time. First just the decorations were removed from inside the cathedral. Then the roof was pulled down to make use of its lead. Without a roof, the

cathedral fell further and further into disrepair, and was quarried by locals for its handy precut stones (which you'll still find in the walls of many old St. Andrews homes). The elements—a big storm in the 1270s and a fire in 1378—also contributed to the cathedral's demise.

The surrounding **graveyard,** dating from the post-Reformation Protestant era, is much more recent than the cathedral. In this golf-obsessed town, the game even infiltrates the cemeteries: Many notable golfers from St. Andrews are buried here (such as Young Tom—or "Tommy"—Morris, four-time British Open winner).

Go through the surviving wall into the former **cloister,** marked by a gigantic grassy square in the center. You can still see the cleats up on the wall, which once supported beams. Imagine the cloister back in its day, its passages filled with strolling monks.

At the end of the cloister is a small **exhibit** (entry fee required), with a relatively dull collection of old tombs and other carved-stone relics that have been unearthed on this site. Your ticket also includes entry to the surviving **tower of St. Rule's Church** (the rectangular tower beyond the cathedral ruins). If you feel like hiking up the 156 very claustrophobic steps for the view over St. Andrews' rooftops, it's worth the price. Up top, you can also look out to sea to find the pier where students traditionally walk out in their robes.

• *Leave the cathedral grounds through the gate on the town side of the cathedral. On your left, bending around the corner, is South Street, and the pointed stone arch of the gate called "the Pends"—which will supposedly collapse should the smartest man in Britain cross under it. Probably best not to test that legend—instead, head right to follow the road around to North Street. Just around the corner is the adorable...*

▲St. Andrews' Preservation Trust Museum and Garden

Filling a 17th-century fishing family's house that was protected from developers, this museum is a time capsule of an earlier, simpler era. The house itself seems built for Smurfs, but once housed 20 family members. The ground floor features replicas of a grocer's shop and a "chemist's" (pharmacy), using original fittings from actual stores. Upstairs are temporary exhibits, and out back is a tranquil garden (dedicated to the memory of a beloved professor) with "great-grandma's washhouse," featuring an exhibit about the history of soap and washing. Lovingly presented, this quaint, humble house provides a nice contrast to the big-money scene around the golf course at the other end of town (free but donation requested, late May–late Sept daily 14:00–17:00, closed off-season, 12 North Street, tel. 01334/477-629, www.standrewspreservation trust.org).

• *From the museum, hang a left around the corner (at the Castle Tavern) to South Castle Street. Just before you hit the top of Market Street, look for the tiny white house on your left, with the cute curved staircase. What's that on the roof?*

Turn right down Market Street (which leads directly to the town's center, but we'll take a curvier route). Notice how the streets and even the buildings are smaller at this end of town, as if the whole city is shrinking as the streets close in on the cathedral. Passing an antique bookstore on your right, turn left onto Baxter Wynd, a.k.a. Baker Lane. You'll pass a tiny garden on your right, before landing on South Street. To take an ice-cream detour, head left and walk 75 yards to the recommended **B. Jannettas.** *Otherwise, head right and immediately cross the street to take in the building marked by a university insignia.*

St. Mary's College
This is the home of the university's School of Divinity (theology). If the gate's open, find the peaceful quad, with its gnarled tree, purportedly planted by Mary, Queen of Scots. To get a feel of student life from centuries past, try poking your nose into one of the old classrooms.

• *Back on South Street, continue to your left. Some of the plainest buildings on this stretch of the street have the most interesting history—several of them were built to fund the Crusades. Our walk ends at charming Church Square, where you'll find the library (with Internet access; see "Helpful Hints," earlier) and recommended Fisher and Donaldson bakery (closed Sun). The TI, grocery store, and ATM are all nearby on North Street (a few yards down Church Street).*

If you want to do more sightseeing, there's one more museum just outside of the town center...

St. Andrews Museum
This small, modest museum, which traces St. Andrews' history from "A to Zed," is an enjoyable way to pass time on a rainy day. It's situated in an old mansion in Kinburn Park, a five-minute walk from the old town (free, daily April–Sept 10:00–17:00, Oct–March 10:30–16:00, café, Doubledykes Road, tel. 01334/659-380).

Golfing in St. Andrews

St. Andrews is the Cooperstown and Mount Olympus of golf, a mecca for the plaid-knickers-and-funny-hats crowd. Even if you're not a golfer, consider going with the flow and becoming one for your visit. While St. Andrews lays claim to founding the sport (the first record of golf being played here was in 1553), nobody knows exactly where and when golf was born. In the Middle Ages, St. Andrews traded with the Dutch, and some historians believe they picked up a golf-like Dutch game on ice, and translated it to the bonnie rolling hills of Scotland's east coast. Since the grassy beachfront strip just outside St. Andrews was too poor to support crops, it was used for playing the game—and, centuries later, it still is. Why do golf courses have 18 holes? Because that's how many fit at the Old Course in St. Andrews, golf's single most famous site.

The Old Course—The Old Course hosts the British Open every five years (next in 2015). At other times it's open to the public for golfing. Fortunately for women golfers, the men-only Royal and Ancient Golf Club doesn't actually own the course, which is public and managed by the St. Andrews Links Trust. Drop by their clubhouse, overlooking the beach near the Old Course (hours change frequently with the season—figure May–Aug daily 7:00–21:00, progressively shorter until 7:30–16:00 in Dec, www .standrews.org.uk).

Teeing Off at the Old Course: Playing at golf's pinnacle course is pricey (£130/person, less off-season), but accessible to the public—subject to lottery drawings for tee times and reserved spots by club members. You can play the Old Course only if you have a handicap of 24 (men) or 36 (women); bring along your certificate or card. If you don't know your handicap—or don't know what "handicap" means—then you're not good enough to play here (they want to keep the game moving, rather than wait for novices to spend 10 strokes on each hole). If you play, you'll do nine holes out, then nine more back in—however, all but four share the same greens.

Reserving a Tee Time: To ensure a specific tee time at the Old Course, it's smart to reserve a full year ahead. Call 01334/466-666 or email reservations@standrews.org.uk. Otherwise, some tee times are determined each day by a lottery. Call or visit in person by 14:00 the day before (or on Saturday, if you're looking to play on Monday) to put your name in (2 players minimum, 4 players max)—then keep your fingers crossed when they post the results online at 16:00 (or call to see if you made it). Note that no advance reservations are taken on Saturdays, and the courses are closed on Sundays—which is traditionally the day when townspeople can walk the course.

Other Courses: The trust manages six other courses (including two right next to the Old Course—the New Course and the Jubilee Course). These are cheaper, and it's much easier to get a tee time (£65 for New and Jubilee, £120 for Castle Course, £12–40 for others). It's usually possible to get a tee time for the same day or next day (if you want a guaranteed reservation, you'll need to make it at least 2 weeks in advance). The Castle Course has great views overlooking the town (but even more wind to blow your ball around).

▲**The Himalayas**—Named for its dramatically hilly terrain, "The Himalayas" is basically a very classy (but still relaxed) game of minigolf. Technically the "Ladies' Putting Green," this cute little patch of undulating grass presents the perfect opportunity for non-golfers (female or male) to say they've played the links at St. Andrews—for less than the cost of a Coke. It's remarkable how the contour of the land can present even more challenging obstacles than the tunnels, gates, and distractions of a corny putt-putt course back home. Flat shoes are required (no high heels). You'll see it on the left as you walk toward the clubhouse from the R&A.

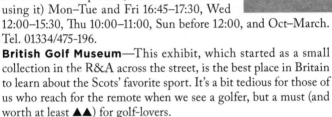

Cost and Hours: £2 for 18 holes. Except when it's open only to members, the putting green is open to the public June–July Mon–Sat 10:30–19:30; May and Aug Mon–Sat 10:30–19:00; April and Sept Mon–Sat 10:30–18:30. It's closed to the public (because members are using it) Mon–Tue and Fri 16:45–17:30, Wed 12:00–15:30, Thu 10:00–11:00, Sun before 12:00, and Oct–March. Tel. 01334/475-196.

British Golf Museum—This exhibit, which started as a small collection in the R&A across the street, is the best place in Britain to learn about the Scots' favorite sport. It's a bit tedious for those of us who reach for the remote when we see a golfer, but a must (and worth at least ▲▲) for golf-lovers.

The compact, one-way exhibit reverently presents a meticulous survey of the game's history—from the monarchs who loved and hated golf (including the king who outlawed it because it was distracting men from church and archery practice), right up to the "Golden Bear" and a certain Tiger. A constant two-and-a-quarter-hour loop film shows highlights of the British Open from 1923 to the present, and other video screens show scratchy black-and-white highlights from the days before corporate sponsorship. At the end, find items donated by the golfers of today, including Tiger Woods' shirt, hat, and glove.

Cost and Hours: £6, ticket good for 2 days and includes informative book about the history of golf; April–Oct Mon–Sat 9:30–17:00, Sun 10:00–17:00; Nov–March daily 10:00–16:00; last entry 45 minutes before closing; Bruce Embankment, in the blocky modern building squatting behind the R&A by the Old Course, tel. 01334/460-046, www.britishgolfmuseum.co.uk.

Sleeping in St. Andrews

Owing partly to the high-roller golf tourists flowing through the town, St. Andrews' accommodations are expensive. Note that during graduation week in June, hotels often require a four-night stay and book up quickly. Solo travelers are at a disadvantage, as many B&Bs don't have singles—and charge close to the double price for one person (I've listed "S" or "Sb" below for those that actually have single rooms). But the quality at my recommendations is

---

Sleep Code

(£1 = about $1.60, country code: 44, area code: 01334)
S = Single, **D** = Double/Twin, **T** = Triple, **Q** = Quad, **b** = bathroom, **s** = shower only. Unless otherwise noted, you can assume credit cards are accepted and breakfast is included.

To help you sort easily through these listings, I've divided the rooms into two categories based on the price for a standard double room with bath (during high season):

$$ Higher Priced—Most rooms £70 or more.
$ Lower Priced—Most rooms less than £70.

Prices can change without notice; verify the hotel's current rates online or by email. For other updates, see www.ricksteves.com/update.

---

high, and budget alternatives—including a hostel—are workable. All of these, except the hostel and the dorms, are on the streets called Murray Park and Murray Place, between North Street and The Scores in the old town. If you need to find a room on the fly, head for this same neighborhood, which has far more options than just the ones I've listed below.

$$ Cameron House has five old-fashioned, paisley, masculine-feeling rooms (including two nice singles that share one bathroom) around a beautiful stained-glass atrium (S-£40, Db-£80, discount for longer stays, prices soft Nov–March, free Wi-Fi, lounge, 11 Murray Park, tel. 01334/472-306, www.cameronhouse-sta.co.uk, elizabeth@cameronhouse-sta.co.uk, Elizabeth and Leonard Palompo).

$$ Lorimer Guest House has five comfortable, tastefully decorated rooms, including one on the ground floor (Db-£94–104 July–Sept, Db-£88–94 spring and fall, cheaper in winter, higher prices are for deluxe top-floor rooms, ask about discount for longer stays, free Internet access and Wi-Fi, 19 Murray Park, tel. 01334/476-599, www.lorimerhouse.com, info@lorimerhouse.com, Mick and Chris Cordner).

$$ Doune Guest House is golfer-friendly, with six straightforward, comfy, plaid-heavy rooms. The helpful owners are happy to arrange early breakfasts and airport transfers (S-£40–47, Db-£80–94, price depends on season, cheaper off-season, cash only, free Internet access and Wi-Fi, 5 Murray Place, tel. 01334/475-195, www.dounehouse.com, info@dounehouse.com).

$$ Arran House has nine modern rooms, including a single with a private bathroom across the hall (S-£50–55, Db-£80–90, three ground-floor rooms, family rooms, free Wi-Fi, 5 Murray

Park, tel. 01334/474-724, mobile 07768-718-237, www.arranhouse standrews.co.uk, jmgmcgrory@btinternet.com, Anne and Jim McGrory).

$$ Glenderran Guest House offers five plush, golf-oriented rooms and a few nice breakfast extras (Sb-£40–50, Db-£80–90, free Internet access and Wi-Fi, same-day laundry-£8, 9 Murray Park, tel. 01334/477-951, www.glenderran.com, info@glenderran .com, Ray and Maggie).

$$ Hoppity House is a recently remodeled, bright, and contemporary place, with neutral tones and built-in furniture that makes good use of space. You may find a stuffed namesake bunny or two hiding out among its six rooms. Golfers appreciate the golf-bag lockers on the ground floor (Sb-£45–55, Db-£75–90, deluxe Db-£90–110, family room, lower prices off-season, fridges in rooms, free Wi-Fi, 4 Murray Park, tel. 01334/461-116, mobile 07701-099-100, www.hoppityhouse.co.uk, enquiries@hoppity house.co.uk, helpful Gordon and Heather).

Hostel: **$ St. Andrews Tourist Hostel** has 44 beds in colorful 4- to 8-bed rooms about a block from the base of Market Street. The high-ceilinged lounge is a comfy place for a break, and the friendly staff is happy to recommend their favorite pubs (£12–14/ bed, no breakfast, kitchen, free Wi-Fi, self-service laundry-£3.50, towels-£1, office open 7:00–23:00, office closed 15:00–18:00 outside of summer, no curfew, St. Mary's Place, tel. 01334/479-911, www.standrewshostel.com, info@standrewshostel.com).

University Accommodations

In the summer (mid-June–early Sept), two of the University of St. Andrews' student-housing buildings are tidied up and rented out to tourists (does not include breakfast; website for both: www .discoverstandrews.com; pay when reserving). **$$ New Hall** has double beds and private bathrooms; it's more comfortable, but also more expensive and less central (Sb-£56, Db-£83, tel. 01334/467-000, new.hall@st-andrews.ac.uk). **$ McIntosh Hall** is cheaper and more central, but it only has twin beds and shared bathrooms (Sb-£35, Db-£60, tel. 01334/467-035, mchall@st-andrews.ac.uk). Because true single rooms are rare in St. Andrews' B&Bs, these dorms are a good option for solo travelers.

Eating in St. Andrews

The first three listings—owned by the same group—are popular and serve up reliably good international cuisine. Comparing their early-dinner specials may help you choose (www.houserestaurants .com).

The Doll's House offers cuisine with a French flair, with two floors of indoor seating and a cozy, colorful, casual atmosphere; the sidewalk seating out front is across from Holy Trinity Church (£7–10 lunches, £9–16 dinners, £13 two-course early-bird special 17:00–18:30, open daily 12:00–15:00 & 17:00–22:00, a block from the TI at 3 Church Square, tel. 01334/477-422).

The Glass House serves pizza, pasta, and salads in a two-story glass building with an open-style layout (£6 lunches, £8-11 dinners, £12 two-course early-bird special 16:00–18:30, open daily 12:00-23:00, second-floor outdoor patio, near the castle on 80 North Street, tel. 01334/473-673).

The Grill House offers Mexican-style food in a vibrantly colored space (£5 lunches, £7-11 dinners, £11 two-course early-bird special 16:00–18:30, open daily 12:00–22:00, St. Mary's Place, tel. 01334/470-500).

The Seafood Restaurant is St. Andrews' favorite splurge. Situated in a modern glassy building overlooking the beach near the Old Course, it's like dining in an aquarium. The place serves locally caught seafood to a room full of tables that wrap around the busy open kitchen. Dinner reservations are recommended (£22 two-course lunch, £26 three-course lunch, £45 three-course dinner, daily 12:00–14:30 & 18:30–22:00, The Scores, tel. 01334/479-475).

On Market Street: In the area around the TI, you'll find a concentration of good restaurants—pubs, grill houses, coffee shops, Asian food, fish-and-chips (see later), and more...take your pick. A block down Market Street, you can stock up for a picnic at **Gregg's** and **Tesco.**

Pubs: There's no shortage in this college town. **Aikmans** features a cozy wood-table ambience and frequent live music (open-mic folk night once weekly, traditional Scottish music upstairs about twice per month, other live music generally Thu–Sat, £5–7 pub grub, open daily 11:00–24:00, 32 Bell Street, tel. 01334/477-425). **The Central** is a St. Andrews standby, with old lamps and lots of brass (£5 sandwiches, £7 burgers, Mon–Sat 11:30–24:00, Sun 12:30–24:00, food until 21:00, 77 Market Street, tel. 01334/478-296). **Ma Bells** is a sleek but friendly place that clings to its (pre-remodel) status as one of Prince William's favorites (£4–7 pub grub, pricier bistro meals, daily 11:00–24:00, a block from the Old Course and R&A at 40 The Scores, tel. 01334/472-622). **Greyfriars** is in a classy, modern hotel near the Murray Park B&Bs (£5 light meals, £7–10 entrées, daily 12:00–20:30, 129 North Street, tel. 01334/474-906).

Fish-and-Chips: **Fritto** is a local favorite for take-away fish-and-chips, centrally located on Market Street near the TI (£4 fish-and-chips, £3 burgers, Mon–Sat 11:00–23:00, Sun 12:00–23:00, at the corner of Union and Market, tel. 01334/476-425). Brave souls will order a can of Irn-Bru with their fish (warning: it doesn't taste like orange soda). For what's considered the country's best chippies, head for the famous place in the East Neuk (described at the end of this chapter).

Dessert: Fisher and Donaldson is beloved for its rich, affordable pastries and chocolates. Listen as the straw-hatted bakers chat with their regular customers, then try their Coffee Tower—like a giant cream puff filled with rich, lightly coffee-flavored cream (£1–2 pastries, Mon–Fri 6:00–17:15, Sat until 17:00, closed Sun, just around the corner from the TI at 13 Church Street, tel. 01334/472-201). **B. Jannettas,** which recently marked its 100th year, features a wide and creative range of 52 tasty ice-cream flavors (£1.30 per scoop, daily 9:00–21:00, 31 South Street, tel. 01334/473-285).

St. Andrews Connections

Remember, trains don't go into St. Andrews—instead, use the Leuchars station (5 miles from St. Andrews, connected by buses coordinated to meet most trains, 2–4/hour). The TI has useful train schedules, which also list bus departure times from St. Andrews.

From Leuchars by Train to: Edinburgh (1–2/hour, 1–1.25 hours), **Glasgow** (2/hour, 2 hours, transfer in Edinburgh), **Inverness** (9/day, 3.25–4 hours, 1 direct, otherwise with 2 changes). Trains run less frequently on Sundays. Train info: toll tel. 0845-748-4950, www.nationalrail.co.uk.

Near St. Andrews: The East Neuk

On the lazy coastline meandering south from St. Andrews, the cute-as-a-pin East Neuk (pronounced "nook") is a collection of tidy fishing villages. While hardly earth-shattering, the East Neuk is a pleasant detour if you've got the time. The villages of Crail and Pittenweem have their fans, but Anstruther is worth most of your attention. The East

Neuk works best as a half-day side-trip (by either car or bus) from St. Andrews, though drivers can use it as a scenic detour between Edinburgh and St. Andrews.

Getting There: It's an easy **drive** from St. Andrews. For the scenic route, follow A917 south of town along the coast, past Crail, on the way to Anstruther and Pittenweem. For a shortcut directly to Anstruther, take B9131 across the peninsula (or return that way after driving the longer coastal route there). **Buses** connect St.

Andrews to the East Neuk: Bus #95 goes hourly from St. Andrews to Crail and Anstruther (50 minutes to Anstruther, catch bus at St. Andrews bus station or from Church Street, around the corner from the TI). The hourly bus #X60 goes directly to Anstruther, then on to Edinburgh (20 minutes to Anstruther, 2.25 hours more to Edinburgh). Bus info: toll tel. 0871-200-2233, www.traveline scotland.com.

▲Anstruther

Stretched out along its harbor, colorful Anstruther (AN-stru-ther; pronounced ENT-ster by locals) is the centerpiece of the East Neuk. The main parking lot and bus stop are both right on the harbor. Anstruther's handy **TI**, which offers lots of useful information for the entire East Neuk area, is located inside the town's main sight, the Scottish Fisheries Museum (April–Sept Mon–Sat 10:00–17:00, Sun 11:00–16:00; Oct Mon–Sat 10:00–16:00, Sun 11:00–16:00; closed Nov–March; tel. 01333/311-073, www.visitfife .com). Stroll the harborfront to the end, detouring inland around the little cove (or crossing the causeway at low tide) to reach some colorful old houses, including one encrusted with seashells.

The **Scottish Fisheries Museum** is true to its slogan: "We are bigger than you think!" The endearingly hokey exhibit sprawls through several harborfront buildings, painstakingly tracing the history of Scottish seafaring from primitive dugout dinghies to modern vessels. You'll learn the story of Scotland's "Zulu" fishing boats and walk through vast rooms filled with boats. For a glimpse at humble fishing lifestyles, don't miss the Fisherman's Cottage, hiding upstairs from the courtyard (£6; April–Sept Mon–Sat 10:00–17:30, Sun 11:00–16:30; Oct–March Mon–Sat 10:00–16:00, Sun 12:00–16:00; last entry one hour before closing, tea room, Harbourhead, tel. 01333/310-628, www.scotfishmuseum.org).

Eating in Anstruther: Anstruther's claim to fame is its fish-and-chips, considered by many to be Scotland's best. Though there are several good "chippies" in town, the famous one is the **Anstruther Fish Bar,** facing the harbor just a block from the TI and Fisheries Museum. As you enter, choose whether you want to get takeout or dine in for a few pounds more. While more expensive than most chippies, the food here is good—so good the place has officially been named "UK's Fish and Chip Shop of the Year" multiple times (£5–7 takeout, £7–9 to dine in, dine-in prices include bread and a drink, daily 11:30–21:30, until 22:00 for take-away, 42–44 Shore Street, tel. 01333/310-518).

GLASGOW

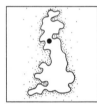

Glasgow (GLAS-goh), though bigger than Edinburgh, lives forever in the shadow of its more popular neighbor. Once a decrepit port city, Glasgow—astride the River Clyde—is both a workaday Scottish city and a cosmopolitan destination with an energetic dining and nightlife scene. The city is also a pilgrimage site of sorts for architecture buffs, thanks to a cityscape packed with Victorian architecture, early-20th-century touches, and modern flair (unfortunately, it also has some truly drab recent construction). Most beloved are the works by hometown boy Charles Rennie Mackintosh, the visionary turn-of-the-20th-century architect who left his mark all over Glasgow.

Edinburgh, a short train-trip away, may have the royal aura, but Glasgow has an unpretentious appeal. As my cab driver said, "The people of Glasgow have a better time at a funeral than the people of Edinburgh have at a wedding." In Glasgow, there's no upper-crust history, and no one puts on airs. Locals call sanded and polished concrete "Glasgow marble." You'll be hard-pressed to find a souvenir shop in Glasgow—and that's just how the natives like it. In this revitalized city, visitors are a novelty, and friendly locals do their best to introduce you to the fun-loving, laid-back Glaswegian (pronounced like "Norwegian") way of life.

Planning Your Time

For most visitors, a few hours are plenty to sample Glasgow. Focus on my self-guided walking tour in the city core, which includes Glasgow's two most interesting sights: Charles Rennie Mackintosh's Glasgow School of Art, and the time-warp Tenement House. With more time, add some of the outlying sights, such as

the cathedral area (to the east), Kelvingrove Gallery and the West End restaurant scene (to the west), and the Burrell Collection (a few miles out of town).

Day Trip from Edinburgh: For a full day, grab breakfast at your B&B in Edinburgh, then catch the 9:30 train to Glasgow (morning trains every 15 minutes; £10.70 same-day round-trip if leaving after 9:15 or on weekend); it arrives at Queen Street Train Station at 10:20. Call to reserve tickets to tour the Glasgow School of Art (aim for an early-afternoon time slot, so you can have lunch beforehand). Once in Glasgow, take my self-guided walk to hit all the major sights, making sure to reach the Tenement House by the last entry time (16:30). For dinner, consider heading out to the thriving West End restaurant scene, then hop the subway back to Queen Street Station (use the Buchanan Street stop) and catch the 21:00 train back to Edinburgh (evening trains every 30 minutes).

Orientation to Glasgow

(area code: 0141)

With a grid street plan, a downtown business zone, and more than its share of boxy office buildings, Glasgow feels more like a midsized American city than a big Scottish one—like Cleveland or Cincinnati with shorter skyscrapers, more sandstone, and more hills. While greater Glasgow is a sprawling city of 1.5 million people, the tourist's Glasgow has three main parts: the city center (including the Merchant City neighborhood), a cluster of minor sights near the cathedral (in the east), and the West End restaurant/nightlife/shopping zone. The easily walkable city center has a hilly northern area and two main drags, both lined with shops and crawling with shoppers: Sauchiehall Street (pronounced "Sockyhall," running west to east) and Buchanan Street (running north to south).

Tourist Information

The TI is opposite Queen Street Station in the southwest corner of George Square (at #11). They hand out an excellent free map, stock other Glasgow brochures, and can book you a room for a £4 fee. The TI sells tickets for the hop-on, hop-off bus tour; the Mackintosh Trail Ticket described below; and several Scotland sightseeing passes (Easter–May Mon–Sat 9:00–18:00, June and Sept until 19:00, July–Aug until 20:00, Oct–Easter until 17:00, Thu opens at 9:30 and Sun 10:00–18:00 year-round, tel. 0141/204-4400, www.seeglasgow.com or www.visitscotland.com). Buses to the West End depart from in front of the TI, and the hop-on, hop-off bus tour leaves from across the square.

Mackintosh Trail Ticket: This ticket, sold by the TI and all Mackintosh sights, covers entry to all "Charles Rennie Mac" sights and public transportation to those outside the city limits (£16/day, www.crmsociety.com).

Arrival in Glasgow

By Train: Glasgow, a major Scottish transportation hub, has two main train stations, which are just a few blocks apart in the very heart of town: **Central Station** (with a grand, genteel interior) and **Queen Street Station** (more functional, with better connections to Edinburgh, and closer to the TI—take the exit marked *George Square* and continue straight across the square). Both stations have pay WCs (£0.30) and baggage storage (Central Station—at the head of track 1, £7/bag for 24 hours; Queen Street Station—near the head of track 7, £5–7/bag). Unless you're packing heavy, it's easier to walk the five minutes between the stations than to take the roundabout "RailLink" bus #398 between them (£0.75, or free if you have a ticket for a connecting train).

By Bus: Buchanan Street Bus Station is at Killermont Street, just two blocks up the hill behind Queen Street Train Station.

By Car: The M8 motorway, which slices through downtown Glasgow, is the easiest way in and out of the city. Ask your hotel for directions to and from M8, and connect with other highways from there.

By Air: For information on Glasgow's two airports, see "Glasgow Connections," at the end of this chapter.

Helpful Hints

Safety: The city center, which is packed with ambitious career types during the day, can feel deserted at night. Avoid the area near the River Clyde entirely (hookers and thugs), and confine yourself to the streets north of Argyle Street if you're in the downtown quarter. The Merchant City area (east of the train stations) and the West End bustle with crowded restaurants well into the evening and feel well-populated in the wee hours.

If you've picked up a football (soccer) jersey or scarf as a souvenir, don't wear it in Glasgow; local passions run very high, and most drunken brawls in town are between supporters of Glasgow's two rival soccer clubs: the Celtic in green and white, and the Rangers in blue and red. (For reasons no one can explain, the Celtic team name is pronounced "sell-tic"—the only place you'll find this pronunciation outside of Boston.)

Sightseeing: Glasgow's city-owned museums—including the sights near the cathedral but not the biggies like the Glasgow School of Art or Tenement House—are free (www.glasgow museums.com).

Sunday Travel: Bus and train schedules are dramatically reduced on Sundays—most routes have only half the departure times they have during the week (though Edinburgh is still easily accessible). If you plan to leave Glasgow for a remote destination on Sunday, check the schedules carefully when you arrive. All trains run less frequently in the off-season; if you want to get to the Highlands by bus on a Sunday in winter, forget it.

Internet Access: You'll see signs advertising Internet cafés around the city core (near Central Station and Buchanan Street). Try **Yeeha Internet Café** (Mon–Fri 9:30–19:00, Sat 10:00–18:00, Sun 11:00–18:00, 48 West George Street, go upstairs to first floor, tel. 0141/332-6543, www.yeeha-internet-cafe.co.uk).

Local Guide: Joan Dobbie, a native Glaswegian and registered Scottish Tourist Guide, will give you the insider's take on Glasgow's sights (£85/half-day, £125/day, tel. 01355/236-749, mobile 07773-555-151, joan.leo@lineone.net).

Getting Around Glasgow

By City Bus: Various companies run Glasgow's buses, but most city-center routes are operated by First (price depends on journey, £3.20 for any two single journeys, £3.75 for all-day ticket, buy ticket from driver, exact change required). Buses run every few minutes down Glasgow's main thoroughfares (such as Sauchiehall Street) to the downtown core (train stations). If you're waiting at a stop and a bus comes along, ask the driver if the bus is headed to Central Station; chances are the answer is yes.

By Hop-on, Hop-off Bus Tour: This tour connects Glasgow's far-flung historic sights in a 1.25-hour loop (£11, ticket valid for 2 days; buy online, from driver, or at TI; daily 9:30–16:30, July–Aug 4/hour, spring and fall 3/hour, winter 2/hour until 16:00; stops in front of Central Station, George Square, and major hotels; tel. 0141/204-0444, www.citysightseeingglasgow.co.uk). If there's a particular sight you want to see, confirm that it's on the route.

By Taxi: Taxis are affordable, plentiful, and often come with nice, chatty cabbies—all speaking in the impenetrable local accent. Just smile and nod. Most taxi rides in the downtown area will cost about £5; from the West End, a one-way trip is about £6. Use taxis or public transport to connect Glasgow's more remote sights; splurge for a taxi (for safety) any time you're traveling late at night.

By Subway: The claustrophobic, orange-line subway runs in a loop around the edge of the city center. The "outer circle" runs clockwise, and the "inner circle" runs counterclockwise. (If you miss your stop, you can just wait it out—you'll come full circle in about 25 minutes. Or hop out and cross to the other side of the platform to go back the way you came.) Though the subway is essentially useless for connecting city-center sightseeing (Buchanan Street is the only downtown stop), it's handy for reaching sights farther out, including the Kelvingrove Gallery (Kelvinhall stop) and West End restaurant/nightlife neighborhood (Hillhead stop; £1.20 single trip, £3.50 Discovery Ticket lets you travel all day; subway runs Mon–Sat 6:30–23:30, Sun 10:00–18:00; www.spt .co.uk/subway).

Self-Guided Walk

Get to Know Glasgow

GLASGOW

Glasgow isn't romantic, but it has an earthy charm, and architecture buffs love it. The trick to sightseeing here is to always look up—above the chain restaurants and mall stores, you'll see a wealth of imaginative facades, complete with ornate friezes and expressive sculptures. These buildings transport you to the heady days around the turn of the 20th century—when the rest of Great Britain was enthralled by Victorianism, but Glasgow set its own course, thanks largely to the artistic bravado of Charles Rennie Mackintosh and his friends (the "Glasgow Four"). This walking tour takes three to four hours, including one hour for Mackintosh's masterpiece, the Glasgow School of Art (in summer, consider calling ahead to reserve your tour there).

• Begin at Central Station. Exit the train station straight ahead from the tracks (to the north, onto Gordon Street), turn right, and cross busy Renfield/Union Street. Continue one block, then turn right down Mitchell Street, and look up on the left side of the street to see a multistory brick water tower topped by a rounded cap. Turn left down a small alley (Mitchell Lane) just in front of the tower. Within about 25 yards, on the right, you'll see the entrance to...

The Lighthouse

This facility, which houses the Scotland Center for Architecture and Design, has two parts: a water tower designed by Charles Rennie Mackintosh in the early 1900s, and a modern glass-and-metal museum built alongside it. The Lighthouse is filled mostly with design exhibitions, lonely floors of conference rooms, and funny icons directing desperate men and women to the bathrooms (free, open Mon and Wed–Sat 10:30–17:00, Tue 11:00–17:00, closed Sun, 11 Mitchell Lane, tel. 0141/276-5365,

www.glasgowarchitecture.co.uk). This sight is skippable for most, but it does offer a fine view over the city. You have two options for scaling the heights: Take the elevator to the sixth-floor windows, or even better, climb up yourself. Head to the third floor, which features information about Mackintosh, along with architectural plans and scale models (linger here only if you're planning to skip the Glasgow School of Art), then climb the 135 spiral steps inside the water tower. The top has a wraparound balcony with 360-degree views.

• *Exit the Lighthouse to the right down the alley, then turn left onto the bustling pedestrian shopping drag called Buchanan Street—Glasgow's outdoor mall. One branch of the Mackintosh-designed Willow Tea Rooms is on your left at 97 Buchanan Street (two recreated Mackintosh interiors, tel. 0141/204-5242, other location described later in this walk). Across the street, find the second alley on the right, called Exchange Place. Before entering, look in the store windows of the former bank building to your left, at 98 Buchanan Street. A thousand antique sewing machines—count 'em—line three sides of the All Saints clothing store in a stunning geometric display worthy of this design-conscious city. Now walk down Exchange Place and pass through the arch, emerging onto the...*

Royal Exchange Square

This square—which marks the entrance to the shopping zone called Merchant City—is home to two interesting buildings. On your left as you enter the square is a stately Neoclassical bank-like building (today housing a Borders bookstore). This was once the **private mansion** of one of the tobacco lords, the super-rich businessmen who reigned here from the 1750s through the 1800s, stomping through the city with gold-tipped canes. During the port's heyday, these entrepreneurs helped make Glasgow Europe's sixth-biggest city.

In the middle of the square is the **Glasgow Gallery of Modern Art,** nicknamed GoMA. Walk around the GoMA building to the main entry (at the equestrian statue), and step back to take in the full Neoclassical facade. On the pediment (above the columns),

Glasgow Walk

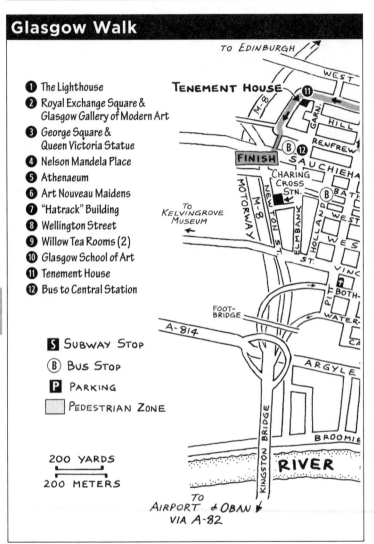

1. The Lighthouse
2. Royal Exchange Square & Glasgow Gallery of Modern Art
3. George Square & Queen Victoria Statue
4. Nelson Mandela Place
5. Athenaeum
6. Art Nouveau Maidens
7. "Hatrack" Building
8. Wellington Street
9. Willow Tea Rooms (2)
10. Glasgow School of Art
11. Tenement House
12. Bus to Central Station

S SUBWAY STOP

B BUS STOP

P PARKING

PEDESTRIAN ZONE

200 YARDS

200 METERS

TO EDINBURGH

TENEMENT HOUSE

FINISH

To KELVINGROVE MUSEUM

CHARING CROSS STN.

FOOT-BRIDGE

A-814

ARGYLE

BROOMIE

RIVER

KINGSTON BRIDGE

TO AIRPORT & OBAN VIA A-82

notice the funky, mirrored mosaic—an example of how Glasgow refuses to take itself too seriously. The temporary exhibits inside GoMA are generally forgettable, but the museum does have an unusual charter: It displays only the work of living artists (free, Mon–Wed and Sat 10:00–17:00, Thu 10:00–20:00, Fri and Sun 11:00–17:00, tel. 0141/287-3050).

• With the facade of GoMA behind you, turn left onto Queen Street. Within a block, you'll be at the southwest corner of…

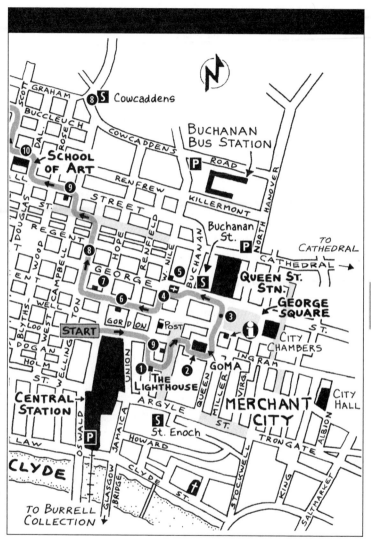

George Square

Here, in the heart of the city, you'll find the TI (just to your right as you come to the square), Queen Street Train Station, the Glasgow City Chambers (the big Neoclassical building to the east, not worth visiting), and—in front of that—a monument to Glaswegians killed fighting in the World Wars. The square is decorated with a *Who's Who* of statues depicting Glaswegians of note. Find James Watt (inventor of the steam engine), as well as Robert Burns and

Sir Walter Scott (Scotland's two most famous poets). Head north along the edge of the square to find a statue of an idealized, surprisingly skinny **Queen Victoria** riding a horse. But you won't see a statue of King George III, for whom the square is named. The stubborn Scots are still angry at George

for losing the colonies (i.e., us), and they never commissioned a statue of him.

• *Just past skinny Vic and Robert Peel, turn left onto West George Street and head for the tall church in the middle of the street (the Yeeha Internet Café—described earlier, under "Helpful Hints"—is on your right at #48). Cross Buchanan Street and go around the church on the left side, entering a little square called...*

Nelson Mandela Place

The area around this church features some interesting bits of architectural detail. First, as you stand along the left side of the church, look up and to the left (across from the church) to find the three circular friezes, on the first floor up, of the former **Stock Exchange** (built in 1875). These idealized heads, which were recently cleaned and restored, represent the industries that made Glasgow prosperous during its heyday: building, engineering, and mining.

• *Continue around to the back of the church and look to the right side of the street for the sandy-colored building at #8 (notice the low-profile label over the door). This is the...*

Athenaeum

Now a law office, this was founded in 1847 as a school and city library during Glasgow's golden age. (Charles Dickens gave the building's inaugural address.) Like Edinburgh, Glasgow was at the forefront of the 17th-century Scottish Enlightenment, a celebration of education and intellectualism. The Scots were known for their extremely practical brand of humanism; all members of society, including the merchant and working classes, were expected to be well-educated. (Tobacco lords, for example, often knew Latin and Greek.) Look above the door to find the symbolic statue of a reader sharing books with young children, an embodiment of this ideal.

• *Continue beyond the church and turn left onto West Nile Street; one block later, turn right onto St. Vincent Street. We'll enjoy more architectural Easter eggs as we continue along this street toward the Glasgow School of Art. After a block, on the left side of the street (at #115), look up to the second floor to see sculptures of...*

Art Nouveau Maidens

Their elongated, melancholy faces and downcast eyes seem to reflect Glasgow's difficult recent past, and decades of economic decline and urban decay. (They mirror similar faces in Art Nouveau paintings in the Glasgow School of Art, particularly in the artwork of Margaret MacDonald, Charles Rennie Mackintosh's wife and artistic partner.) As you walk along this street, keep your eyes above street level to take in classic Glaswegian sandstone architecture and the Mackintosh-influenced modern takes on it.

• *Another block down on the right (at #144) is the slender building locals have nicknamed the...*

"Hatrack" Building

At first glance it looks like most other sandstone buildings in the city. But look up at the very top to see the ornate rooftop and elaborate ironwork (Glasgow had roaring iron forges back in the day). The Hatrack is a prime example of the adventurous turn-of-the-century Glaswegian architecture: The building's internal framework bears all the weight, so the facade can use very little load-bearing stone. This "curtain wall" method allows for architectural creativity—here the huge bay windows let in plenty of light and contrast nicely with the recessed arches, making the building both unusual and still quintessentially Glaswegian. (The same method gave Antoni Gaudí the freedom to create his fantastical buildings in Barcelona.) Above the left doorway as you face the building, notice the stained-glass ship in turbulent seas, another fitting icon for a city that's seen more than its share of ups and downs.

• *At the end of the block, turn right up...*

Wellington Street

Climb this street to the crest of the hill, where the two- and three-story buildings have a pleasing, uniform look. These sandstone structures were the homes of Glasgow's upper-middle class, the factory managers who worked for the city's barons (such as the titan who owned the mansion back on Royal Exchange Square). In the strict Victorian class structure, the people who lived here were distinctly higher on the social scale than the people who lived in the tenements (which we'll see at the end of this tour).

• *Turn left onto Bath Street and then right onto West Campbell Street. It opens onto Sauchiehall, Glasgow's main commercial street. Turn left onto Sauchiehall. Half a block later, at #217 (on the left), you'll see a black-and-white Art Nouveau building with a sign reading...*

Willow Tea Rooms

Charles Rennie Mackintosh made his living from design commissions, including multiple tearooms for businesswoman Kate

Charles Rennie Mackintosh
(1868–1928)

During his lifetime, Charles Rennie Mackintosh brought an exuberant Art Nouveau influence to the architecture of his hometown. His designs challenged the city planners of this otherwise practical, working-class port city to create beauty in the buildings they commissioned. A radical thinker, he freely shared credit with his artist wife, Margaret MacDonald. (He once famously said, "I have the talent...Margaret has the genius.")

When Mackintosh was a young student at the Glasgow School of Art, the Industrial Age dominated life here. Factories belched black soot into the city as they burned coal and forged steel. Mackintosh and his circle of artist friends drew their solace and inspiration from nature (just as the Romantics had before them) and created some of the original Art Nouveau buildings, paintings, drawings, and furniture.

As a student traveling abroad in Italy, Mackintosh ignored the famous Renaissance paintings inside the museum walls, and set up his easel to paint the exteriors of churches and buildings instead. He rejected the architectural traditions of ancient Greece and Rome. In Venice and Ravenna, he fell under the spell of Byzantine design, and in Siena he saw a unified, medieval city design he would try to import—but with a Scottish flavor and Glaswegian palette—to his own hometown.

His first commission came in 1893, to design an extension to the Glasgow Herald building. More work soon followed, including the Glasgow School of Art and the Willow Tea Rooms 10 years later. Mackintosh envisioned a world without artistic borders, where an Islamic flourish could find its way onto a workaday building in a Scottish city. Inspired by the great buildings of the past and by his Art Nouveau peers, he in turn influenced others, such as painter Gustav Klimt and Bauhaus founder Walter Gropius. A century after Scotland's greatest architect set pencil to paper, his hometown is at last celebrating his unique vision.

Cranston. (You might also see fake "Mockintosh" tearooms sprinkled throughout the city— ignore them.) A well-known control freak, Mackintosh designed everything here—down to the furniture, lighting, and cutlery. He took his theme for the café from the name of the street it's on—*saugh* is Scots for willow, and

haugh for meadow.

In the design of these tearooms, there was a meeting of the (very modern) minds. Cranston wanted a place for women to be able to gather while unescorted, in a time when traveling solo could give a woman a less-than-desirable reputation. An ardent women's rights supporter, Cranston requested that the rooms be bathed in white, the suffragists' signature color.

Enter the Willow Tea Rooms and make your way past the tacky jewelry and trinket store that now inhabits the bottom floor. On the open mezzanine level you'll find 20 crowded tables run like a diner from a corner kitchen, serving bland meals to middle-class people—just as this place has since it opened in 1903 (£4–7 breakfasts, £4–5 sandwiches, £7 salads and entrées, £12.25 afternoon tea served all day). Don't leave without poking your head into the almost-hidden Room de Luxe. Head up the stairs (following signs for the toilet) to the first landing, and go left down the hall to see this peaceful tearoom space (only open for tea at certain times—call ahead). While some parts of the Room de Luxe are reproductions (such as the chairs and the doors, which were too fragile to survive), the rest is just as it was in Mackintosh's day (Mon–Sat 9:00–16:30, Sun 11:00–16:15, last orders 30 minutes before closing, 217 Sauchiehall Street, second location at 97 Buchanan Street, tel. 0141/332-0521, www.willowtearooms.co.uk).

• *From here it's a five-minute, mostly uphill walk to the only must-see Mackintosh sight within the town center. Walk a block and a half west on Sauchiehall, and make a right onto Dalhousie Street; the big reddish-brown building on the left at the top of the hill is the Glasgow School of Art. Enter at the Dalhousie Street entrance.*

If you have time to kill before your tour starts, consider eating lunch at one of my recommended restaurants: the student café **Where the Monkey Sleeps** *(closed Sat-Sun; go to the corner, cross Renfrew Street, and head left) or the* **CCA Terrace Bar and Courtyard Café** *(closed Sun-Mon; go around the corner, walk a block past the school, then turn left and go one block downhill). Or, if you have at least an hour before your tour, you can head to the Tenement Museum (listed at the end of this walk, closed mornings and Nov–Feb), a preserved home from the early 1900s—right when Mackintosh was doing his most important work.*

▲Glasgow School of Art

A pinnacle of artistic and architectural achievement, the Glasgow School of Art presented a unique opportunity for Charles Rennie Mackintosh to design a massive project entirely to his own liking, down to every last detail. These details—from a fireplace that looks like a kimono to windows that soar for multiple stories—are the beauty of the Glasgow School of Art.

Mackintosh loved the hands-on ideology of the Arts and Crafts movement, but he was also a practical Scot. Study the

outside of the building. Those protruding wrought-iron brackets that hover outside the multipaned windows were a new invention during the time of the Industrial Revolution; they reinforce the big, fragile glass windows, allowing natural light to pour in to the school. Mackintosh brought all the most recent technologies to this work and added them to his artistic palate—which also merged clean Modernist lines, Asian influences, and Art Nouveau flourishes.

Because the Glasgow School of Art is still a working school, the interior can only be visited by one-hour **guided tour,** though several exhibition galleries in the school are free and open to the public, even without a tour. Enter at the Dalhousie Street entrance, and buy your tour ticket at the shop.

Cost and Hours: £8.75 guided tour, April–Sept tours generally depart daily at the top of the hour 10:00–17:00, Oct–March tours daily at 11:00 and 15:00, no tours for one week in late May/early June during final exams; tip the starving students a pound or two if they give a good spiel. In the summer, tours are frequent, but they fill up quickly—it's smart to call or email the shop to confirm times and reserve a spot (shop open daily April–Sept 9:30–18:30, Oct–March 10:00–17:00). Tel. 0141/353-4526 (leave call-back number if leaving a message), www.gsa.ac.uk, shop@gsa.ac.uk. No cameras are allowed on the tour.

Background: When the building first opened, it was modern and minimalist. Other elements were added later, such as the lobby's tile mosaics depicting the artistic greats, including mustachioed Mackintosh (who hovers over the gift shop). As you tour the building, you'll see how Mackintosh—who'd been a humble art student himself not too long before he designed this building—strove to create a space that was both artistically innovative and completely functional for students. The plaster replicas of classical sculptures lining the halls were part of Mackintosh's vision to inspire students by the greats of the past. You'll likely see students and their canvases lining the halls. Do you smell oil paint?

Linking these useable spaces are clever artistic patterns and puzzles that Mackintosh embedded to spur creative thought. A resolute pagan in a very Protestant city, he romanticized the ideals of nature and included an abstract icon of a spiral-within-a-circle rose design on many of his works. In some cases, he designed a little alcove just big enough for a fresh, single-stem rose and placed it next to one of his stained-glass roses—so students could compare reality with the artistic form. (You'll even find these roses on the swinging doors in the bathroom.)

Mackintosh cleverly arranged the school so that every one of the cellar studios is bathed in intense natural light. And yet, as you climb to the top of the building—which should be the brightest, most light-filled area—the space becomes dark and gloomy, and the stairwell is encumbered by a cage-like structure. Then, reaching the top floor, the professors' offices are again full of sunrays—a literal and metaphorical "enlightenment" for the students after slogging through a dark spell.

During the tour, you'll be able to linger a few minutes in the major rooms, such as the remarkable forest-like library and the furniture gallery (including some original tables and chairs from the Willow Tea Rooms). Walking through the GSA, remember that all of this work was the Art Nouveau original, and that Frank Lloyd Wright, the Art Deco Chrysler Building, and everything that resembles it came well after "Charles Rennie Mack's" time.

• *To finish this walk, we'll do a wee bit of urban "hillwalking" (a popular Scottish pastime). Head north from the Glasgow School of Art on Scott Street (from the shop's exit, turn left, then left again on Renfrew Street; one block later, turn right onto Scott Street). Huff and puff your way over the crest of the hill, and make a left onto Buccleuch Street. After three blocks, the last house on the left is the...*

▲Tenement House

Packrats of the world, unite! A strange quirk of fate—the 10-year hospitalization of a woman who never redecorated—created this perfectly preserved middle-class residence. The Scottish National Trust bought this otherwise ordinary row home, located in a residential neighborhood, because of the peculiar tendencies of Miss Toward. For five decades, she kept her home essentially unchanged. The kitchen calendar is still set for 1935, and canisters of licorice powder (a laxative) still sit on the bathroom shelf. It's a time-warp experience, where Glaswegian old-timers enjoy coming to reminisce about how they grew up.

Buy your ticket on the main floor, and poke around the little museum. You'll learn that in Glasgow, a "tenement" isn't a slum—it's simply a stone apartment house. In fact, tenements like these were typical for every class except the richest. But with the city's economic decline, tenements went the way of the dodo bird as the city's population shrank.

Head upstairs to the apartment, which is staffed by caring volunteers. Ring the doorbell to be let in. Ask them why the bed is in the kitchen or why the rooms still smell like natural gas.

As you look through the rooms stuffed with lace and Victorian trinkets—such as the ceramic dogs on the living room's fireplace mantle—consider how different they are from Mackintosh's stark, minimalist designs from the same period.

Cost and Hours: £5.50, £3.50 guidebook, March–Oct 13:00–17:00, last entry 30 minutes before closing, closed Nov–Feb, 145 Buccleuch Street down off the top of Garnethill, toll tel. 0844-493-2197, www.nts.org.uk. No photos allowed.

• *Exit the Tenement House, cross the street, go left, and follow the sidewalk down the hill. Pass the pedestrian bridge on your left and curve around to arrive at the far end of Sauchiehall Street.*

To return to Central Station, turn left, walk to the second bus shelter, and take bus #44 (every 10 minutes, other buses also go to station—ask the driver if another bus pulls up while you're waiting). Taxis zip by on Sauchiehall; a ride to the station costs about £3.

To catch the bus from here straight out to the recommended restaurants in the West End, cross Sauchiehall Street, turn left, and walk two blocks to Holland Street. Turn right and walk one short block to the bus stop near the corner of Holland and Bath streets, and wait for bus #16 (every 20 minutes, ask driver to let you off near the Hillhead subway stop).

GLASGOW

More Sights in Glasgow

Away from the Center

▲**Kelvingrove Art Gallery and Museum**—This museum is like a Scottish Smithsonian—with everything from a pair of stuffed elephants to fine artwork by the great masters. The well-described collection is impressively displayed in an impressive 100-year-old Spanish Baroque-style building. It's divided into two sections. The "Life" section, in the West Court, features a menagerie of stuffed animals (including a giraffe, kanga-

roo, ostrich, and moose) with a WWII-era Spitfire fighter plane hovering overhead. Branching off are halls with exhibits ranging from Ancient Egypt to "Scotland's First Peoples" to weaponry ("Conflict and Consequence"), as well as several fine paintings (find Salvador Dalí's *Christ of St. John of the Cross*). The more serene "Expression" section, in the East Court, focuses on artwork, including Dutch, Flemish, French, and Italian paintings. It also has exhibits on "Scottish Identity in Art" and on Charles Rennie Mackintosh and the Glasgow School. The Kelvingrove claims to be one of the most-visited museums in Britain—presumably because of all the field-trip groups you'll see here. Watching all the excited Scottish kids—their imaginations ablaze—is as much fun as the collection itself (free, Mon–Thu and Sat 10:00–17:00, Fri and Sun 11:00–17:00, Argyle Street; subway to Kelvinhall stop—when you exit, turn left and walk 5 minutes; buses #9, #16, #23, #42, and #62 all stop nearby; tel. 0141/276-9599, www.glasgowmuseums.com).

▲**Burrell Collection**—This eclectic art collection of a wealthy local shipping magnate is one of Glasgow's top destinations, but

it's three miles outside the city center. If you'd like to visit, plan to make an afternoon of it, and leave time to walk around the surrounding park, where Highland cattle graze. The diverse contents of this museum include sculptures (from Roman to Rodin), stained glass, tapestries, furniture, Asian and Islamic works, and halls of paintings—starring Cézanne, Renoir, Degas, and a Rembrandt self-portrait (free, Mon–Thu and Sat 10:00–17:00, Fri and Sun 11:00–17:00, Pollok Country Park, 2060 Pollokshaws Road, tel. 0141/287-2550, www.glasgowmuseums.com). To get here from downtown, take bus #45, #47, #48, or #57 to Pollokshaws Road, or take a train to the Pollokshaws West train station; the entrance is a 10-minute walk from the bus stop and the train station. By car, follow M8 to exit at junction 22 onto M77 Ayr; exit junction 1 on M77 and follow signs.

East of Downtown: The Cathedral and Nearby

To reach these sights from the TI on George Square, head up North Hanover Street, turn right on Cathedral Street, and walk about 20 minutes (or hop a bus along the main drag—confirm with driver that the bus stops at the cathedral). All sights are free.

Glasgow Cathedral—This blackened, Gothic-to-the-extreme cathedral is a rare example of an intact pre-Reformation Scottish cathedral. Currently under renovation to remove dark soot and replace its mortar, the cathedral is open but covered with scaffolding until 2014. Inside, look up to see the wooden barrel-vaulted ceiling, and notice the beautifully decorated section over the choir ("quire"). Standing at the choir, turn around to look down the nave at the west wall, and notice how the right wall lists. (Don't worry; it's been standing for 800 years.) Peek into the lower church, and don't miss the Blacader Aisle (stairs down to the right as you face the choir), where you can look up to see the ceiling bosses— colorful carved demons, dragons, skulls, and more (April–Sept

Mon–Sat 9:30–17:30, Sun 13:00–17:00; Oct–March Mon–Sat 9:30–16:00, Sun 13:00–16:00, last entry 45 minutes before closing; near junction of Castle and Cathedral Streets, tel. 0141/552-6891, www.glasgowcathedral.org.uk).

Provand's Lordship—With low beams and medieval decor, this creaky home—supposedly the "oldest house in Glasgow"—displays the *Lifestyles of the Rich and Famous*...circa 1471. The interior shows off a few pieces of furniture from the 16th, 17th, and 18th centuries. Out back, explore the St. Nicholas Garden, which was once part of a hospital that dispensed herbal remedies. The plaques in each section show the part of the body each plant is used to treat (Tue–Thu and Sat 10:00–17:00, Fri and Sun 11:00–17:00, closed Mon, across the street from St. Mungo Museum at 3 Castle Street, tel. 0141/552-8819, www.glasgowmuseums.com).

St. Mungo Museum of Religious Life and Art—This museum, next to the cathedral, aims to promote religious understanding. Taking an ecumenical approach, it provides a handy summary of major and minor world religions, showing how each faith handles various rites of passage through the human life span: birth, puberty, marriage, death, and everything in between (same hours as Provand's Lordship, cheap ground-floor café, 2 Castle Street, tel. 0141/276-1625, www.glasgowmuseums.com).

Necropolis—Built to resemble Paris' Père Lachaise cemetery, Glasgow's huge burial hill next to the cathedral has a similarly wistful, ramshackle appeal, along with an occasional deer. Its gravestones seem poised to slide down the hill (open year-round, www.glasgownecropolis.org; if main black gates are closed, walk around to the side and see if you can get in and out through a side alleyway).

Nightlife in Glasgow

Glasgow is a young city, and its nightlife scene is renowned. Walking through the city center, you'll pass at least one club or bar on every block. For the latest, pick up a copy of *The List* (sold at newsstands).

In the West End: **Òran Mòr,** a converted 1862 church overlooking a busy intersection, is one of Glasgow's most popular hangouts. In addition to hosting an atmospheric bar, outdoor beer garden, and brasserie, the building's former nave (now decorated with funky murals) has a nightclub featuring everything from rock shows to traditional Scottish music nights (brasserie serves £10–20 entrées; pub with dressy conservatory or outdoor beer garden serves £7–10 pub grub; daily 9:00–very late, food served 12:00–15:00 & 17:00–22:00, top of Byres Road at 731–735 Great Western Road, tel. 0141/357-6226, www.oran-mor.co.uk).

In the City Center: **The Pot Still** is an award-winning malt whisky bar from 1835 that boasts a formidable selection of more than 300 choices. You'll see locals of all ages sitting in its leathery interior, watching football (soccer) and discussing their drinks. They have whisky aged in sherry casks, whisky preferred by wine drinkers, and whisky from every region of Scotland. Give the friendly bartenders a little background on your beverage tastes, and they'll narrow down a good choice for you from their long list (whisky runs £2–250 a glass, average price £4–5, no food served, Mon–Sat 11:00–24:00, Sun 12:30–24:00, 154 Hope Street, tel. 0141/333-0980).

Sleeping in Glasgow

On Renfrew Street

A batch of basic B&Bs lines Renfrew Street, a block away from the Glasgow School of Art. From here you can walk downhill into the downtown core in about 15 minutes (or take a £3–4 taxi). If approaching by car, you can't drive down one-way Renfrew Street from the city center. Instead, from busy Sauchiehall Street, go up Scott Street or Rose Street, turn left onto Buccleuch Street, and circle around to Renfrew Street.

$$ Rennie Mackintosh Art School Hotel has 24 nice-enough rooms and public spaces inspired by Glasgow's favorite architect (slippery rates change with demand, but generally Sb-£32–35; Db-£48–55 Sun–Thu, £55 Fri–Sat; includes breakfast, free Wi-Fi on ground floor, laundry services, 218–220 Renfrew Street, tel. 0141/333-9992, fax 0141/333-9995, www.rmghotels .com, rennie@rmghotels.com).

GLASGOW

Sleep Code

(£1 = about $1.60, country code: 44, area code: 0141)
S = Single, **D** = Double/Twin, **T** = Triple, **Q** = Quad, **b** = bathroom, **s** = shower only. You can assume credit cards are accepted unless otherwise noted.

To help you sort easily through these listings, I've divided the rooms into two categories based on the price for a standard double room with bath (during high season):

$$ Higher Priced—Most rooms £50 or more.
$ Lower Priced—Most rooms less than £50.

Prices can change without notice; verify the hotel's current rates online or by email. For other updates, see www .ricksteves.com/update.

Central Glasgow Hotels & Restaurants

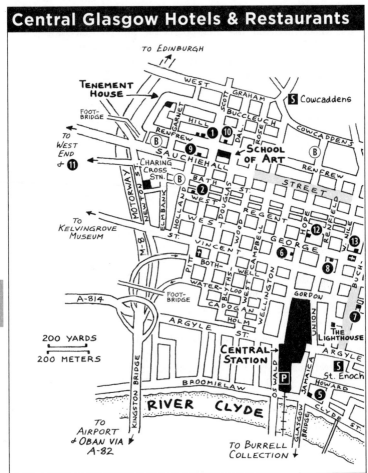

$$ **Victorian House Hotel** is a crank-'em-out place with a friendly staff and 58 worn but workable rooms sprawling through several old townhouses (S-£32, Sb-£39, Db-£60, lots of stairs and no elevator, 212 Renfrew Street, tel. 0141/332-0129, www.the victorian.co.uk, info@thevictorian.co.uk).

Elsewhere in Central Glasgow

$$ **Ibis Glasgow,** part of the modern hotel chain, has 141 cookie-cutter rooms with blond wood and predictable comfort just three blocks downhill from the Renfrew Street B&Bs. It's a 10-minute, slightly uphill walk from downtown (Sb/Db-£55 on weeknights, £60 on weekends, £85 "event rate" during festivals and in Aug, breakfast-£7, air-con, pay Internet access and free Wi-Fi, eleva-

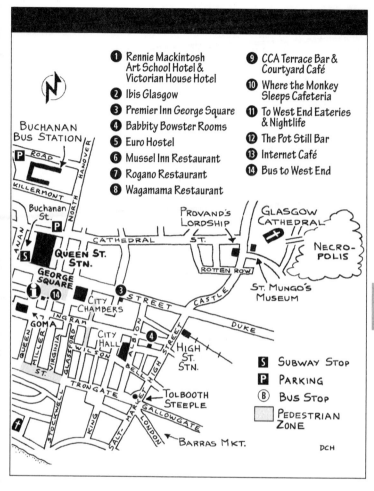

tor, restaurant, hiding behind a big Novotel at 220 West Regent Street, tel. 0141/225-6000, fax 0141/225-6010, www.ibishotel.com, h3139@accor.com).

$$ Premier Inn George Square is a family-friendly chain hotel in the Merchant City district, close to Queen Street Station (Db for up to 2 adults and 2 kids-£69, cheaper in winter, elevator, pay Wi-Fi, 187 George Street, tel. 08715-278-440, www.premier-inn.com).

$$ Babbity Bowster, named for a traditional Scottish dance, is a pub and restaurant renting six basic rooms up top. It's located in the trendy Merchant City on the eastern fringe of downtown, near several clubs and restaurants (Sb-£45, Db-£60, lots of stairs and no elevator, 10-minute walk from Central Station, 16–18

Blackfriars Street, tel. 0141/552-5055, babbity@btinternet.com). The ground-floor pub serves £5–9 pub grub (daily 12:00–22:00); the first-floor restaurant, run by a French chef, offers £14–17 entrées (Thu–Sat only 18:30–21:30, closed Sun–Wed).

$ Euro Hostel is the best bet for hostel beds in the city center. Part of a chain, this place is a lively hive of backpacker activity, with 365 beds on nine floors, plus pay Internet access, free Wi-Fi in the bar, a kitchen, and friendly staff (request a room on a higher floor and in the back for maximum quiet; very slippery rates, but figure Sb-£29–40, Db-£36–52, £13–16 bunk in 4- to 14-bed dorm with bathroom, couples should request a double or you'll get a bunk-bed, includes continental breakfast, elevator, laundry-£4/load, 318 Clyde Street, tel. 0141/222-2828, www.euro-hostels .co.uk, reservations@euro-hostels.co.uk). It's on the busy main thoroughfare past Central Station, along the River Clyde, near some seedy areas.

Eating in Glasgow

Many of Glasgow's fancier eateries serve "pre-theatre menus"— affordable, fixed-price meals served before 19:00.

In the City Center

Mussel Inn offers light, good-value fish dinners and seafood plates in an airy, informal environment. The restaurant is a cooperative, owned and run by shellfish farmers. Their £10 "kilo pot" of Scottish mussels is popular with locals and big enough to share (£7 small grilled platters, £11–17 meals, Mon–Fri 12:00–14:30 & 17:00–22:00, Sat 12:00–22:00, Sun 12:30–22:00, 157 Hope Street, between St. Vincent and West George Streets, tel. 0141/572-1405).

Rogano is a time-warp Glasgow institution that retains much of the same classy Art Deco interior it had when it opened in 1935. You half-expect to see Bacall and Bogart at the next table. The restaurant has three parts. The bar in front has outdoor seating (£6 lunch sandwiches, £9–10 meals). The fancy dining room at the back of the main floor smacks of the officers' mess on the *Queen Mary*, which was built here on the Clyde during the same period (£20–24 meals with a focus on seafood). A more casual yet still dressy bistro in the cellar is filled with 1930s-Hollywood glamour (£11–14 meals, £15 afternoon tea; daily 12:00–22:30, fancy restaurant closed 14:30–18:00, 11 Exchange Place—just before giant archway from Buchanan Street, reservations smart, tel. 0141/248-4055).

Wagamama is part of a reliably good UK chain that serves delicious Asian noodle dishes at a reasonable price (£6–10 entrées, Mon–Sat 12:00–23:00, Sun 12:30–22:00, 97–103 West George Street, tel. 0141/229-1468).

And More: Dozens of restaurants line the main commercial areas of town: Sauchiehall Street, Buchanan Street, and the Merchant City area. Most are very similar, with trendy interiors, Euro disco-pop soundtracks, and dinner for about £15–20 per person.

Budget Options near the Glasgow School of Art

CCA Terrace Bar and Courtyard Café, located on the first floor of Glasgow's edgy contemporary art museum, has delicious designer food at art-student prices. An 18th-century facade, discovered when the site was excavated to build the museum, looms over the courtyard restaurant (£5–7 salads, sandwiches, and entrées; £9–13 early-bird specials 17:00–19:00; food served Tue–Thu 10:00–19:30, Fri–Sat 10:00–21:00; closed Sun–Mon, 350 Sauchiehall Street, tel. 0141/332-7959).

Where the Monkey Sleeps is a cheap student cafeteria across the street from the entrance to the Glasgow School of Art. This is a good spot for a subsidized lunch (open to the public, choice of two hot meals a day for £2–4, soups for £2, and sandwiches for £1–3). Nothing is ever more than £4. It's your chance to mingle with the city's next generation of artists and hear more of that lilting Glaswegian accent (Sept–June Mon–Fri 8:00–17:00, closed Sat–Sun, outside of the school year fewer foods to choose from, entrance is on the left as you face the multicolored windows, follow *refectory* signs, 166 Renfrew Street, tel. 0141/353-4728).

In the West End

The hip, lively residential neighborhood called the West End is worth exploring, particularly at dinnertime. A collection of fine and fun eateries lines Ashton Lane, a small street just off bustling Byres Road (the scene continues north along Cresswell Lane). Before choosing a place, make a point of strolling the whole scene to comparison-shop.

Local favorites (all open long hours daily) include the landmark **Ubiquitous Chip** (with various pubs and restaurants sprawling through a deceptively large building; £5–7 pub grub, £8–20 restaurant meals, tel. 0141/334-5007) and **The Loft** (£7–9 pizzas and pastas in the lobby of Grosvenor Cinema, a grand old movie theater; tel. 0141/339-0686). Up at Cresswell Lane, consider **Café Andaluz,** which offers £4–7 tapas and sangria behind lacy wooden screens, as the waitstaff clicks past on the cool tiles (2 Cresswell Lane, tel. 0141/339-1111). Back on Byres Road, **La Vallée Blanche** serves French cuisine with a Scottish twist, in a romantic dining area that resembles an upscale mountain lodge (£11–18 entrées, closed Mon, 360 Byres Road, tel. 0141/334-3333). Also note that the church-turned-pub **Òran Mòr**—described earlier, under "Nightlife in Glasgow"—is a five-minute walk away (at the intersection of Byres and Great Western Road).

Getting to the West End: It's easiest to take the subway to Hillhead, which is a two-minute walk from Ashton Lane (exit the station to the left, then take the first left to find the lane). From the city center, you can also take a £5–6 taxi or catch bus #20 or #66 (stops just in front of the TI and on Hope Street, near recommended Renfrew Street hotels, runs every 10 minutes; get out when you reach Byres Road).

Glasgow Connections

Traveline Scotland has a journey planner that's linked to all of Scotland's train and bus schedule info. Go online (www .travelinescotland.com); call them at toll tel. 0871-200-2233; or use the individual websites listed below. If you're connecting with Edinburgh, note that the train is faster but the bus is cheaper.

From Glasgow's Central Station by Train to: Keswick in the Lake District (about hourly, 1.5 hours to Penrith, then catch a bus to Keswick, roughly hourly, only 8/day on Sun, 40 minutes), **Stranraer** and ferry to Belfast (7/day, 2.5 hours, some direct, others with change in Ayr), **Troon** and ferry to Belfast (2/hour, 45 minutes), **Blackpool** (1–2/hour, 3–3.5 hours, transfer in Preston), **Liverpool** (1–2/hour, 3.5 hours, change in Wigan or Preston), **Durham** (1–2/hour, 2.75–3 hours, may require change in Edinburgh), **York** (2/hour, 3.5 hours, may require change in Edinburgh), **London** (1–2 hour, 4.5–5 hours direct). Train info: toll tel. 0845-748-4950, www.nationalrail.co.uk.

From Glasgow's Queen Street Station by Train to: Oban (3–5/day, just 1/day Sun in winter, 3.25 hours), **Inverness** (9/day, 3.25–3.5 hours, 3 direct, the rest change in Perth), **Edinburgh** (4/hour, 50 minutes), **Stirling** (3/hour, 30–45 minutes), **Pitlochry** (9/day, 1.5–1.75 hours, some with transfer in Perth).

From Glasgow by Bus to: Edinburgh (4/hour, 1.25 hour), **Oban** (6/day, 2.75 hours, some with transfer in Tyndrum), **Fort William** (buses #914, #915, and #916; 8/day, 3 hours), **Glencoe** (buses #914, #915, and #916; 8/day, 2.5 hours), **Inverness** (every 1–2 hours, 3.5–4.5 hours, some transfer in Perth), **Portree** on the Isle of Skye (buses #915 and #916, 3/day, 6.25 hours), **Pitlochry** (5/day, 2.25 hours, transfer in Perth). Bus info: toll tel. 0871-266-3333, www.citylink.co.uk.

Glasgow International Airport: Located eight miles west of the city, this airport has currency-exchange desks, a TI, Internet access, luggage storage, and ATMs (toll tel. 0844-481-5555, www .glasgowairport.com). Taxis connect downtown to the airport for about £20. Glasgow Flyer Bus #500 zips to central Glasgow (daily at least 4/hour 5:00–23:00, then hourly through the night, £4.50/one-way, £7/round-trip, 15–20 minutes to both train stations, 25 minutes to the bus station, catch at bus stop #1, www.glasgow flyer.com).

Prestwick Airport: A hub for Ryanair (as well as the US military, which refuels planes here), this airport is about 30 miles southwest of the city center (toll tel. 0871-223-0700, ext. 1006, www.gpia.co.uk). The best connection is by train, which runs between the airport and Central Station (Mon–Sat 2/hour, 45 minutes, half-price with Ryanair ticket). Stagecoach buses link the airport with Buchanan Street Station (£4–7, daily 1–2/hour plus a few nighttime buses, 45–60 minutes, check schedules at www .travelinescotland.com).

OBAN AND THE SOUTHERN HIGHLANDS

Oban • Mull • Iona • Glencoe • Fort William

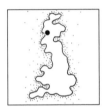

The area north of Glasgow offers a fun and easy dip into the southern part of the Scottish Highlands. Oban is a fruit crate of Scottish traditions, with a handy pair of wind-bitten Hebrides islands (Mull and Iona) just a hop, skip, and jump away. Nearby, the evocative "Weeping Glen" of Glencoe aches with both history and natural beauty. Beyond that, Fort William anchors the southern end of the Caledonian Canal, offering a springboard to more Highlands scenery—this is where Britain's highest peak, Ben Nevis, keeps its head in the clouds, and where you'll find a valley made famous by a steam train carrying a young wizard named Harry.

Planning Your Time

Oban is a smart place to spend the night on a blitz tour of central Scotland; with more time to linger (and an interest in a day trip to the islands), spend two nights—Iona is worthwhile but adds a day to your trip. If you have a third night to spare, you can sleep in Iona and give yourself time to roam around Mull. Glencoe is worth considering as a very sleepy, rural overnight alternative to Oban, or if you have plenty of time and want a remote village experience on your way north.

Oban works well if you're coming from Glasgow, or even all the way from England's Lake District (for driving tips, see the end of this chapter). Assuming you're driving, here's an ambitious two-day plan for the Highlands.

Day 1

Morning Drive up from the Lake District, or linger in Glasgow.

11:30 Depart Glasgow.

12:00 Rest stop on Loch Lomond, then joyride on.

13:00 Lunch in Inveraray.

16:00 Arrive in Oban, tour whisky distillery, and drop by the TI.

20:00 Dine in Oban.

Day 2

9:00 Leave Oban.

10:00 Visit Glencoe museum and the valley's Visitors Centre.

12:00 Drive to Fort William and follow the Caledonian Canal to Inverness, stopping at Fort Augustus to see the locks and along Loch Ness to search for monsters.

16:00 Visit the Culloden Battlefield (closes earlier off-season) near Inverness.

17:00 Drive south.

20:00 Arrive in Edinburgh.

With More Time

While you'll see the Highlands on the above itinerary, you'll whiz past them in a misty blur. With more time, head north from Fort William to the Isle of Skye, spend a night or two there, head over to Inverness via Loch Ness, and consider a stop in Pitlochry.

Getting Around the Highlands

By Car: Drivers enjoy flexibility and plenty of tempting stopovers. Barring traffic, you'll make great time on good, mostly two-lane roads. Be careful, but don't be too timid about passing; otherwise, diesel fumes and large trucks might be your main memory of driving in Scotland. As you drive along Loch Ness, antsy locals may ride your bumper. For step-by-step instructions, read the "Route Tips for Drivers" at the end of this chapter.

By Public Transportation: Glasgow is the gateway to this region (so you'll most likely have to transfer there if coming from Edinburgh). The **train** zips from Glasgow to Fort William, Oban, and Kyle of Lochalsh in the west; and up to Stirling, Pitlochry, and Inverness in the east. For more remote destinations (such as Glencoe), the bus is better.

Most of the **buses** you'll need are operated by Scottish Citylink. Buy tickets at local TIs, pay the driver in cash when you board, or purchase tickets in advance online at www.citylink.co.uk. The nondescript town of Fort William serves as a hub for Highlands buses. Note that bus frequency is substantially reduced on Sundays and off-season—during these times, always carefully confirm schedules locally. Unless otherwise noted, I've listed bus information for summer weekdays.

These buses are particularly useful for connecting the sights in this book:

Buses **#976** and **#977** connect Glasgow with Oban (6/day, 2.75 hours, some with transfer in Tyndrum).

Bus **#913** runs one daily direct bus from Edinburgh to this region—stopping at Glasgow, Stirling, and Glencoe on the way to Fort William (allow 4 hours from Edinburgh to Fort William; 5 more/day with change in Glasgow on buses #900 and #914, 5 hours).

Bus **#978** connects Edinburgh with Oban, stopping in Stirling, but not Glencoe (1/day direct, 3.75 hours; 6 more/day with changes in Glasgow and/or Tyndrum, 4.75 hours).

Bus **#914** goes from Glasgow to Fort William, stopping at Glencoe (5/day, 3 hours).

Buses **#915** and **#916** follow the same route (Glasgow–Glencoe–Fort William), then continue all the way up to Portree on the Isle of Skye (3/day, 6.75 hours for the full run).

Bus **#918** goes from Oban to Fort William, stopping en route at Ballachulish near Glencoe (3/day in summer, 2/day off-season, never on Sun; 1 hour to Ballachulish, 1.5 hours total to Fort William).

Bus **#919** connects Fort William with Inverness (5/day, 2 hours).

By Plane: Seaplane service connects downtown Glasgow (on the River Clyde) and Oban Bay. While pricey—about £169 round-trip—the flight takes only about half an hour and provides a unique view of the Highlands you won't see any other way (on-demand morning or afternoon flights March–Nov, weather permitting, office hours daily 8:30–18:00, book far ahead in summer, tel. 0870-242-1457 or 01436/675-030, www.lochlomondsea planes.com).

Oban

Oban (pronounced OH-bin) is called the "gateway to the isles." Equal parts functional and scenic, this busy little ferry-and-train terminal has no important sights, but makes up the difference in character. It's a low-key resort, with a winding promenade lined by gravel beaches, ice-cream stands, fish-and-chip take-away shops, and a surprising diversity of fine restaurants. When the rain clears, sun-starved Scots sit on benches along The Esplanade, leaning back to catch some rays. Wind, boats, gulls, layers of islands, and the promise of a wide-open Atlantic beyond give Oban a rugged charm.

Orientation to Oban

(area code: 01631)

Oban's business action, just a couple of streets deep, stretches along the harbor and its promenade. (The island just offshore is Kerrera,

with Mull looming behind it.) Everything in Oban is close together, and the town seems eager to please its many visitors. There's live music nightly in several bars and restaurants; wool and tweed are perpetually on sale (tourist shops stay open later than usual in summer—until 20:00—and many are even open on Sundays); and posters announce a variety of day tours to Scotland's wild and rabbit-strewn western islands.

Tourist Information

Oban's impressive TI, located in a former church, sells bus and ferry tickets and has a fine bookshop. Stop by to get brochures and information on everything from bike rental to golf courses to horseback riding to rainy-day activities and more. They also offer coin-operated Internet access (£1/20 minutes) and can book you a room for a £4 fee (flexible hours, generally July–Aug daily 9:00–19:00; April–June Mon–Sat 9:00–17:30, Sun 10:00–17:00; Sept–Oct daily 10:00–17:00; Nov–March Mon–Sat 10:00–17:00, Sun 12:00–17:00; on Argyll Square, just off the harbor a block from the train station, tel. 01631/563-122, www.oban.org.uk). Wander through the TI's free exhibit (in the back) on the area, and pick up a few phones to hear hardy locals talk about their life on the wild western edge of Scotland. Check the "What's On" board for the latest on Oban's small-town evening scene (free live entertainment downstairs in the bar at the Great Western Hotel on the Esplanade—nightly at 20:30 generally year-round, Scottish Night generally every Thu, call for details, tel. 01631/563-101).

Helpful Hints

Internet Access: One option is at the **TI** (see above). **Fancy That** is a souvenir shop on the main drag with seven high-speed Internet terminals and Wi-Fi in the back room (£1/20 minutes, daily 9:30–17:00, until 22:00 July–Aug, 108 George

OBAN

Oban

1. Strathaven Terrace Accommodations
2. To Glenburnie House, The Barriemore & Kilchrenan House
3. The Rowantree Hotel
4. Oban Backpackers
5. Oban Backpackers Annex
6. IYHF Hostel
7. Jeremy Inglis' Hostel
8. Ee'usk & Piazza Restaurants
9. To The Seafood Temple
10. Coast Restaurant
11. Cuan Mòr Gastro-Pub
12. Room 9 Restaurant
13. Ferry to Waypoint Bar & Grill
14. The Lorne Pub
15. Shellfish Shack
16. The Kitchen Garden Deli & Café
17. Tesco Supermarket
18. Skipinnish Ceilidh House
19. Great Western Hotel (Live Shows)
20. Fancy That Shop (Internet)
21. Bowman's Tours & West Coast Motors (Bag Storage)
22. Laundry
23. To Bike Rental
24. Whisky Distillery

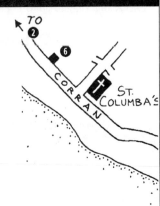

OBAN BAY

100 YARDS
100 METERS

||||| STAIRS

P PARKING

BOATS TO MULL & IONA

FERRY TERMINAL

SOUTH PIER

TO 9 & KERREA FERRY

ST. COLUMBA'S

CORRAN

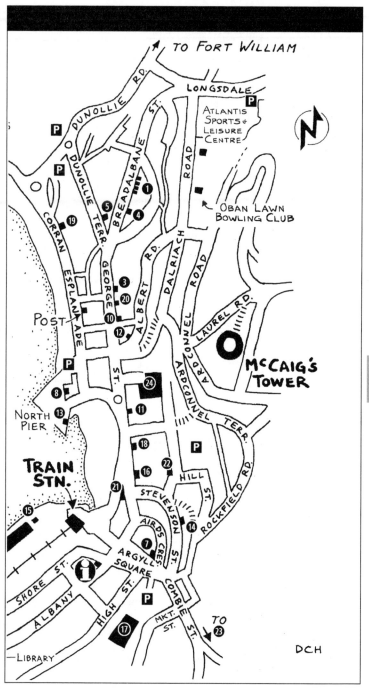

OBAN

Street, tel. 01631/562-996). To surf for free, get online at the **library** just above the ferry terminal; you can just show up, but it's smart to call ahead to book a 30-minute time slot (Mon and Wed 10:00–13:00 & 14:00–19:00, Thu until 18:00, Fri until 17:00, closed Sat afternoon and all day Tue and Sun, 77 Albany Street, tel. 01631/571-444, www.argyll-bute.gov.uk).

Baggage Storage: The train station has luggage lockers (£3–4 depending on bag size), but these have been known to close for security reasons. In this case, **West Coast Motors**, which sells bus tickets, has a pricey left-luggage service (£1/hour per piece, unsecured in main office, Mon–Fri 8:00–13:00 & 14:00–16:00, Sat 9:00–14:00, closed Sun, July–Aug open during lunch, can be sporadically closed Oct–May, next to Bowman's Tours at Queens Park Place, www.westcoast motors.co.uk).

Laundry: You'll find **Oban Quality Laundry** tucked a block behind the main drag, at the intersection of Stevenson and Tweedle Streets (£6–9 per load for same-day drop-off service, no self-service, Mon–Fri 9:00–17:00, Sat 9:00–13:00, closed Sun, tel. 01631/563-554). The **Oban Backpackers** and **IYHF** hostels have laundry service or facilities for guests.

Supermarket: Tesco is a five-minute walk from the TI (Mon–Fri 8:00–22:00, Sat 8:00–24:00, Sun 9:00–18:00, WC in front by registers, inexpensive cafeteria, look for entrance to large parking lot a block past TI on right-hand side, Lochside Street).

Bike Rental: Try **Flit Self Drive** (£10/half-day, £14/day, Mon–Fri 9:00–17:30, Sat 9:00–12:00, closed Sun, Glencruitten Road, tel. 01631/566-553, www.flitselfdrive.co.uk).

Tours near Oban

▲▲**Nearby Islands**—For the best day trip from Oban, tour the islands of Mull and Iona (offered daily Easter–Oct)—or consider staying overnight on remote and beautiful Iona. With more time or other interests, consider one of many other options you'll see advertised.

Wildlife Tours—Those more interested in nature than church history will enjoy trips to the wildly scenic Isle of Staffa with Fingal's Cave. The journey to Treshnish Island brims with puffins, seals, and other sea critters. Several groups, including Sealife Adventures and SeaFari, run whale-watching tours that feature rare minke whales, basking sharks, bottlenose dolphins, and porpoises. Departures and options abound—check at the TI for information.

Open-Top Bus Tours—If there's good weather and you don't have a car, take a spin out of Oban for views of nearby castles and

OBAN

islands, plus a stop at McCaig's Tower (£8, valid for 24 hours, late May–late Sept daily at 11:00 and 14:00, no tours off-season, 2.5 hours, departs from rail station, tel. 01586/552-319, www.citysight seeingoban.com).

Sights in Oban

In Oban

▲West Highland Malt Scotch Whisky Distillery Tours—The 200-year-old Oban Whisky Distillery produces more than 16,000 liters a week. They offer serious and fragrant one-hour tours explaining the process from start to finish, with two smooth samples, a whisky glass (normally sells for £6), and a discount coupon for the shop. This is the handiest whisky tour you'll see, just a block off the harbor and better than anything in Edinburgh. The exhibition that precedes the tour gives a quick, whisky-centric history of Scotland (£7; July–Sept Mon–Fri 9:30–19:30, Sat-Sun 9:30–17:00; Easter–June and Oct Mon–Sat 9:30–17:00, closed Sun; March–Easter and Nov Mon–Fri 10:00–17:00, closed Sat–Sun; Dec and Feb Mon–Fri 12:30–16:00, closed Sat–Sun; closed Jan; last tour 1.25 hours before closing, tel. 01631/572-004). In high season, these very popular tours (which are limited to 15 people every 15 minutes) fill up quickly. Call or stop by the day before to reserve your time slot.

Skipinnish Ceilidh House—On most nights mid-June through mid-September, you can stroll into Skipinnish on the main drag for Highland music and storytelling. This venue, owned by professional musicians, invests in talented musicians and puts on a good show, with live bands, songs sung in Gaelic, and Highland dancing. For many, the best part is the chance to learn some *ceilidh* dancing. These group dances are a lot of fun—wallflowers and bad dancers are warmly welcomed, and the staff is happy to give you pointers (£8 music session, pricier for concerts with visiting big-name *ceilidh* bands, music 4–5 nights/week mid-June–mid-Sept at 20:00, Thu only in late May and late Sept, 2 hours, sidewalk ticket stall open daily 12:00–17:00, 34–38 George Street, tel. 01631/569-599, www.skipinnish.com).

McCaig's Tower—The unfinished "colosseum" on the hill overlooking town was an employ-the-workers-and-build-me-a-fine-memorial project undertaken by an early Oban tycoon in 1900. While the structure itself is nothing to see close-up, a 10-minute hike through a Victorian residential neighborhood leads you to a peaceful garden and a mediocre view.

Atlantis Leisure Centre—This industrial-type sports center is a good place to get some exercise on a rainy day or let the kids run wild for a few hours. There's an indoor swimming pool with a big water slide, a rock-climbing wall, tennis courts, and two playgrounds (Mon–Fri 7:00–21:00, Sat–Sun 8:30–18:00; open-swim pool hours vary by season—call or check online for exact times; pool entry: adults-£3.50, kids-£2.20, no rental towels or suits, lockers-£0.20, on the north end of Dalriach Road, tel. 01631/566-800, www.atlantisleisure.co.uk). The center's outdoor playground is free and open all the time; the indoor "soft play centre" for children under five costs £2 per kid.

Oban Lawn Bowling Club—The club has welcomed visitors since 1869. This elegant green is the scene of a wonderfully British spectacle of old men tiptoeing wishfully after their balls. It's fun to watch, and—if there's no match and the weather's dry—for £4 each, anyone can rent shoes and balls and actually play (informal hours, but generally daily 10:00–16:00 & 17:00 to "however long the weather lasts," just south of sports center on Dalriach Road, tel. 01631/570-808).

Near Oban

Kerrera—Just offshore from Oban, this stark but very green island offers a quick, easy opportunity to get that romantic island experience. Although Kerrera (KEH-reh-rah) dominates Oban's sea view, you'll have to head two miles south of town (follow the coast road past the ferry terminal) to catch the boat to the middle of the island (ferry-£5 round-trip, bikes free, 5-minute trip; Easter–Sept first ferry Mon–Sat at 8:45, then daily 2/hour 10:30–12:30 & 14:00–17:00, last ferry at 18:00; Oct–Easter 5–6/day, last ferry Mon–Fri at 17:50, Sat–Sun at 17:00—but changes with demand; at Gallanach's dock; tel. 01631/563-665, if no answer contact Oban TI for info; www.kerrera-ferry.co.uk). Bus #431 runs between the Oban train station and the Kerrera ferry twice a day in summer (late May–late Sept only, www.westcoastmotors.co.uk). The free shuttle service between Oban's North Pier and the Kerrera Marina is for customers of the Waypoint Bar & Grill, but you could always take a walk around the island after lunch.

Sleeping on Kerrera: To spend the night on the island, your only option is the **$ Kerrera Bunkhouse,** a converted 18th-century stable that has seven bunk beds in four compartments (£14 per person, £70 for the entire bunkhouse, includes bedding but not towels, cheaper for 2 nights or more, open year-round but book ahead in winter, kitchen, tel. 01631/570-223, ferry info at www.kerrerabunkhouse.co.uk, info@kerrerabunkhouse.co.uk, Susan). They also run a tea garden that serves meals (April–mid-Oct Wed–Sun 10:30–16:30, closed Mon–Tue and mid-Oct–March).

Isle of Seil—Enjoy a drive, a walk, some solitude, and the sea. Drive 12 miles south of Oban on A816 to B844 to the Isle of Seil (pronounced "seal"), connected to the mainland by a bridge (which, locals like to brag, "crosses the Atlantic"...well, maybe a small part of it).

Just over the bridge on the Isle of Seil is a pub called **Tigh-an-Truish** ("House of Trousers"). After a 1745 English law forbade the wearing of kilts on the mainland, Highlanders on the island used this pub to change from kilts to trousers before they made the crossing. The pub serves great meals and good seafood dishes to those either in kilts or pants (pub open daily April–Oct 11:00–23:00—food served 12:00–14:00 & 18:00–20:30, July–Aug all day until 21:00, Nov–March shorter hours and soup/sandwiches only, darts anytime, tel. 01852/300-242).

Five miles across the island, on a tiny second island and facing the open Atlantic, is **Easdale**, a historic, touristy, windy little slate-mining town—with a slate-town museum and incredibly tacky egomaniac's "Highland Arts" shop (shuttle ferry goes the 300 yards). An overpriced direct ferry runs from Easdale to Iona; but, at twice the cost of the Mull–Iona trip, the same time on the island, and very little time with a local guide, it's hardly worth it.

Sleeping in Oban

(area code: 01631)

B&Bs

Oban's B&Bs offer a better value than its hotels. All of the places below are a very short walk from the town center. None of these B&Bs accepts credit cards.

On Strathaven Terrace

The following B&Bs line up on a quiet, flowery street that's nicely located two blocks off the harbor, three blocks from the center, and a 10-minute walk from the train station. By car, as you enter town, turn left after King's Knoll Hotel, and take your first right onto Breadalbane Street. ("Strathaven Terrace" is actually just the name for this row of houses on Breadalbane Street.) The alley behind the buildings has parking for all of these places.

$$ Sandvilla B&B rents six fine rooms—including one on the ground floor—with sleek contemporary decor (Db-£55, £65 in July–Aug, Tb-£83–90, free Wi-Fi, at #4, tel. 01631/562-803, www.holidayoban.co.uk, sandvilla@holidayoban.co.uk, Joyce and Scott).

$$ Gramarvin Guest House has five fresh and cheery rooms (Db-£55–60, £65 in Aug, Tb-£95, free Wi-Fi, at #5, tel. 01631/564-622, www.gramarvin.co.uk, mary@gramarvin.co.uk, Mary).

$$ Raniven Guest House has five simple, tastefully decorated rooms (Sb-£30–35, Db-£55–60, price depends on season,

Sleep Code

(£1 = about $1.60, country code: 44, area code: 01631)
S = Single, D = Double/Twin, T = Triple, Q = Quad, b = bathroom, s = shower only. Unless otherwise noted, you can assume credit cards are accepted at hotels and hostels—but not B&Bs—and breakfast is included.

To help you sort easily through these listings, I've divided the rooms into three categories based on the price for a standard double room with bath (during high season):

$$$ Higher Priced—Most rooms £70 or more.
 $$ Moderately Priced—Most rooms between £30-70.
  $ Lower Priced—Most rooms £30 or less.

Prices can change without notice; verify the hotel's current rates online or by email. For other updates, see www.ricksteves.com/update.

free Wi-Fi, at #1, tel. 01631/562-713, www.raniven.co.uk, info @raniven.co.uk, Moyra and Stuart).

$$ Tanglin B&B, with five Grandma's house–homey rooms, comes with lively, chatty hosts Liz and Jim Montgomery, who create an easygoing atmosphere (S-£25, tiny D-£44, Db-£50, flexible rates and family deals, free Wi-Fi, at #3, tel. 01631/563-247, mobile 0774/8305-891, jimtanglin@aol.com).

Guest Houses and Small Hotels

These options are a step up from the B&Bs—in terms of both amenities and price. The first three, which are along The Esplanade that stretches north of town above a cobble beach (with beautiful bay views), are a 5- to 10-minute walk from the center. The last one is on the main drag in town.

$$$ Glenburnie House, a stately Victorian home, has an elegant breakfast room overlooking the bay. Its 12 spacious, comfortable, classy rooms feel like plush living rooms. There's a nice lounge and a tiny sunroom with a stuffed "hairy coo" head (Sb-£50, Db-£84–100, price depends on size and view, closed mid-Nov–Easter, free Wi-Fi, free parking, The Esplanade, tel. & fax 01631/562-089, www.glenburnie.co.uk, graeme.strachan@bt internet.com, Graeme).

$$$ The Barriemore is the last place on Oban's grand waterfront esplanade. Its woody, bright front-facing rooms—some with bay views—are well-appointed, with furnishings that fit the house's grand Victorian feel. Rooms in the modern addition in the back have no views and simple furnishings, but are cheaper (Sb-£65–75,

Db-£92–102, Tb-£105–126, less off-season, price depends on view, free Wi-Fi, The Esplanade, tel. 01631/566-356, fax 01631/571-084, www.barriemore-hotel.co.uk, reception@barriemore-hotel.co.uk, friendly Nic and Sarah Jones, and Mara the complacent Great Dane).

$$$ Kilchrenan House, the turreted former retreat of a textile magnate, has 14 tastefully renovated, large rooms, most with bay views (Sb-£45, Db-£70–90, 2-night minimum, higher prices are for seaview rooms in June–Aug, lower prices are for back-facing rooms and Sept–May, stunning room #5 is worth the few extra pounds, welcome drink of whisky or sherry, different "breakfast special" every day, closed Dec–Jan, a few houses past the cathedral on The Esplanade, tel. 01631/562-663, www.kilchrenanhouse .co.uk, info@kilchrenanhouse.co.uk, Colin and Frances).

$$$ The Rowantree Hotel is a group-friendly place with 24 freshly renovated rooms reminiscent of a budget hotel in the US, and a central locale right on Oban's main drag (Sb-£50, Db-£90, prices may be soft for walk-ins and off-season, easy parking, George Street, tel. 01631/562-954, www.rowantreehoteloban.co.uk).

Hostels

Oban offers plenty of cheap dorm beds. Your choice: easygoing, institutional (but with fantastic views), or New Age.

$ Oban Backpackers is the most central, laid-back, and fun, with a wonderful, sprawling public living room and 48 beds. The giant mural of nearby islands in the lobby is useful for orientation, and the staff is generous with travel tips (£16/bed, 6–12 bunks per room, includes breakfast, pay Internet access, free Wi-Fi, £2.50 laundry service for guests only, 10-minute walk from station, on Breadalbane Street, tel. 01631/562-107, www.obanbackpackers .com, info@obanbackpackers.com, Peter). Their bunkhouse across the street has several basic but cheerful private rooms that share a kitchen (S-£19-22, D-£43, T-£57, same contact info as hostel).

$ The orderly **IYHF hostel,** on the scenic waterfront Esplanade, is in a grand building with 110 beds and smashing views of the harbor and islands from the lounges and all of the rooms. The smaller, private rooms—including several that can usually be rented as doubles—are in a separate newer building out back (£15–18/bed in 5- to 10-bed rooms, bunk-bed Db-£40–55, T-£55–65, Q-£70–85, price varies with demand, also has 8-bed apartment with kitchen, disabled access, £2 cheaper for members, breakfast-£4–6, pay Internet access and Wi-Fi, great facilities and public rooms with cushy sofas, one laundry machine, tel. 01631/562-025, www.syha.org.uk, oban@syha.org.uk).

$ Jeremy Inglis' Hostel has 37 beds located two blocks from the TI and train station. This loosely run place feels more like a commune than a youth hostel...and it's cheap (£15/bed, S-£22, D-£30, cash only, includes linens, kitchen, free Wi-Fi, breakfast comes with Jeremy's homemade jam, no curfew, second floor at 21 Airds Crescent, tel. 01631/565-065, jeremyinglis@mctavishs .freeserve.co.uk).

Eating in Oban

Oban calls itself the "seafood capital of Scotland," and there are plenty of good fish places in town.

Ee'usk (a phonetic rendering of *iasg*, Scottish Gaelic for "fish") is a popular, stylish, family-run place on the waterfront. It has tall tables, a casual-chic atmosphere, a bright and glassy interior, sweeping views on three sides, and fish dishes favored by both locals and tourists. Reservations are recommended every day in summer and on weekends off-season; if you have to wait for a table, find a seat on one of the comfy sofas in the loft bar (£5–9 lunches, £13–20 dinners, daily 12:00–15:00 & 18:00–21:00, North Pier, tel. 01631/565-666, MacLeod family).

Piazza, next door and also run by the MacLeods, has similar decor but serves Italian cuisine and offers a more family-friendly ambience (£7–10 pizzas and pastas, daily 12:00–15:00 & 17:30–21:00, smart to reserve ahead July–Aug, tel. 01631/563-628).

The Seafood Temple is worth the 15-minute walk from the town center (follow the road past the ferry terminal, or take a £3 taxi ride). This small eatery is situated in a beautifully restored former public toilet building from the Victorian era (no joke), with panoramic views across the bay to the Isle of Kerrera. Owner/chef John—who also runs the shellfish shack at the ferry dock (listed later)—prides himself on creating the best seafood dishes in town, listed on a limited, handwritten menu. Reservations are a must: To book a table, make a £10-per-person deposit at the shellfish shack (£12–21 meals, large portions, Thu–Sun seatings at 18:00 and 20:00, closed Mon–Wed, tel. 01631/566-000).

Coast proudly serves fresh local fish, meat, and veggies in a mod pine-and-candlelight atmosphere. As everything is prepared and presented with care by husband-and-wife team Richard and Nicola—who try to combine traditional Scottish elements in innovative new ways—come here only if you have time for a slow meal (£7–10 lunches, £13–18 dinners, £12 two-course and £15 three-course specials served for lunch and at 17:30–18:30, open daily 12:00–14:00 & 17:30–21:00, closed Sun for lunch, 104 George Street, tel. 01631/569-900).

Cuan Mòr is a popular gastropub that combines traditional Scottish with modern flair—both in its tasty cuisine and in its furnishings, made entirely of wood, stone, and metal scavenged from

OBAN

the beaches of Scotland's west coast (£6 lunches, £8–13 entrées, food served daily 12:00–22:00, brewery in the back, 60 George Street, tel. 01631/565-078).

Room 9 seats just 24 diners in one tiny light-wood room, and has a select menu of homemade nouvelle-cuisine dishes. It's owned and run with care by the chef (dinner only, £13–17 meals, Mon–Sat 17:30–21:30, closed Sun, reservations smart Fri–Sat, 9 Craigard Road, tel. 01631/564-200).

Waypoint Bar & Grill, just across the bay from Oban, is a laid-back patio at the Kerrera Marina with a no-nonsense menu of grilled seafood. It's not fancy, but the food is fresh and inexpensive, and on a nice day the open-air waterside setting is unbeatable (£8–10 plates, £15 seafood platter, May–Sept daily 12:00–14:00 & 17:00–21:00, closed Oct–April, tel. 08740/650-669). A free-for-customers eight-minute ferry to the marina leaves from Oban's North Pier—look for the sign near the recommended Piazza restaurant (departs hourly at :10 past each hour).

Pub Grub: **The Lorne** is a lively high-ceilinged pub known for its good grub and friendly service. After hours, it becomes the most happening nightspot in town...which isn't saying much (£7–9, food served Mon–Sat 12:00–15:00 & 17:30–21:00, Sun 12:30–15:30 & 17:30–21:00, outside seating, free Wi-Fi, tucked a couple of blocks off the main drag behind the stream at Stevenson Street, tel. 01631/570-020).

Lunch

The green **shellfish shack** at the ferry dock is the best spot to pick up a seafood sandwich or a snack (often free salmon samples, inexpensive coffee, meal-size £3 salmon sandwiches, picnic tables nearby, open daily from 10:00 until the boat unloads from Mull around 17:45). This is a good place to pick up a sandwich for your island day—or get a light, early dinner (or "appetizer") when you return from the isles. For a full meal, check out the same folks' Seafood Temple restaurant, described earlier.

The Kitchen Garden is fine for soup, salad, or sandwiches. It's a deli and gourmet-foods store with a charming café upstairs (£3.50 sandwiches to go, £5–8 dishes upstairs, Mon–Sat 9:00–17:00, Sun 11:00–16:00, closed Sun Jan–mid-Feb, 14 George Street, tel. 01631/566-332).

Oban Connections

By Train from Oban: Trains link Oban to the nearest transportation hub in **Glasgow** (3–5/day, just 1/day Sun in winter, 3.25 hours); to get to **Edinburgh,** you'll have to transfer in Glasgow (3–5/day, 4.25 hours). To reach **Fort William** (a transit hub for the Highlands), you'll take the same Glasgow-bound train, but transfer in Crianlarich—the direct bus is easier (see below). Oban's small train station has limited hours (ticket window open Mon–Sat 7:15–18:00, Sun 10:45–18:00, same hours apply to lockers, train info tel. 08457-484-950, www.nationalrail.co.uk).

By Bus: Bus #918 passes through Ballachulish—a half-mile from **Glencoe**—on its way to **Fort William** (3/day in summer, 2/day off-season, never on Sun; 1 hour to Ballachulish, 1.5 hours total to Fort William). Take this bus to Fort William, then transfer to bus #919 to reach **Inverness** (3.75 hours total, with a 20-minute layover in Fort William) or **Portree** on the Isle of Skye (2/day, 4.5–5 hours total). A different bus (#976 or #977) connects Oban with **Glasgow** (6/day, 2.75 hours, some with transfer in Tyndrum), from where you can easily connect by bus or train to **Edinburgh** (figure 4.5 hours total). Buses arrive and depart in front of the Caledonian Hotel, across from the train station (toll tel. 08712/663-333, www.citylink.co.uk).

By Boat: Ferries fan out from Oban to the **southern Hebrides** (see information on the islands of Iona and Mull, later). Caledonian MacBrayne Ferry info: tel. 01631/566-688, free booking tel. 0800-066-5000, www.calmac.co.uk.

Between Glasgow and Oban

Drivers coming from the south can consider these stopovers, which are listed in order from Glasgow to Oban.

Loch Lomond
Leaving Glasgow on A82, you'll soon be driving along the scenic lake called Loch Lomond. The first picnic turnout has the best lake views, benches, a park, and a playground. Twenty-four miles long and speckled with islands, Loch Lomond is second in size only to Loch Ness. It's well-known mostly because of its easy proximity to Glasgow (about 15 miles away)—and also because its bonnie, bonnie banks inspired a beloved folk song: *Ye'll take the high road, and I'll take the low road, and I'll be in Scotland afore ye...* (You'll be humming that one all day. You're welcome.)
• *Halfway up the loch, at Tarbet, take the "tourist route" left onto A83, driving along Loch Long toward Inveraray.*

Rest-and-Be-Thankful Pass
A low-profile pull-out on A83 just west of A82 offers a pleasant opportunity to stretch your legs and get your first taste of that rugged Scottish countryside. The colorful name comes from the 1880s, when second- and third-class coach passengers got out and pushed the coach and first-class passengers up the hill.

Inveraray

Nearly everybody stops at this lovely, seemingly made-for-tourists castle town on Loch Fyne. Park near the pier and browse the wide selection of restaurants and tourist shops.

Inveraray's **TI** sells bus and ferry tickets, has Internet access, and offers a free mini-guide and an exhibit about the Argyll region (May–June Mon–Sat 9:00–17:00, Sun 12:00–17:00; July–Aug daily 9:00–8:00; April and Sept–Oct Mon–Sat 10:00–17:00, Sun 12:00–17:00; Nov–March daily 10:00–15:00; last entry to exhibit one hour before closing, Front Street, tel. 01499/302-063). Public WCs are at the end of the nearby pier (£0.20).

The town's main "sight" is the **Inveraray Jail,** an overpriced, corny, but mildly educational former jail converted into a museum. This "living 19th-century prison" includes a courtroom where mannequins argue the fate of the accused. You'll have the opportunity to be locked up for a photo op by a playful guard (£8.25, daily April–Oct 9:30–18:00, Nov–March 10:00–17:00, last entry one hour before closing, Church Square, tel. 01499/302-381, www.inveraryjail.co.uk).

You'll spot the dramatic **Inveraray Castle** on the right as you cross the bridge coming from Glasgow. This impressive-looking stronghold of one of the more notorious branches of the Campbell clan is striking from afar but dull inside; save your time for better Highlands castles elsewhere.

• *To continue on to Oban, leave Inveraray through a gate (at the Woolen Mill) to A819, and go through Glen Aray and along Loch Awe. A85 takes you into Oban.*

OBAN

Islands near Oban: Mull and Iona

For the easiest one-day look at two of the dramatic and historic Hebrides (HEB-rid-eez) Islands, take the Iona/Mull tour from Oban. (For a more in-depth look, head north to Skye—see next chapter.)

Here's the game plan: You'll take a ferry from Oban to Mull (45 minutes), ride a Bowman's bus across Mull (1.25 hours), then board a quick ferry from Mull to Iona. The total round-trip travel time is 5.5 hours (all of it incredibly

Oban & the Southern Highlands

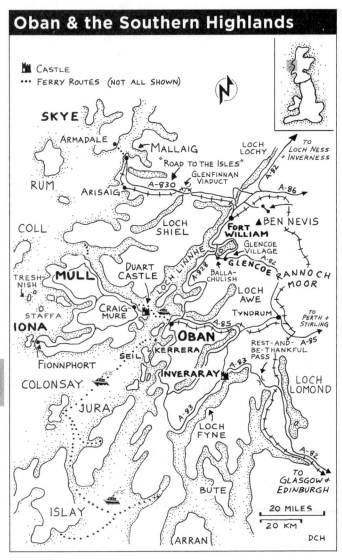

CASTLE
FERRY ROUTES (NOT ALL SHOWN)

SKYE

ARMADALE

MALLAIG

RUM

"ROAD TO THE ISLES"

GLENFINNAN
VIADUCT

ARISAIG

A-830

LOCH
LOCHY

TO
LOCH NESS
+ INVERNESS

A-82

A-86

COLL

LOCH
SHIEL

FORT
WILLIAM

▲BEN NEVIS

GLENCOE
VILLAGE

GLENCOE

RANNOCH
MOOR

TRESH-
NISH

MULL

DUART
CASTLE

LOCH LINNHE

A-828

BALLA-
CHULISH

LOCH
AWE

A-82

STAFFA

CRAIG-
MURE

TYNDRUM

A-85

TO
PERTH +
STIRLING

IONA

OBAN

REST-AND-
BE-THANKFUL
PASS

A-85

FIONNPHORT

SEIL

KERRERA

INVERARAY

A-83

LOCH
LOMOND

COLONSAY

JURA

A-83

LOCH
FYNE

A-82

TO
GLASGOW +
EDINBURGH

BUTE

ISLAY

20 MILES

20 KM

ARRAN

DCH

scenic), plus about two hours of free time on Iona. Buy your set of six tickets—one for each leg—at the Bowman's office in Oban (£34, £2 discount with this book in 2011 for Iona/Mull tour, no tours Nov–Easter, book one day ahead in July–Sept if possible, bus tickets can sell out during busy summer weekends, office open daily 8:30–17:30, 1 Queens Park Place, a block from train station, tel. 01631/566-809 or 01631/563-221, www.bowmanstours.co.uk).

You'll leave in the morning from the Oban pier on the huge

Oban–Mull ferry run by Caledonian MacBrayne (boats depart Sun–Fri at 9:50, Sat at 9:30, board at least 20 minutes before departure; boats return daily around 17:45). As the schedule can change slightly from year to year, confirm your departure time carefully in Oban. The best inside seats on the ferry—with the biggest windows—are in the sofa lounge on the uppermost deck (Level 4) on the back end of the boat. (Follow signs for the toilets, and look for big staircase to the top floor; this floor also has its own small snack bar with £3 sandwiches and £4 box lunches.) On board, if it's a clear day, ask a local or a crew member to point out Ben Nevis, the tallest mountain in Great Britain. The ferry has a fine cafeteria and a bookshop (though guidebooks are cheaper in Oban). Five minutes before landing on Mull, you'll see the striking 13th-century Duart Castle on the left (www.duartcastle.com).

Upon arrival in Mull, find your tour company's bus for the entertaining and informative ride across the Isle of Mull. All drivers spend the entire ride chattering away about life on Mull. They are hardworking local boys who make historical trivia fascinating—or at least fun. Your destination is Mull's westernmost ferry terminal (Fionnphort), where you'll board a small, rocking ferry for the brief ride to Iona. Unless you stay overnight, you'll have only about two hours to roam freely around the island before taking the ferry–bus–ferry ride in reverse back to Oban.

Mull

The Isle of Mull, the third-largest in Scotland, has 300 scenic miles of coastline and castles and a 3,169-foot-high mountain. Called Ben More ("Big Mountain" in Gaelic), it was once much

bigger. The last active volcano in northern Europe, it was 10,000 feet tall—making up the entire island of Mull—before it blew. It's calmer now, and, similarly, Mull has a notably laid-back population. My bus driver reported that there are no deaths from stress, and only a few from boredom.

With steep, fog-covered hillsides topped by cairns (piles of stones, sometimes indicating graves) and ancient stone circles, Mull has a gloomy, otherworldly charm. Bring plenty of rain protection and wear layers in case the sun peeks through the clouds. As my driver said, Mull is a place of cold, wet, windy winters and mild, wet, windy summers.

On the far side of Mull, the caravan of tour buses unloads at Fionnphort, a tiny ferry town. The ferry to the island of Iona takes about 200 walk-on passengers. Confirm the return time with your bus driver, then hustle to the dock to make the first trip over (otherwise, it's a 30-minute wait). There's a small ferry-passenger building/meager snack bar (and a pay WC); if it's closed, just buy your ticket from the ferry worker at the dock (cash or credit/debit cards accepted; leaving Iona, do the same as there's no ferry office). After the 10-minute ride, you wash ashore on sleepy Iona (free WC on this side), and the ferry mobs that crowded you on the boat seem to disappear up the main road and into Iona's back lanes.

The **About Mull Tours and Taxi** service can also get you around Mull (tel. 01681/700-507 or mobile 0788-777-4550, www .aboutmull.co.uk). They also do day tours of Mull (£35), focusing on local history and wildlife (half-day tours also available, shorter Mull tours can drop you off at Iona ferry dock at 15:00 for a quick Iona visit and pick you up at 18:00, minimum 2 people, smart to book ahead).

For directions on how to just buy ferry tickets to Mull and Iona (but not take the Bowman's bus tour), see "Staying Longer on Iona," later.

Iona

The tiny island of Iona, just 3 miles by 1.5 miles, is famous as the birthplace of Christianity in Scotland. You'll have about two hours here on your own before you retrace your steps (your driver will tell you which return ferry to take back to Mull—don't miss this boat); you'll dock back in Oban about 17:45. And though the day is spectacular when it's sunny, it's worthwhile in any weather.

A pristine quality of light and a thoughtful peace pervade the stark, (nearly) car-free island and its tiny community. With buoyant clouds bouncing playfully off distant bluffs, sparkling-white crescents of sand, and lone tourists camped thoughtfully atop huge rocks just looking out to sea, Iona is a place perfect for meditation. Climb a peak—nothing's higher than 300 feet above the sea.

Staying Longer on Iona: For a chance to really experience peaceful, idyllic Iona, consider spending a night or two. Scots bring their kids and stay on this tiny island for a week. If you want to overnight in Iona, don't buy your tickets at Bowman's in Oban—they require a same-day return. Instead, buy each leg of the ferry–bus–ferry (and return) trip separately. Get your Oban–

Mull ferry ticket in the Oban ferry office (one-way for walk-on passengers-£4.65, round-trip-£7.90, ticket good for 5 days). Once you arrive in Mull (Craignure), follow the crowds to the Bowman buses and buy a ticket directly from the driver (£10 round-trip). When you arrive at the ferry terminal (Fionnphort), walk into the small trailer ferry office to buy a ticket to Iona (£2.15 each way).

If you want to spend more time on Iona (about four hours) and return to Oban the same day, you have another option. Although taking the Bowman's tour bus guarantees a seat back the same day, you can also take an earlier Bowman's service bus (no tour narration, same price, buy each leg separately as described above) from the Mull ferry terminal to Fionnphort. Ask at the Bowman's office for details.

Orientation to Iona

The village, Baile Mòr, has shops, a restaurant/pub, enough beds, and no bank (get cash back with a purchase at the grocery store). The **Finlay Ross Shop** rents bikes (to the left as you depart the ferry, £4.50/4 hours, £8/day, £10 deposit per bike; open April–Oct Mon–Sat 9:30–17:00, Sun 11:30–16:00; shorter hours off-season, tel. 01681/700-357, www.finlayrossiona.co.uk). The only taxi on Iona is **Iona Taxi** (tel. 07810-325-990, www.ionataxi.co.uk). Up the road from the ferry dock is a little **Spar** grocery (Mon–Sat 9:00–17:15, Sun 12:00–16:00, shorter hours off-season and closed Sun, free island maps). Iona's official website (www.isle-of-iona .com) has good information about the island.

Sights on Iona

A single paved road leads from the ferry, passing through the village and up a small hill to the **nunnery ruins** (one of the best-preserved medieval nunneries in Britain) before heading to the **abbey,** with its graveyard. **St. Oran's Chapel** (next to the graveyard) is the oldest church building on the island. Inside you'll find several grave slabs carved in the distinctive Iona School style, developed by local stonecarvers in the 14th century. Look for the depictions of medieval warrior aristocrats. Many more of these carved graves have been moved to the abbey, where you can see them in its cloisters and old infirmary. It's free to see the nunnery ruins, graveyard, and chapel; the abbey itself has an admission fee, but it's worth the cost just to sit in the stillness of its lovely, peaceful interior courtyard (£4.70, not covered by bus tour ticket, includes 30-minute guided tour, £14 guidebook, daily April–Sept 9:30–17:00, Oct–March 9:30–16:00, tel. 01681/700-512, www .historic-scotland.gov.uk). While the present abbey, nunnery, and

OBAN

History of Iona

St. Columba, an Irish scholar, soldier, priest, and founder of monasteries, got into a small war over the possession of an illegally copied psalm book. Victorious but sickened by the bloodshed, Columba left Ireland, vowing never to return. According to legend, the first bit of land out of sight of his homeland was Iona. He stopped here in 563, and established an abbey.

Columba's monastic community flourished, and Iona became the center of Celtic Christianity. Missionaries from Iona spread the gospel throughout Scotland and northern England, while scholarly monks established Iona as a center of art and learning. The *Book of Kells*—perhaps the finest piece of art from "Dark Ages" Europe—was probably made on Iona in the eighth century. The island was so important that it was the legendary burial place for ancient Scottish and even Scandinavian kings (including Shakespeare's Macbeth).

Slowly, the importance of Iona ebbed. Vikings massacred 68 monks in 806. Fearing more raids, the monks evacuated most of Iona's treasures to Ireland (including the *Book of Kells*, which is now in Dublin). Much later, with the Reformation, the abbey was abandoned, and most of its finely carved crosses were destroyed. In the 17th century, locals used the abbey only as a handy quarry for other building projects.

Iona's population peaked at about 500 in the 1830s. In the 1840s, a potato famine hit, and in the 1850s, a third of the islanders emigrated to Canada or Australia. By 1900, the population was down to 210, and today it's only around 100.

But in our generation, a new religious community has given the abbey fresh life. The Iona Community is an ecumenical gathering of men and women who seek new ways of living the Gospel in today's world, with a focus on worship, peace and justice issues, and reconciliation.

graveyard go back to the 13th century, much of what you'll see was rebuilt in the 20th century. (There may be scaffolding on the abbey tower during your visit, as the mortar is being replaced.)

Across from the abbey is the **Iona Community's information center** (free WCs), which runs the abbey with Historic Scotland and hosts modern-day pilgrims who come here to experience the birthplace of Scottish Christianity. Its gift shop is packed with books on the island's important role in Christian history.

If you have extra time, the **Heritage Center** is small but well done, with displays on local and natural history and a tiny tea room (£3, Mon–Sat 10:30–16:30, closed Sun; on the left past the nunnery ruins). You can also catch a **worship service** at the abbey (get times from Iona Community's information center, tel. 01681/700-404, www.iona.org.uk).

Sleeping and Eating on Iona

(£1 = about $1.60, country code: 44, area code: 01681)
In addition to the options listed below, there are many B&Bs, apartments, and a hostel on the island (see www.isle-of-iona.com /accommodation.htm).

$$$ Argyll Hotel, built in 1867, proudly overlooks the water-front, with 16 rooms and pleasingly creaky hallways lined with bookshelves (Sb-£55-60, D-£70, Db-£96, larger Db-£130, cheaper off-season, extra bed for kids-£15, includes continental breakfast, closed Nov–March, free Wi-Fi, comfortable lounge and sunroom, tel. 01681/700-334, fax 01681/700-510, www.argyllhoteliona.co.uk, reception@argyllhoteliona.co.uk, Daniel and Claire). Its white-linen dining room is open to the public for lunch (12:30–13:30) and dinner (£12–16 entrées, 19:00–20:00).

$$$ St. Columba Hotel, situated in the middle of a peace-ful garden with picnic tables, has 27 pleasant rooms and spa-cious lodge-like common spaces (Sb-£55–70, Db-£90–120, huge view Db-£150, front rooms have sea views but windows are small, includes continental breakfast, discounts for stays of 4 or more nights, extra bed for kids-£15, free Internet access, next door to abbey on road up from dock, open Easter–Oct only, tel. 01681/700-304, fax 01681/700-688, www.stcolumba-hotel.co.uk, info@stcolumba-hotel.co.uk). Their fine 14-table restaurant, open to the public, overlooks the water (£5–10 lunches, £10–13 dinners, daily 12:00–14:30 & 18:30–20:00). Even if you're not staying here, you can stop by to use the Internet (£0.50/15 minutes).

$$ Calva B&B, near the abbey, has three spacious rooms (Db-£55, second house on left past the abbey, look for sign in win-dow and gnomes on porch, tel. 01681/700-340, friendly Janetta and Jack the bearded collie).

Glencoe

This valley is the essence of the wild, powerful, and stark beauty of the Highlands. Along with its scenery, Glencoe offers a good dose of bloody clan history: In 1692, British Redcoats (led by a local Campbell commander) came to the valley, and were sheltered and fed for 12 days by the MacDonalds—whose leader had been late in swearing an oath to the British monarch. Then, the morning of February 13, the soldiers were ordered to rise up early and kill their sleeping hosts, violating the rules of Highland hospitality and earning the valley the name "The Weeping Glen." It's fitting that such an epic, dramatic incident should be set in this equally epic, dramatic valley, where the cliffsides seem to weep (with running streams) when it rains.

Orientation to Glencoe

(area code: 01855)
The valley of Glencoe is just off the main A828/A82 road between Oban and points north (such as Fort William and Inverness). (If you're coming from the north, the signage can be tricky—at the roundabout south of Fort William, follow signs to *Crianlarich* and *A82*.) The most appealing town here is the one-street Glencoe village, while the slightly larger and more modern town of Ballachulish (a half-mile away) has more services. Though not quite quaint, the very sleepy village of Glencoe is worth a stop for its folk museum and its status as the gateway to the valley. The town's hub of activity is its grocery store (ATM, daily 8:00–20:00).

Tourist Information
Your best source of information (especially for walks and hikes) is the **Glencoe Visitors Centre,** described later. The nearest **TI** is well-signed in Ballachulish (daily 9:00–17:00, opens at 10:00 on Sun in winter, bus timetables, free phone to call area B&Bs, café, shop, tel. 01855/811-866, www.glencoetourism.co.uk or www.discoverglencoe.com).

Sights in Glencoe

Glencoe Village
Glencoe village is just a line of houses sitting beneath the brooding mountains. Two tiny thatched-roof, early-18th-century croft

houses are jammed with local history at the huggable **Glencoe and North Lorn Folk Museum.** It's filled with humble exhibits gleaned from the town's old closets and attics. When one house was being rethatched, its owner found a cache of 200-year-old swords and pistols hidden there from the British Redcoats after the disastrous battle of Culloden. Don't miss the museum's little door that leads out back, where you'll find more exhibits on the Glencoe Massacre, local slate, farm tools, and an infamous local murder that inspired Robert Louis Stevenson to write *Kidnapped* (£3, call ahead for hours—generally Easter–Oct Mon–Sat 10:00–17:30, closed Sun and off-season, tel. 01855/811-664).

In Glencoe Valley

▲▲**Driving Through Glencoe Valley**—If you have a car, spend an hour or so following A82 through the valley, past the Glencoe Visitors Centre (see next listing), into the desolate moor beyond, and back again. You'll enjoy grand views, flocks of "hairy coos" (shaggy Highland Cattle), and a chance to hear a bagpiper in the wind—roadside Highland buskers (most often seen on good-weather summer weekends). If you play the recorder (and no other tourists are there), ask to finger a tune while the piper does the hard work. At the end of the valley you hit the vast Rannoch Moor—500 desolate square miles with barely enough decent land to graze a sheep.

OBAN

Glencoe Visitors Centre—This modern facility, a mile up A82 past Glencoe village (off to the left) into the dramatic valley, is designed to resemble a *clachan,* or traditional Highlands settlement. The information desk inside the shop is your single best resource for advice (and maps or guidebooks) about local walks and hikes, some of which are described next. At the back of the complex you'll find a viewpoint with a handy 3-D model of the hills for orientation. There's also a pricey £5.50 exhibition about the surrounding landscape, local history, mountaineering, and conservation. It's worth the time to watch the more-interesting-than-it-sounds video on geology and the 14-minute film on the Glencoe Massacre, which thoughtfully traces the events leading up to the tragedy rather than simply recycling romanticized legends (April–Aug daily 9:30–17:30; Sept–Oct daily 10:00–17:00; Nov–mid-Dec and Feb-March Thu–Sun 10:00–16:00, closed Mon–Wed; closed mid-Dec–Jan; last entry 45 minutes before closing, café, tel. 01855/811-307, www.nts.org.uk).

Walks—For a steep one-mile hike, climb the Devil's Staircase (trailhead just off A82, 8 miles east of Glencoe). For a three-hour hike, ask at the Visitors Centre about the Lost Valley of the MacDonalds (trailhead just off A82, 3 miles east of Glencoe). For an easy walk above Glencoe, head to the mansion on the hill (over the bridge, turn left, fine loch views). This mansion was built in 1894 by Canadian Pacific Railway magnate Lord Strathcona for his wife, a Canadian with First Nations (Native American) ancestry. She was homesick for the Rockies, so he had the grounds landscaped to represent the lakes, trees, and mountains of her home country. It didn't work, and they eventually returned to Canada. The house originally had 365 windows, to allow a different view each day.

Glencoe's Burial Island and Island of Discussion—In the loch just outside Glencoe (near Ballachulish), notice the burial island—where the souls of those who "take the low road" are piped home. (Ask a local about "Ye'll take the high road, and I'll take the low road.") The next island was the Island of Discussion—where those in dispute went until they found agreement.

Sleeping in Glencoe

(£1 = about $1.60, country code: 44, area code: 01855)

Glencoe is an extremely low-key place to spend the night between Oban or Glasgow and the northern destinations. These places are accustomed to one-nighters just passing through, but some people stay here for several days to enjoy a variety of hikes. All of these B&Bs are along the main road through the middle of the village, and all are cash-only.

$$ Inchconnal B&B is a cute, renovated house with a bonnie wee potted garden out front, renting two bright rooms with views—one cottage-style, the other woodsy (Db-£48, £50 July–Aug, tel. 01855/811-958, warm Caroline Macdonald).

$$ Heatherlea B&B, at the end of the village, has three pleasant, modern rooms, homey public spaces, and a big board-game collection (Sb-£26–28, Db-£52–56, £52 in July–Aug, closed Nov–Easter, tel. 01855/811-799, heatherleaglencoe@gmail.com, friendly Ivan and Thea).

$$ Tulachgorm B&B has two comfortable rooms that share a bathroom in a modern house with fine mountain views (D-£42, tel. 01855/811-391, mellow Ann Blake and friendly West Highland terrier Jo).

$$$ Clachaig Inn, outside of town, works well for hikers who want a comfy mountain inn (Db-£88–92; see description below, under "Eating in Glencoe").

Eating in Glencoe

The choices in and near Glencoe are slim—this isn't the place for fine dining. But three options offer decent food a short walk or drive away. For evening fun, take a walk or ask your B&B host where to find music and dancing.

In Glencoe: The only choice in Glencoe village is **The Glencoe Hotel,** with lovely dining areas and a large outdoor deck (£8–10 entrées, food served daily 12:00–14:00 & 18:00–20:30, at junction of A82 and Glencoe village, tel. 01855/811-140).

Near Glencoe: **Clachaig Inn** is a Highlands pub in a stunning valley setting whose clientele is half locals and half tourists. This unpretentious and very popular social hub features billiards, jukeboxes, and pub grub (£5–13 entrées, open daily for lunch and dinner, tel. 01855/811-252, www.clachaig.com). Drive to the end of Glencoe village, cross the bridge, and follow the little single-track road for three miles, past campgrounds and hostels, until you reach the inn on the right.

In Ballachulish, near Glencoe: **Laroch Bar & Bistro,** in the next village over from Glencoe (toward Oban), is family-friendly (£6–9 pub grub, food served 12:00–14:30 & 17:30–21:00, tel. 01855/811-900). Drive into Ballachulish village, and you'll see it on the left.

Glencoe Connections

Unfortunately, buses don't actually drive down the main road through Glencoe village. Some buses (most notably those going between Glasgow and Fort William) stop near Glencoe village at a place called **"Glencoe Crossroads"**—a short walk into the village center. Other buses (such as those between Oban and Fort William) stop at the nearby town of **Ballachulish,** which is just a half-mile away (or a £3 taxi ride). Tell the bus driver where you're going ("Glencoe village") and ask to be let off as close to there as possible.

From **Glencoe Crossroads,** you can catch bus #914, #915, or #916 (8/day) to **Fort William** (30 minutes) or **Glasgow** (2.5 hours).

From **Ballachulish,** you can take bus #918 (3/day in summer, 2/day off-season, never on Sun) to **Fort William** (30 minutes) or **Oban** (1 hour). Bus info: Toll tel. 08712/663-333, www.citylink .co.uk.

To reach **Inverness** or **Portree** on the Isle of Skye, transfer in Fort William. To reach **Edinburgh,** transfer in Glasgow.

Near Glencoe: Fort William

Laying claim to the title of "outdoor capital of the UK," Fort William is well-positioned between Oban, Inverness, and the Isle of Skye. This crossroads town is a transportation hub and has a pleasant-enough, shop-studded, pedestrianized main drag, but few charms of its own. Most visitors just pass through...and should. But while you're here, consider buying lunch and stopping by the TI to get your questions answered.

Tourist Information: The TI is on the car-free main drag (June–Aug Mon–Sat 9:00–18:00, Sun 9:30–17:00; Easter–May and Sept–Oct Mon–Sat 9:00–17:00, Sun 10:00–16:00; shorter hours and closed Sun off-season; Internet access, free public WCs up the street next to parking lot, 15 High Street, tel. 01397/701-801).

Sights in and near Fort William

Fort William has no real sights, aside from a humble-but-well-presented **West Highland Museum,** with exhibits on local history, wildlife, dress, Jacobite memorabilia, and more (£4, guidebook-£2.50; June–Sept Mon–Sat 10:00–17:00, July–Aug also Sun 10:00–16:00; Oct–May Mon–Sat 10:00–16:00, closed Sun; on Cameron Square, tel. 01397/702-169, www.westhighlandmuseum .org.uk).

The appealing options described below lie just outside of town.

Ben Nevis

From Fort William, take a peek at Britain's highest peak, Ben Nevis (4,409 feet). Thousands walk to its summit each year. On a clear day, you can admire it from a distance. Scotland's only mountain cable cars—at the **Nevis Range Mountain Experience**—can take you to a not-very-lofty 2,150-foot perch on the slopes of Aonach Mor for a closer look (£10.50, daily July–Aug 9:30–18:00, Sept–June 10:00–17:00, 15-minute ride, shuts down in high winds and mid-Nov–mid-Dec—call ahead, signposted on A82 north of Fort William, tel. 01397/705-825, www.nevisrange.co.uk). They also have high-wire obstacle courses (£20, under age 17-£14, daily 10:00–16:00).

Toward the Isle of Skye: The Road to the Isles and the Jacobite Steam Train

The magical steam train that scenically transports Harry Potter to the wizarding school of Hogwarts runs along a real-life train line. The West Highland Railway Line chugs 42 miles from Fort William west to the ferry port at Mallaig. Along the way, it passes

OBAN

the iconic **Glenfinnan Viaduct,** with 416 yards of raised track over 21 supporting arches. This route is also graced with plenty of loch-and-mountain views and, near the end, passes along a beautiful stretch of coast with some fine sandy beaches. While many people take the Jacobite Steam Train to enjoy this stretch of Scotland, it can be more rewarding to drive the same route—especially if you're headed for the Isle of Skye.

By Train: The **Jacobite Steam Train** (they don't actually call it the "Hogwarts Express") offers a small taste of the Harry Potter experience...but many who take this trip for that reason alone are disappointed. Although one of the steam engines and some of the coaches were used in the films, don't expect a Harry Potter theme ride. However, you can expect beautiful scenery. Along the way, the train stops for 20 minutes at Glenfinnan station (just after the Glenfinnan Viaduct), and then gives you way too much time (1.75 hours) to poke around the dull port town of Mallaig before heading back to Fort William (one-way—£23.50 adults, £13.50 kids; round-trip—£31 adults, £17.50 kids; £2.50 booking fee, more for first class, tickets must be purchased in advance—see details next, 1/day Mon–Fri mid-May–late Oct, also Sat–Sun July–Aug, departs Fort William at 10:20 and returns at 16:00, about a 2-hour ride each way, WCs on board, tel. 08451/284-681 or 08451/284-685, www.westcoastrailways.co.uk).

Note: Trains leave Fort William from the main train station, but you must book ahead online or by phone—you cannot buy tickets for this train at the Fort William or Mallaig train-station ticket offices. There may be a limited amount of seats available each day on a first-come, first-served basis (cash only, buy from conductor), but in summer, trips are often sold out.

The 84-mile round-trip from Fort William takes the better part of a day to show you the same scenery twice. Modern "Sprinter" trains follow the same line—consider taking the steam train one-way to Mallaig, then speeding back on a regular train to avoid the long Mallaig layover and slow return (1.25 hours, 2-3/day, book at least two days ahead July–Aug, tel. 08457-550-033, www.scotrail.co.uk). Note that you can use this train to reach the Isle of Skye: Take the train to Mallaig, walk onto the ferry to Armadale (on Skye), then catch a bus in Armadale to your destination on Skye (toll tel. 08712/663-333, www.citylink.co.uk).

There are lockers for storing luggage at the Fort William train station (£4–5/24 hours, station open Mon–Sat 7:20–22:10, Sun 11:30–22:10).

By Car: While the train is time-consuming and expensive, driving the same **"Road to the Isles"** route (A830)—ideally on your way to Skye—can be a fun way to see the same famous scenery more affordably and efficiently. The key here is to be sure you leave enough time to make it to Mallaig before the Skye ferry departs—get timing advice from the Fort William TI. I'd allow at least 1 hour and 20 minutes to get from Fort William to the ferry landing in Mallaig (if you keep moving, with no stops en route)—and note that vehicles are required to arrive 30 minutes before the boat departs. As you leave Fort William on A830, a sign on the left tells you what time the next ferry will depart Mallaig.

Sleeping in Fort William

These two B&Bs are on Union Road, a five-minute walk up the hill above the main pedestrian street that runs through the heart of town. Each place has three rooms, one of which has a private bathroom on the hall.

$$ Glenmorven Guest House is a friendly, flower-bedecked, family-run place renting rooms with views of Loch Linnhe (Db-£60, free pick-up from train or bus station with advance notice, laundry service, Union Road, Fort William, tel. 01397/703-236, www.glenmorven.co.uk, glenmorven@yahoo.com, Anne and Colin Jamieson).

$$ Gowan Brae B&B ("Hill of the Big Daisy") has antique-filled rooms with loch or garden views in a hobbit-cute house (Db-£64 in high season, £50 off-season, Union Road, tel. 01397/704-399, www.gowanbrae.co.uk, gowan_brae@btinternet.com, Jim and Ann Clark).

Eating in Fort William

All three places listed below are on the main walking street, near the start of town; the first two serve only lunch.

Hot Roast Company sells beef, turkey, ham, or pork sandwiches, topped with some tasty extras (£3 take-away, a bit more for sit-down service, Mon–Sat 9:30–15:30, closed Sun, 127 High Street, tel. 01397/700-606).

Café 115 features good food and modern bistro decor (£4–8 meals, £8 fish-and-chips, daily 10:00–17:30, mid-July–Aug until 21:30, 115 High Street, tel. 01397/702-500).

The Grog & Gruel serves real ales, good pub grub, and Tex-Mex and Cajun dishes, with unusual meals such as vegetarian haggis with Drambuie sauce, boar burgers, and venison chili (£5–12 meals, food served daily 12:00–21:00, Sun in winter 17:00–21:00, free Wi-Fi, 66 High Street, tel. 01397/705-078). Their upstairs restaurant features the same menu (daily 17:00–21:00).

Fort William Connections

Fort William is a major transit hub for the Highlands, so you'll likely change buses here at some point during your trip.

From Fort William by Bus to: Glencoe (all Glasgow-bound buses—#914, #915, and #916; 8/day, 30 minutes), **Ballachulish** near Glencoe (Oban-bound bus #918, 3/day in summer, 2/day off-season, never on Sun, 30 minutes), **Oban** (bus #918, 3/day in summer, 2/day off-season, never on Sun, 1.5 hours), **Portree** on the Isle of Skye (buses #915 and #916, 4/day, 3 hours), **Inverness** (Citylink bus #919 or Stagecoach bus #19, 8/day, 2 hours), **Glasgow** (buses #914, #915, and #916; 8/day, 3 hours, some with change in Tyndrum), **Edinburgh** (bus #913, 3/day in evening, 4 hours, 1 direct, 2 with change in Tyndrum; more with transfer in Glasgow on buses #900 and #914/915, 5 hours). Bus info: toll tel. 08712/663-333, www.citylink.co.uk or www.stagecoachbus.com.

Route Tips for Drivers

From England's Lake District to Glasgow: From Keswick, take A66 for 18 miles to M6 and speed north nonstop (via Penrith and Carlisle), crossing Hadrian's Wall into Scotland. The road becomes M74 south of Glasgow. To slip through Glasgow quickly, leave M74 at Junction 4 onto M73, following signs to *M8/Glasgow*. Leave M73 at Junction 2, exiting onto M8. Stay on M8 west through Glasgow, exit on Junction 30, cross Erskine Bridge, and turn left on A82, following signs to *Crianlarich* and *Loch Lomond*. (For a scenic drive through Glasgow, take exit 17 off M8 and stay on A82 toward Dumbarton.)

From Oban to Glencoe and Fort William: From Oban, follow coastal A828 toward Fort William. After about 20 miles, you'll see the photogenic Castle Staulker marooned on a lonely island. At North Ballachulish, you'll reach a bridge spanning Loch Leven; rather than crossing the bridge, turn off and follow A82 into the Glencoe valley. After exploring the valley, make a U-turn and return through Glencoe. To continue on to Fort William, backtrack to the bridge at North Ballachulish and cross it, following A82 north. (For a scenic shortcut directly back to Glasgow or Edinburgh, head north only as far as Glencoe, and then cut to Glasgow or Edinburgh on A82 via Rannoch Moor and Tyndrum.)

From Fort William to Loch Ness and Inverness: Follow the Caledonian Canal north along A82, which goes through Fort Augustus (and its worthwhile Caledonian Canal Heritage Centre) and then follows the west side of Loch Ness on its way to Inverness. Along the way, A82 passes Urquhart Castle and two Loch Ness Monster exhibits in Drumnadrochit. These attractions are described

OBAN

in the Inverness and the Northern Highlands chapter.

From Fort William to the Isle of Skye: You have two options for this journey: Head west on A830 (the Road to the Isles), then catch the ferry from Mallaig to Armadale on the Isle of Skye; or head north on A82 to Invergarry, and turn left (west) on A87, which you'll follow (past Eilean Donan Castle) to Kyle of Lochalsh and the Skye Bridge to the island. Consider using one route one way, and the other on the return trip—for example, follow the "Road to the Isles" from Fort William to Mallaig, and take the ferry to Skye; later, leaving Skye, take A87 east from the Skye Bridge past Eilean Donan Castle to Loch Ness and Inverness.

ISLE OF SKYE

The rugged, remote-feeling Isle of Skye has a reputation for unpredictable weather ("Skye" means "cloudy" in Old Norse, and locals call it "The Misty Isle"). But it also offers some of Scotland's best scenery, and it rarely fails to charm its many visitors. Narrow, twisty roads wind around Skye in the shadows of craggy, black, bald mountains.

Skye seems to have more sheep than people; 200 years ago, many human residents were forced to move off the island to make room for more livestock during the Highland Clearances. The people who remain are some of the most ardently Gaelic Scots in Scotland. The island's Sleat Peninsula is home to a rustic but important Gaelic college. Half of all native island residents speak Gaelic (which they pronounce "gallic") as their first language. A generation ago, it was illegal to teach Gaelic in schools; today, Skye offers its residents the opportunity to enroll in Gaelic-only education, from primary school to college.

Set up camp in one of the island's home-base towns, Portree or Kyleakin. Then dive into Skye's attractions. Drive around the appealing Trotternish Peninsula, enjoying stark vistas of jagged rock formations with the mysterious Outer Hebrides looming on the horizon. Explore a gaggle of old-fashioned stone homes, learn about Skye's ancient farming lifestyles, and pay homage at the grave of a brave woman who rescued a bonnie prince. Climb the dramatic Cuillin Hills, and drive to a lighthouse at the end of the world. Visit a pair of castles—run-down but thought-provoking Dunvegan, and nearby but not on Skye, the photo-perfect Eilean Donan.

Planning Your Time

With a week in Scotland, Skye merits two nights, with a full day to hit its highlights (Trotternish Peninsula, Dunvegan Castle, Cuillin Hills, Talisker Distillery). Mountaineers enjoy extra time for hiking and hillwalking. Because it takes time to reach, Skye (the northernmost destination in this book) is skippable if you only have a few days in Scotland—instead, focus on Edinburgh and the more accessible Highlands sights near Oban.

Skye fits neatly into a Highlands itinerary between Oban/Glencoe and Loch Ness/Inverness. To avoid seeing the same scenery twice, it works well to drive the "Road to the Isles" from Fort William to Mallaig, then take the ferry to Skye; later, leave Skye via the Skye Bridge and follow A87 east toward Loch Ness and Inverness, stopping at Eilean Donan Castle en route.

Orientation to the Isle of Skye

The Isle of Skye is big (over 600 square miles), with lots of ins and outs—but you're never more than five miles from the sea. The island is punctuated by peninsulas and inlets (called "sea lochs"). Skye is covered with hills, but the most striking are the mountain-like Cuillin Hills in the south-central part of the island.

There are only about 11,000 people on the entire island; roughly a quarter live in the main village, Portree. Other population centers include Kyleakin (near the bridge connecting Skye with the mainland) and Broadford (a tidy string of houses on the road between Portree and the bridge, with the biggest and handiest grocery store on the island). A few of the villages—including Broadford and Dunvegan—have TIs, but the most useful one is in Portree.

Getting to the Isle of Skye

By Car: Your easiest bet is the slick, free **Skye Bridge** that crosses from Kyle of Lochalsh on the mainland to Kyleakin on Skye.

The island can also be reached from the mainland via a pair of **car ferry** crossings. The major ferry line connects the mainland town of Mallaig (west of Fort William along the "Road to the Isles" and the Harry Potter steam-train line) to Armadale on Skye (£20.30/car, £3.85/passenger, late March–late Oct 8/day each way, 4-6/day on Sun, late Oct–late March very limited Sat–Sun connections, check-in closes 30 minutes before sailing, can be cancelled in rough weather, 30-minute trip, operated by Caledonian MacBrayne, www.calmac.co.uk). A tiny six-car, proudly local "turntable" ferry crosses the short gap between the mainland Glenelg and Skye's Kylerhea (£12/car with up to 4 passengers, £15 round-trip, Easter–Oct daily every 20 minutes 10:00–18:00, June–Aug until 19:00, no need to book ahead, no boats off-season,

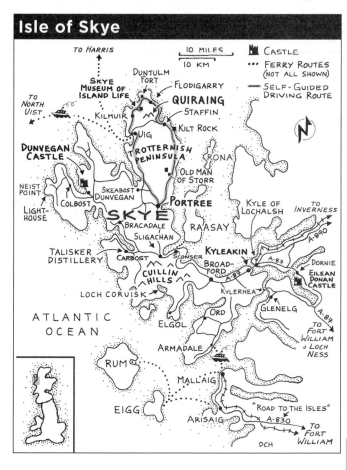

Isle of Skye

TO HARRIS

10 MILES
10 KM

■ CASTLE
••• FERRY ROUTES (NOT ALL SHOWN)
— SELF-GUIDED DRIVING ROUTE

DUNTULM FORT
SKYE MUSEUM OF ISLAND LIFE
FLODIGARRY
QUIRAING
STAFFIN

TO NORTH UIST

KILMUIR
UIG
KILT ROCK

TROTTERNISH PENINSULA
RONA

DUNVEGAN CASTLE
OLD MAN OF STORR

NEIST POINT
SKEABOST DUNVEGAN
PORTREE

LIGHTHOUSE
COLBOST
SKYE
KYLE OF LOCHALSH
TO INVERNESS

BRACADALE
RAASAY
SLIGACHAN

TALISKER DISTILLERY
CARBOST
SCONSER
KYLEAKIN
A-87
DORNIE

CUILLIN HILLS
BROADFORD
EILEAN DONAN CASTLE

LOCH CORUISK
KYLERHEA

A-83

ATLANTIC OCEAN
ELGOL
ORD
GLENELG
TO FORT WILLIAM & LOCH NESS

ARMADALE

RUM
MALLAIG

EIGG
"ROAD TO THE ISLES"
A-830
TO FORT WILLIAM

ARISAIG

DCH

Skye Ferry, www.skyeferry.co.uk).

By Public Transportation: Skye is connected to the outside world by a series of Scottish CityLink **buses** (www.citylink.co.uk), which use Portree as their Skye hub. From Portree, buses connect to **Inverness** (bus #917, 2–3/day, 3.25 hours, via Loch Ness), **Glasgow** (buses #915 and #916, 3/day, 6.25 hours, also stops at **Fort William** and **Glencoe**), and **Edinburgh** (3/day, 7.5–8 hours, transfer in Fort William or Glasgow).

There are also some more complicated connections possible for the determined: Take the train from Edinburgh, Glasgow, or Inverness to Fort William; transfer to the steam train to Mallaig; take the ferry across to Armadale; and catch a bus to Portree. Alternatively, you can take the train from Edinburgh or Glasgow to Inverness, take the train to Kyle of Lochalsh, then take the bus to Portree.

Getting Around the Isle of Skye

By Car: Once on Skye, you'll need a car to enjoy the island. (Even if you're doing the rest of your trip by public transportation, a car rental is worthwhile to bypass the frustrating public-transportation options.) If you're driving, a good map is a must (look for a 1:130,000 map that covers the entire island with enough detail to point out side roads and attractions). You'll be surprised how long it takes to traverse this "small" island. Here are driving-time estimates for some likely trips: Kyleakin and Skye Bridge to Portree—45 minutes; Portree to Dunvegan—30 minutes; Portree to the tip of Trotternish Peninsula and back again—1.5–2 hours; Uig (on Trotternish Peninsula) to Dunvegan—45 minutes.

By Bus: Skye is frustrating by bus, especially on Sundays, when virtually no local buses run (except for a few long-distance buses to the ferry dock and mainland destinations). Portree is the hub for local bus traffic. Most Skye buses are operated by Stagecoach (www.stagecoachbus.com/highlands, timetable info from Traveline, toll tel. 0871-200-2233, www.traveline.org.uk). If you'll be using local buses a lot, consider a Skye Dayrider ticket (£6.50/1 day) or the Skye Megarider (£41/7 days, covers all of Skye plus trip to Eilean Donan, cheaper options available for just part of the island). You can buy either of these tickets from any driver. From Portree you can go around the **Trotternish Peninsula** (#57, Mon–Sat 4–5/day in each direction—clockwise and counterclockwise; none on Sun), to **Dunvegan** (#56, 5/day Mon–Fri, 3/day Sat, none on Sun, goes right to the castle, catch a bus that leaves no later than 12:35 to have enough time at the castle), and to **Kyleakin** (#50, 5/day Mon–Sat, 2/day Sun, transfer in Broadford).

By Tour: If you're without a car, consider taking a tour. Several operations on the island take visitors to hard-to-reach spots on a half-day or full-day tour. Some are more educational, while others are loose and informal. Look for brochures around the island, or ask locals for tips. The **Aros Centre** near Portree leads three-hour tours twice daily (£14, mid-April–mid-Oct Mon–Sat at 10:00 and 14:00, can pick you up in Portree, reserve ahead by calling 01478/613-649 or in person at the Portree TI, www.aros.co.uk). **Kathleen MacAskil** with Skye Tours gives private tours by car or minibus (about £100/4 hours, minimum 2 people, tel. 01470/582-306, kathleenmacaskil@aol.com).

The Trotternish Peninsula

This inviting peninsula north of Portree is packed with windswept castaway scenery, unique geological formations, and some offbeat sights. In good weather, a spin around Trotternish is the single best Skye activity (and you'll still have time to visit Dunvegan Castle or the Cuillin Hills later on).

Self-Guided Driving Tour

The following loop tour starts and ends in Portree, circling the peninsula counterclockwise. If you did it without stopping, you'd make it back to Portree within two hours—but it deserves the better part of a day.

Begin in the island's main town, Portree. (If you're heading up from Kyleakin, you'll enjoy some grand views of the Cuillin Hills on your way up.) Note that from Portree to Uig, you'll be driving on a paved single-track road, with occasional "passing places" to allow cars to pull over.

• *Head north of Portree on A855, following signs for* Staffin. *About three miles out of town, you'll begin to enjoy some impressive views of the Trotternish Ridge. As you pass the small loch on your right, straight ahead is the distinctive feature called the...*

Old Man of Storr: This 160-foot-tall tapered slab of basalt stands proudly apart from the rest of the Storr. The unusual land-

scape of the Trotternish Peninsula is due to massive landslides (the largest that have ever occurred in Britain). This block slid down the cliff about 6,500 years ago and landed on its end, where it was slowly whittled by weather into a pinnacle. The lochs on your right have been linked together to spin the turbines at a nearby hydro-electric plant that once provided all of Skye's electricity.

ISLE OF SKYE

• *After passing the Old Man, enjoy the scenery on your right, over-looking...*

Nearby Islands and the Mainland: Some of Skye's most appealing scenery isn't of the island itself, but of the surrounding terrain. In the distance, craggy mountains recede into the horizon. The long island in the foreground, a bit to the north, is called Rona. This military-owned island, and the channel behind it, were used to develop and test one of Margaret Thatcher's pet projects, the Sting Ray remote-control torpedo.

• *After about five miles, keep an eye out on the right for a large parking lot near a wee loch. Park and walk to the viewpoint to see...*

Kilt Rock: So named because of its resemblance to a Scotsman's tartan kilt, this 200-foot-tall sea cliff has a layer of

volcanic rock with vertical lava columns that resemble pleats, sitting atop a layer of horizontal sedimentary rock.

• *After continuing through the village of Staffin (whose name means "the pinnacle place"), you'll begin to see interesting rock formations high on the hill to your left. When you get to the crossroads, head left toward Quiraing (a rock formation). This crossroads is a handy pit stop—there's a public WC in the little white building behind the red phone box just up the main road.*

Now twist your way up the road to...

Quiraing: As you drive up, notice (on your left) a couple of modern cemeteries high in the hills, far above the village. It seems like a strange spot to bury the dead, in the middle of nowhere, but the earth here is less valuable for development, and (since it's not clay, like down by the water) it provides better drainage.

You'll enjoy fine views on the right of the jagged, dramatic northern end of the Trotternish Ridge, called the Quiraing—rated

▲▲. More landslides caused the dramatic scenery in this area, and each rock formation has a name, such as "The Needle" or "The Prison." As you approach the summit of this road, you'll reach a parking area on the left. This marks a popular trailhead for hiking out to get a closer look at

the formations. If you've got the time, energy, and weather for a sturdy 30-minute uphill hike, here's your chance. You can either follow the trail along the base of the rock formations, or hike up to the top of the plateau and follow it to the end (both paths are faintly visible from the parking area). Once up top, your reward is a view of the secluded green plateau called "The Table," another landslide block, which isn't visible from the road.

• *You could continue on this road all the way to Uig, at the other end of the peninsula, but it's worth backtracking, then turning left onto the main road (A855), to see the...*

Tip of Trotternish: A few miles north, you'll pass a hotel called **Flodigarry**, with a cottage on the premises that was once home to Bonnie Prince Charlie's rescuer, Flora MacDonald (for her story, read "Monument to Flora MacDonald," later; cottage is now part of the hotel and not open to the public).

Soon after, at the top of the ridge at the tip of the peninsula, you'll see the remains of an old **fort**—not from the Middle Ages or the days of Bonnie Prince Charlie, but from World War II, when the Atlantic was monitored for U-boats from this position.

Then you'll pass (on the right) the crumbling remains of another fort, this one much older: **Duntulm Castle,** which was the first stronghold on Skye of the influential MacDonald clan. The castle was abandoned around 1730 for Armadale Castle on the southern end of Skye; according to a legend, the family left after a nursemaid accidentally dropped the infant heir out a window onto the rocks below. In the distance beyond, you can see the **Outer Hebrides**—the most rugged, remote, and Gaelic part of Scotland. (Skye, a bit closer to the mainland, belongs to the Inner Hebrides.)

• *A mile after the castle, you'll come to a place called Kilmuir. Watch for the turn-off on the left to the excellent...*

Skye Museum of Island Life: This fine little stand of seven thatched stone huts, organized into a family-run museum and

worth ▲▲, explains how a typical Skye family lived a century and a half ago (£2.50, Easter–Oct Mon–Sat 10:00–16:30, closed Sun and Nov–Easter, tel. 01470/552-206, www.skyemuseum.co.uk). Though there are ample posted explanations, the £1.25 guidebook is worthwhile.

The three huts closest to the sea are original (more than 200 years old). Most interesting is the one called The Old Croft House, which was the residence of the Graham family until 1957. Inside you'll find three rooms: kitchen (with peat-burning fire) on the right, parents' bedroom in the middle, and a bedroom for the 12 kids on the left. Nearby, The Old Barn displays farm implements, and the Ceilidh House contains some dense but very informative displays about crofting (the traditional tenant-farmer lifestyle on Skye—explained later), Gaelic, and other topics.

The four other huts were reconstructed here from elsewhere on the island, and now house exhibits about weaving and the village smithy (which was actually a gathering place for villagers). As you explore, admire the smart architecture of these humble but deceptively well-planned structures. Rocks hanging from the roof keep the thatch from blowing away, and the streamlined shape of the structure embedded in the ground encourages strong winds to deflect around the hut rather than hit it head-on.

ISLE OF SKYE

• After touring the museum, drive out to the very end of the small road that leads past the parking lot, to a lonesome cemetery. The tallest Celtic cross at the far end of the cemetery (you can enter the gate to reach it) is the...

Monument to Flora MacDonald: This local heroine sup-posedly rescued beloved Scottish hero Bonnie Prince Charlie

at his darkest hour. After his loss at Culloden, and with a hefty price on his head, Charlie retreated to the Outer Hebrides. But the Hanover dynasty, which controlled the islands, was clos-ing in. Flora MacDonald rescued the prince, disguised him as her Irish maid, Betty Burke, and sailed him to safety on Skye. (Charlie pulled off the ruse thanks to his soft, feminine features—hence the nickname "Bonnie," which means "beautiful.") The flight inspired a popu-lar Scottish folk song: *Speed bonnie boat like a bird on the wing, / Onward, the sailors cry. / Carry the lad that's born to be king / Over the sea to Skye.*

• Return to the main road and proceed about six miles around the pen-insula. On the right, notice the big depression.

The Missing Loch: This was once a large loch, but it was drained in the mid-20th century to create more grazing land for sheep. If you look closely, you may see a scattering of stones in the middle of the field. Once an island, this is the site of a former mon-astery...now left as high, dry, and forgotten as the loch. Beyond the missing loch is Prince Charlie's Point, where the bonnie prince supposedly came ashore on Skye with Flora MacDonald.

• Soon after the loch, you'll drop down over the town of...

Uig: Pronounced "OO-eeg," this village is the departure point for ferries to the Outer Hebrides (North Uist and Harris islands, 3/day). It's otherwise unremarkable, but does have a café with good £3 sandwiches (follow *Uig Pier* signs into town, blue building with white *café* sign, next to ferry terminal at entrance to town).

• Continue past Uig, climbing the hill across the bay. Near the top is a large parking strip on the right. Pull over here and look back to Uig for a lesson about Skye's traditional farming system.

Crofting: You'll hear a lot about crofts during your time on Skye. Traditionally, arable land on the island was divided into plots. If you look across to the hills above Uig, you can see strips of demar-cated land running up from the water—these are crofts. Crofts were generally owned by landlords (mostly English aristocrats or Scottish clan chiefs, and later the Scottish government) and rented to tenant farmers. The crofters lived and worked under very difficult

conditions, and were lucky if they could produce enough potatoes, corn, and livestock to feed their families. Rights to farm the croft were passed down from father to son over generations, but always under the auspices of a wealthy landlord.

Finally, in 1976, new legislation kicked off a process of privatization called "decrofting." Suddenly crofters could have their land decrofted, then buy it for an affordable price (£130 per quarter-hectare, or about £8,000 for one of the crofts you see here). Many decroftees would quickly turn around and sell their old family home for a huge profit, but hang on to most of their land and build a new house at the other end. In the crofts you see here, notice that some have a house at the top of a strip of land, and another house at the bottom. Many crofts (like most of these) are no longer cultivated, but a new law might require crofters to farm their land...or lose it. In many cases, families who have other jobs still hang on to their traditional croft, which they use to grow produce for themselves or to supplement their income.

• *Our tour is finished. From here, you can continue along the main road south toward Portree (and possibly continue from there on to the Cuillin Hills). Or, take the shortcut road just after Kensaleyre (B8036), and head west on A850 to Dunvegan and its castle (both options described later in this chapter).*

More Sights on the Isle of Skye

ISLE OF SKYE

▲▲Cuillin Hills

These dramatic, rocky "hills" (which look more like mountains to me) stretch along the southern coast of the island, dominating Skye's landscape. More craggy and alpine than anything else you'll see in Scotland, the Cuillin seem to rise directly from the deep. You'll see them from just about anywhere on the southern two-thirds of the island, but no roads actually take you through the heart of the Cuillin—that's reserved for hikers and climbers, who love this area. To get the best views with a car, consider these options:

Near Sligachan: The road from the Skye Bridge to Portree is the easiest way to appreciate the Cuillin (you'll almost certainly drive along here at some point during your visit). These mountains are all that's left of a long-vanished volcano. As you approach, you'll clearly see that there are three separate ranges (from right to left): red, gray, and black. The steep and challenging Black Cuillin is the most popular for serious climbers; the granite Red Cuillin ridge is more rounded.

The crossroads of Sligachan, with an old triple-arched bridge and a landmark hotel, is nestled at the foothills of the Cuillin, and is a popular launch pad for mountain fun. The 2,500-foot-tall cone-shaped hill looming over Sligachan, named Glamaig ("Greedy Lady"), is the site of an annual competition in July (www.carnethy. com): Speed hikers begin at the door of the Sligachan Hotel, race to the summit, run around a bagpiper, and scramble back down to the hotel. The record: 44 minutes (30 minutes up, 13 minutes down, 1 minute dancing a jig up top).

Elgol: For the best view of the Cuillin, locals swear by the drive from Broadford (on the Portree–Kyleakin road) to Elgol, at the tip of a small peninsula that faces the Black Cuillin head-on. While it's just 12 miles as the crow flies from Sligachan, give it a half-hour each way to drive into Elgol from Broadford. To get an even better Cuillin experience, take a boat excursion from Elgol into Loch Coruisk, a "sea loch" (fjord) surrounded by the Cuillin (April–Oct, various companies do the trip several times a day, fewer on Sun and off-season, generally 3 hours round-trip including 1.5 hours free time on the shore of the loch, figure £15–20 round-trip).

▲Dunvegan Castle

Perched on a rock overlooking a sea loch, this past-its-prime castle is a strange and intriguing artifact of Scotland's antiquated, nearly extinct clan system. Dunvegan Castle is the residence of the MacLeod (pronounced "McCloud") clan—along with the MacDonalds, one of Skye's preeminent clans. Worth ▲▲▲ to people named MacLeod, and mildly interesting to anyone else, this is a good way to pass the time on a rainy day. The owners claim

it is the oldest continuously inhabited castle in Scotland. They are restoring it, so the roof may be under a blue tarp during your visit.

Cost and Hours: £8, April–mid-Oct daily 10:00–17:30, last entry 30 minutes before closing, mid-Oct–March Mon–Fri open by appointment only, no photos, tel. 01470/521-206, www.dunvegan castle.com. Consider picking up the £2 guidebook by the late chief.

Getting There: It's near the small town of Dunvegan in the northwestern part of the island, well-signposted from A850. As you approach Dunvegan on A850, the two flat-topped plateaus you'll see are nicknamed the "MacLeod Tables."

You can also get to the castle by bus from Portree (#56, 5/day Mon–Fri, 3/day Sat, none on Sun; leave Portree no later than the 12:35 departure to have time to tour the castle).

Background: In Gaelic, *clann* means "children," and the clan system was the traditional Scottish way of passing along power—similar to England's dukes, barons, and counts. Each clan traces its roots to an ancestral castle, like Dunvegan. The MacLeods (or, as they prefer, "MacLeod of MacLeod") have fallen on hard times. Having run out of male heirs in 1935, Dame Flora MacLeod of MacLeod became the 28th clan chief. Her grandson, John MacLeod of MacLeod, became the 29th chief after her death in 1976. Their castle is rough around the edges, and to raise money to fix the leaky roof, John MacL of MacL actually pondered selling the Black Cuillin ridge of hills (which technically belong to him) to an American tycoon for £10 million a few years back. The deal fell through, and the chief passed away in early 2007. Now his son Hugh Magnus MacLeod of MacLeod, in his mid-thirties, has become clan chief of the MacLeods.

❸ Self-Guided Tour: The interior feels a bit worn, but the MacLeods proudly display their family heritage—old photographs and portraits of former chiefs. You'll wander through halls, the dining room, the library, and look down into the dungeon's deep pit. Pick up the laminated flyer in each room to discover some of the history. In the **Drawing Room,** look for the tattered silk remains of the Fairy Flag, a mysterious swatch with about a dozen different legends attached to it (most say that it was a gift from a fairy, and somehow it's related to the Crusades). It's said that the clan chief can invoke the power of the flag three times, in the clan's darkest moments. It's worked twice before on the battlefield—which means there's just one use left.

The most interesting historical tidbits are in the **North Room,** which was built in 1360 as the original Great Hall. The family's coat of arms (in the middle of the carpet) has a confused-looking bull and the clan motto, "Hold Fast"—recalling an incident where a MacLeod saved a man from being gored by a bull when he grabbed its horns and forced it to stop. In the case nearby, find the Dunvegan Cup and the Horn of Rory Mor. Traditionally, this horn would be filled with nearly a half-gallon of claret (Bordeaux wine), which a potential heir had to drink without stopping (or falling) to prove himself fit for the role. (The late chief, John MacLeod of MacLeod, bragged that he did it in less than two minutes...but you have to wonder if Dame Flora chug-a-lugged.) Other artifacts in the North Room include bagpipes and several

ISLE OF SKYE

relics related to Bonnie Prince Charlie (including a lock of his hair and his vest). Look for a portrait of Flora MacDonald and some items that belonged to her.

At the end of the tour, you can wander out onto the **terrace** (overlooking a sea loch) and, in the cellar, watch a stuffy **video** about the clan. Between the castle and the parking lot are five acres of enjoyable **gardens** to stroll through while pondering the fading clan system. You can also take a boat ride on Loch Dunvegan to visit a seal colony on a nearby island (£5, 25-minute trip, mid-April–Sept only).

The flaunting of inherited wealth and influence in some English castles rubs me the wrong way. But here, seeing the rough edges of a Scottish clan chief's castle, I had the opposite feeling: sympathy and compassion for a proud way of life that's slipping into the sunset of history. You have to admire the way that they "hold fast" to this antiquated system (in the same way the Gaelic tongue is kept on life support). Paying admission here feels more like donating to charity than padding the pockets of a wealthy family. In fact, watered-down McClouds and McDonalds from America, eager to reconnect with their Scottish roots, help keep the Scottish clan system alive.

▲Neist Point and Lighthouse

To get a truly edge-of-the-world feeling, consider an adventure on the back lanes of the Duirinish Peninsula, west of Dunvegan. This trip is best for hardy drivers looking to explore the most remote corner of Skye and undertake a strenuous hike to a lighthouse. (The lighthouse itself is a letdown, so do this only if you believe a journey is its own reward.) Although it looks close on  the map, give this trip 30 minutes each way from Dunvegan, plus 30 minutes or more for the lighthouse hike.

Head west from Dunvegan, following signs for *Glendale*. You'll cross a moor, then twist around the Dunvegan sea loch, before heading overland and passing through rugged, desolate hamlets that seem like the setting for a BBC sitcom about backwater Britain. After passing through Glendale, carefully track *Neist Point* signs until you reach an end-of-the-road parking lot. The owner of this private property has signs on his padlocked gate stating that you enter at your own risk—which many walkers happily do. (It's laughably easy to walk around the unintimidating "wall.") From here you enjoy sheep and cliff views, but can't see the light-

ISLE OF SKYE

house itself unless you do the sturdy 30-minute hike (with a steep uphill return). After hiking around the cliff, the lighthouse springs into view, with the Outer Hebrides beyond.

It's efficient and fun to combine this trek with lunch or dinner at the recommended **Three Chimneys Restaurant,** on the road to Neist Point at Colbost.

▲Talisker Distillery

Opened in 1830, Talisker is a Skye institution. If you've only tried mainland whisky, island whisky is worth a dram to appreciate the differences. Island whisky is known for having a strong smoky flavor, due to the amount of peat smoke used during the roasting of the barley. The Isle of Islay has the smokiest, and Talisker workers describe theirs as "medium smoky," which may be easier for non-connoisseurs to take. Talisker produces single-malt whisky only, so it's a favorite with whisky purists: On summer days, this tiny distillery down a tiny road in Carbost village swarms with visitors from all over the world (£5 for an hour-long tour and wee dram; Easter–Oct Mon–Sat 9:30–17:00, closed Sun except in July–Aug when it's open 11:00–17:00, last tour one hour before closing; Nov–Easter Mon–Fri 10:00–17:00, tours at 10:30, 12:00, 14:00 and 15:30, closed Sat–Sun, call ahead; no photos or cell phones, tel. 01478/614-308, www.taliskerwhisky.com).

Skye Bridge

Connecting Kyleakin on Skye with Kyle of Lochalsh on the mainland, the Skye Bridge severely damaged B&B business in the towns it connects. And environmentalists worry about the bridge disrupting the habitat for otters—keep an eye out for these furry native residents. But it's been a boon for Skye tourism—making a quick visit to the island possible without having to wait for a ferry.

The bridge, which was Europe's most expensive toll bridge when it opened in 1995, has stirred up a remarkable amount of controversy among island-dwellers. Here's the Skye natives' take on things: A generation ago, Lowlanders (city folk) began selling their urban homes and buying cheap property on Skye. Natives had grown to enjoy the slow-paced lifestyle that came with living life according to the whim of the ferry, but these new transplants found their commute into civilization too frustrating by boat. They demanded a new bridge be built. Finally a deal was struck to privately fund the bridge, but the toll wasn't established before construction began. So when the bridge opened—and the ferry line it replaced closed—locals were shocked to be charged upward of £5 per car each way to go to the mainland. A few years ago, the bridge was bought by the Scottish Executive, the fare was abolished, and the Skye natives were appeased...for now.

▲▲Near the Isle of Skye: Eilean Donan Castle

This postcard castle, watching over a sea loch from its island perch, is conveniently and scenically situated on the road between the Isle of Skye and Loch Ness. Famous from such films as Sean Connery's *Highlander* (1986) and the James Bond movie *The World Is Not Enough* (1999), Eilean Donan (EYE-lan DOHN-an) might be Scotland's most photogenic

countryside castle. Though it looks ancient, the castle is actually less than a century old. The original castle on this site (dating from 800 years ago) was destroyed in battle in 1719, then rebuilt between 1912 and 1932 by the MacRae family as their residence.

Even if you're not going inside, the castle warrants a five-minute photo stop. But the interior—with cozy rooms—is worth a peek if you have time. Walk across the bridge and into the castle complex, and make your way into the big, blocky keep. First you'll see the claustrophobic, vaulted Billeting Room (where soldiers had their barracks), then head upstairs to the inviting Banqueting Room. Docents posted in these rooms can tell you more. Another flight of stairs takes you to the circa-1930 bedrooms. Downstairs is the cute kitchen exhibit, with mannequins preparing a meal (read the recipes posted throughout). Finally, you'll head through a few more assorted exhibits to the exit.

Cost and Hours: £5.50, good £3.50 guidebook, early March–Oct daily 10:00–18:00, June opens at 9:30, July–Aug opens at 9:00, last entry one hour before closing; generally closed Nov–early March but may be open a few times a week—call; tel. 01599/555-202, www.eileandonancastle.com.

Getting There: It's not actually on the Isle of Skye, but it's quite close, in the mainland town of Dornie. Follow A87 about 15 minutes east of Skye Bridge, through Kyle of Lochalsh and toward Loch Ness and Inverness. The castle is on the right side of this road, just after a long bridge.

ISLE OF SKYE

Portree

Skye's main attraction is its natural beauty, not its villages. But
among them, the best home
base is Portree (say poor-
TREE fast, comes from
Port Righ, literally, "Royal
Port"). This village (with
3,000 people, too small to
be considered a "town") is
Skye's largest settlement
and the hub of activity and
transportation.

Orientation to Portree

(area code: 01478)
This functional village has a small harbor and, on the hill above it,
a tidy main square (from which buses fan out across the island and
to the mainland). Surrounding the central square are just a few
streets. Homes, shops, and B&Bs line the roads to other settlements on the island.

Tourist Information
Portree's helpful TI is a block off the main square, along Bridge
Road. They can help you sort through bus schedules, give you maps,
and book you a room for a £4 fee (June–early Sept Mon–Sat 9:00–
18:00, Aug until 20:00, Sun 10:00–16:00; early Sept–May Mon–Fri
9:00–17:00, Sat 10:00–16:00, closed Sun; just south of Bridge Street,
tel. 01478/612-137 or toll tel. 0845-225-5121). Public WCs are across
the street and down a block, across from the hostel.

Helpful Hints
Internet Access: The TI has two terminals in the back (£1/20
   minutes), and the **Aros Centre** has four (£2/hour). You can
   get online at the **library** in Portree High School (free, picture
   ID required, Mon–Fri 9:15–17:00, Tue and Thu until 20:00,
   Sat 10:00–16:00, closed Sun, Viewfield Road, tel. 01478/614-
   823).
Laundry: The **Independent Hostel,** just off the main square, has
   a self-service launderette down below (about £4 self-service,
   £8 full-service, usually 11:00–21:00, last load starts at 20:00,
   tel. 01478/613-737).
Supermarket: A **Co-op** is on Bank Street (Mon–Sat 8:00–22:00,
   Sun 9:00–19:00).

Bike Rental: Island Cycles rents bikes at the lower parking lot, along the water (£7.50/half-day, £14/24 hours, Mon–Sat 9:00–17:00, closed Sun, tel. 01478/613-121, www.isbuc.co.uk).

Car Rental: M2 Motors will pick you up at your B&B or the bus station (£35/day, half-day available, Dunvegan Road, tel. 01478/613-344, www.m2motors.co.uk). Other places to rent a car are the **MacRae Dealership,** a 10-minute walk from downtown Portree on the road toward Dunvegan (£38–42/day, Mon–Fri 8:30–17:30, Sat 9:00–12:30, closed Sun, call at least a week in advance in summer, tel. 01478/612-554). Farther along the same road are two more options: **Jansvans** (£43/day, Mon–Sat 8:00–17:30, closed Sun, tel. 01478/612-087, www.jans.co.uk) and **Portree Coachworks** (£38/day, Mon–Fri 8:30–17:30, weekends by appointment, tel. 01478/612-688, www.portreecoachworks.co.uk).

Parking: As you enter town, a free parking lot is off to the right; look for the sign.

Sights in Portree

Harbor—There's little to see in Portree itself, other than to wander along the colorful harbor, where boat captains offer £14 90-minute excursions out to the sea-eagle nests and around the bay (ask at TI).

Aros Centre—This visitors center and cinema, a mile outside of town on the road to Kyleakin and Skye Bridge, overlooks the sea loch. It offers a humble but earnest exhibit about the island's natural history and wildlife (when I visited it, there was a heron nest in the trees at the end of the parking lot). Enjoy the 20-minute movie with aerial photos of otherwise-hard-to-reach parts of Skye, and chat with the ranger. The exhibit also describes the local sea eagles. These raptors were hunted to extinction on Skye and have been reintroduced to the ecosystem from Scandinavia. A live webcam shows their nests nearby—or, if there are no active nests, a "greatest hits" video show of past fledglings (£4.50, daily 9:00–17:00, last entry 30 minutes before closing, café, gift shop, Internet access, a mile south of town center on Viewfield Road, tel. 01478/613-649, www.aros.co.uk).

Sleeping in Portree

(area code: 01478)

$$$ Almondbank Guest House, on the road into town from Kyleakin, works well for drivers and has great views of the loch from the public areas. It has four tidy, homey rooms (two with sea

---

Sleep Code

(£1 = about $1.60, country code: 44)

S = Single, **D** = Double/Twin, **T** = Triple, **Q** = Quad, **b** = bathroom, **s** = shower only. Unless otherwise noted, you can assume credit cards are accepted at hotels and hostels—but not B&Bs—and breakfast is included.

To help you sort easily through these listings, I've divided the rooms into three categories based on the price for a standard double room with bath (during high season):

$$$ Higher Priced—Most rooms £65 or more.
$$ Moderately Priced—Most rooms between £45–65.
$ Lower Priced—Most rooms £45 or less.

Prices can change without notice; verify the hotel's current rates online or by email. For other updates, see www .ricksteves.com/update.

---

views for no extra charge) run by friendly Effie Nicolson (Sb-£65, D-£64, Db-£72, free Wi-Fi, Viewfield Road, tel. 01478/612-696, fax 01478/613-114, j.n.almondbank@btconnect.com). She also rents a three-bedroom cottage next door that sleeps up to six (4-night minimum, www.fisherfield-self-catering.co.uk).

$$ Braeside B&B has three comfortable rooms at the top of town, up from the Bosville Hotel (Db-£55, cash only, closed Nov–Feb, steep stairs, Stormyhill, tel. 01478/612-613, www .braesideportree.co.uk, mail@braesideportree.co.uk, Judith and Philip Maughan).

$$ Bayview House has seven small, sterile, and basic rooms, well-located on the main road just below the square (Db-£50, no breakfast, tel. 01478/613-340, www.bayviewhouse.co.uk, info@bayviewhouse.co.uk, Murdo and Alison). If there's no answer, walk down the stairs to Bayfield Backpackers, described below.

$$ Marine House, run by sweet Skye native Fiona Stephenson, has two simple, homey rooms (one with a private bathroom down the hall) and great views of the harbor (Db-£60–65, cash only, 2 Beaumont Crescent, tel. 01478/611-557).

Hostel: **$ Bayfield Backpackers**—run by Murdo and Alison from the Bayview House, above—is a modern-feeling, institutional, cinderblock-and-metal hostel with 24 beds in four- to eight-bed rooms (£15 per bunk, pay Wi-Fi, kitchen, laundry, tel. 01478/612-231, www.skyehostel.co.uk, info@skyehostel.co.uk).

ISLE OF SKYE

Sleeping near Portree, in Sligachan

$$$ Sligachan Hotel—actually a compound of related sleeping and eating options—is a local institution and a haven for hikers. It's been in the Campbell family since 1913. The hotel's 21 renovated rooms are comfortable, if a bit simple for the price, while the nearby campground and bunkhouse offer a budget alternative. The setting—surrounded by the mighty Cuillin Hills—is remarkably scenic (Db-£118 May–Sept, £98 March–April and Oct, closed Nov–Feb, campground-£5 per person, bunkhouse-£16 per person, pay Internet access in pub, on A87 between Kyleakin and Portree in Sligachan, tel. 01478/650-204, www.sligachan.co.uk, reservations@sligachan.co.uk).

Eating in Portree

Note that Portree's few eateries tend to close early (21:00 or 22:00), and during busy times, lines begin to form soon after 19:00. Eating early works best here.

On the Waterfront: A pair of good eateries vie for your attention along Portree's little harbor. **Lower Deck** feels like a salty sailor's restaurant, decorated with the names of local ships (£5–9 lunches, £9–16 dinners, daily 12:30–14:30 & 18:00–21:30, closed Nov–March, tel. 01478/613-611).

Sea Breezes, with a more contemporary flair, serves tasty cuisine with an emphasis on seafood (£7–9 lunches, £13–18 dinners, £16 two-course early-bird specials 17:00–18:00, open daily 12:00–14:00 & 17:00–21:00, sometimes closed Sun, reserve ahead for dinner, tel. 01478/612-016).

Café Arriba tries hard to offer eclectic flavors in this small Scottish town. With an ambitious menu that includes local specialties, Mexican, Italian, and more, this youthful, colorful, easygoing eatery's hit-or-miss cuisine is worth trying. Drop in to see what's on the blackboard menu today (£4–7 lunches, £8–15 dinners, lots of vegetarian options, daily 7:00–17:00 & 18:00–21:00, Quay Brae, tel. 01478/611-830).

The Café, a few steps off the main square, is a busy, popular hometown diner serving good crank-'em-out food to an appreciative local crowd. The homemade ice-cream stand in the front is a nice way to finish your meal (£8–9 lunches and burgers, £10–15 dinners, also does take-away, daily 8:30–15:30 & 17:30–21:00, tel. 01478/612-553).

The Bosville Hotel has, according to locals, the best of Portree's many hotel restaurants. There are two parts: the inexpensive, casual **bistro** (£5 lunch sandwiches, £9–16 lunches and dinners, June–Aug daily 12:00–14:00 & 17:30–21:30, shorter hours off-season), and the well-regarded formal **Chandlery Restaurant**

(£36 two-course meal, £44 three-course meal, nightly 18:30–20:30). While pricey, it's a suitable splurge (just up from the main square, 9–11 Bosville Terrace, tel. 01478/612-846). Their 19 rooms, also expensive, are worth considering (Db-£128, www.bosville hotel.co.uk).

Eating Elsewhere on the Isle of Skye

In Sligachan

Sligachan Hotel (described earlier) has a restaurant and a micro-brew pub serving up mountaineer-pleasing grub in an extremely scenic setting nestled in the Cuillin Hills (traditional dinners in restaurant—£25 for three courses, served nightly 18:30–21:00; pub grub served until 21:00—£7–11; closed Nov–Feb, on A87 between Kyleakin and Portree in Sligachan, tel. 01478/650-204).

In Colbost, near Dunvegan

Three Chimneys Restaurant is your big-splurge-on-a-small-island meal. The high-quality Scottish cuisine, using local ingredients, earns rave reviews. Its 16 tables fill an old three-chimney croft house, with a stone-and-timbers decor that artfully melds old and new. It's cozy, classy, and candlelit, but not stuffy. Because of its remote location—and the fact that it's almost always booked up—reservations are absolutely essential, ideally several weeks ahead, although it's worth calling in case of last-minute cancellations (lunch: £27.50 for two courses, £35 for three courses; dinner: £55 for three courses, £80 for seven-course "showcase menu"; dinner served nightly 18:15–21:45, lunch mid-March–Oct Mon–Sat 12:15–13:45, no lunch Sun or Nov–mid-March, closed for 3 weeks in Jan, tel. 01470/511-258, Eddie and Shirley Spear). They also rent six swanky, pricey suites next door (Db-£285, less off-season, www.threechimneys.co.uk).

Getting There: It's in the village of Colbost, about a 10- to 15-minute drive west of Dunvegan on the Duirinish Peninsula (that's about 45 minutes each way from Portree). To get there, first head for Dunvegan, then follow signs toward *Glendale*. This single-track road with "passing places" twists you through the countryside, over a moor, and past several dozen sheep before passing through Colbost. You can combine this with a visit to the Neist Point Lighthouse (described earlier), which is at the end of the same road.

Kyleakin

Kyleakin (kih-LAH-kin), the last town in Skye before the bridge, used to be a big tourist hub...until the bridge connecting it to the mainland made it much easier for people to get to Portree and other areas deeper in the island. Today this unassuming little village with a ruined castle (Castle Moil), a cluster of lonesome fishing boats, and a forgotten ferry slip still works well as a home base.

If you want to pick up information on the island before you drive all the way to Portree, stop by the tiny **TI** in Broadford, about 15 minutes up the road from Kyleakin (Mon–Fri 10:00–17:00, Sat 11:00–16:00, closed Sun and off-season, maps and hiking books, next to Co-op, WCs across street next to church, toll tel. 08452-255-121).

Helpful Hints

Internet Access: If you're desperate, **Saucy Mary's** store/bar has one laptop available for visitors to rent (Main Street, tel. 01599/534-845).

Laundry: There's none in town, but a launderette is in Broadford, next to the Co-op supermarket (daily 6:00–20:00, less in winter).

Supermarkets: A **Co-op** is across the bridge in Kyle of Lochalsh (Mon–Sat 8:00–22:00, Sun 9:00–18:00, Bridge Road, tel. 01599/530-190) or up the road in Broadford (Mon–Sat 8:00–22:00, Sun 9:00–18:00, Main Street, tel. 01471/820-420).

Car Rental: You can rent a car for the day from **Kyle Taxi** (about £45/day, Mon–Sat 9:00–17:00, closed Sun, will deliver in Kyleakin, tel. 01599/534-323, www.lochalsh.net/taxi).

Sleeping in Kyleakin

(£1 = about $1.60, country code: 44, area code: 01599)

$$$ MacKinnon Country House Hotel is my favorite countryside home base on Skye. It sits quietly in the middle of five acres of gardens just off the bustling Skye Bridge. Ian and the Tongs family have lovingly restored this old 1912 country home with Edwardian antiques and 18 clan-themed rooms, an inviting overstuffed-sofa lounge, and a restaurant with garden views in nearly every direction (Sb-£50, Db-£100–135 depending on room size and amenities, 10 percent discount when you mention this book in 2011, about 20 percent cheaper Oct–Easter, room fridges, tel. 01599/534-180, www.mackinnonhotel.co.uk, info@mackinnon hotel.co.uk, a 10-minute walk from Kyleakin, at the turnoff for the bridge). Ian also serves a delicious dinner to guests and non-guests alike (see "Eating in Kyleakin," later). Moss, the border collie, will try to take you for a walk.

$$$ White Heather Hotel, run by friendly and helpful Gillian and Craig Glenwright, has nine small but nicely decorated rooms with woody pine bathrooms, across from the waterfront and the castle ruins (Sb-£50, Db-£70, family rooms, cheaper for stays longer than 2 nights, free Internet access and Wi-Fi, lounges, closed Nov–mid-March, The Harbour, tel. 01599/534-577, fax 01599/534-427, www.whiteheatherhotel.co.uk, info@whiteheather hotel.co.uk).

$$ Cliffe House B&B rents three rooms in a white house perched at the edge of the water. All of the rooms, and the breakfast room, enjoy wonderful views over the strait and the bridge (Db-£60, £70 in July–Aug, cash only, tel. 01599/534-019, www .cliffehousebedandbreakfast.co.uk, i.sikorski@btinternet.com, Ian and Mary Sikorski).

Hostel: **$ Dun-Caan Hostel,** named for a dormant volcano on a nearby island, is mellow and friendly. With woody ambience and 15 beds in three rooms, it's quieter and cozier than most hostels—enjoying a genuine camaraderie without an obnoxious party atmosphere (£16/bed, includes sheets, towels-£0.50, pleasant kitchen and lounge, free Wi-Fi, laundry service, The Pier Road, tel. 01599/534-087, www.skyerover.co.uk, info@skyerover.co.uk, Terry and Laila).

Eating in and near Kyleakin

Locals like the **Taste of India,** just past the roundabout outside Kyleakin on A87 toward Broadford (£6–10 entrées, also does takeaway, daily 12:00–14:00 & 17:00–23:00, tel. 01599/534-134). For a nice dinner, head up to the recommended **MacKinnon Country House Hotel** (listed earlier; £13–15 entrées, nightly 19:00–21:00, just outside Kyleakin at roundabout, tel. 01599/534-180). And there are a few pubs in little Kyleakin; ask your B&B host for advice.

In Kyle of Lochalsh: If you can get reservations, eat fresh Scottish cuisine at the **Waverly Restaurant,** a tiny six-table place with locally sourced food across the bridge from Kyleakin in Kyle of Lochalsh (£12–17 entrées, £11.50 two-course dinner special 17:30–19:00, open Fri–Wed 17:30–21:30, closed Thu, reservations essential, Main Street, across from Kyle Hotel and up the stairs, tel. 01599/534-337, Dutch chef/owner Ank).

In Broadford: Up the road in Broadford are more eateries, including the newly renovated **Broadford Hotel** overlooking the bay (£9–12 entrées, many Drambuie drinks, Torrin Road at junction with Elgol, tel. 01471/822-204). It was here that a secret elixir—supposedly once concocted for Bonnie Prince Charlie—caught on in the 19th century. Now known as Drambuie, the popular liqueur is made with Scottish whisky, honey, and spices.

ISLE OF SKYE

INVERNESS AND THE NORTHERN HIGHLANDS

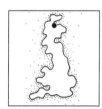

Filled with more natural and historical mystique than people, the northern Highlands are where Scottish dreams are set. Legends of Bonnie Prince Charlie linger around crumbling castles as tunes played by pipers in kilts swirl around tourists. Explore the locks and lochs of the Caledonian Canal while the Loch Ness monster plays hide-and-seek. Hear the music of the Highlands in Inverness and the echo of muskets at Culloden, where the English drove Bonnie Prince Charlie into exile and conquered his Jacobite supporters.

I've focused my coverage on the handy hub of Inverness, with several day-trip options into the surrounding countryside. For Highlands sights to the south and west, see the Oban and the Southern Highlands chapter; for the Isle of Skye off Scotland's west coast, see the previous chapter.

Planning Your Time

Though it has little in the way of sights, Inverness does have a workaday charm and is a handy spot to spend a night or two en route to other Highland destinations. One night here gives you time to take a quick tour of nearby attractions. With two nights, you can find a full day's worth of sightseeing nearby.

Note that Loch Ness is on the way toward Oban or the Isle of Skye. If you're heading to one of those places, it makes sense to see Loch Ness en route, rather than as a side trip from Inverness.

Getting Around the Highlands

With a car, the day trips around Inverness are easy. Without a car, you can get to Inverness by train (better from Edinburgh or

Pitlochry) or by bus (better from Skye, Oban, and Glencoe), then side-trip to Loch Ness, Culloden, and other nearby attractions by public bus or with a package tour.

Inverness

The only city in the north of Scotland, Inverness is pleasantly situated on the River Ness at the base of a castle (now a courthouse, not

a tourist attraction). Inverness' charm is its normalcy—it's a nice, midsize Scottish city that gives you a palatable taste of the "urban" Highlands, and is well-located for enjoying the surrounding countryside sights. Check out the bustling, pedestrian downtown or meander the picnic-friendly riverside paths—best at sunset, when the light hits the castle and couples hold hands while strolling along the water and over the many footbridges.

Orientation to Inverness

(area code: 01463)

Inverness, with about 70,000 people, is the fastest-growing city in Scotland. Marked by its castle, Inverness clusters along the River Ness. Where the main road crosses the river at Ness Bridge, you'll find the TI; within a few blocks (away from the river) are the train and bus stations and an appealing pedestrian shopping zone. The best B&Bs huddle atop a gentle hill behind the castle (a 15-minute mostly uphill walk, or a £5 taxi ride, from the city center).

Tourist Information

At the centrally located TI, you can pick up activity and day-trip brochures, the self-guided *Historic Trail* walking-tour leaflet, and the *What's On* events booklet for the latest theater, music, and film showings (both free). The office also books rooms for a £4 fee and tours for a £1 fee (July–mid-Sept Mon–Sat 9:00–18:30, Sun 9:30–18:30; mid-Sept–June Mon–Sat 9:00–17:00, Sun 10:00–16:00; Internet access, free WCs up behind TI, Castle Wynd, tel. 01463/234-353).

INVERNESS

Tattoos and the Painted People

In Inverness, as in other Scottish cities such as Glasgow and Edinburgh, hip pubs are filled with tattooed kids. In parts of Scotland, however, tattoos aren't a recent phenomenon—this form of body art has been around longer than the buildings and sights. Some of the area's earliest known settlers of the Highlands were called the Picts, dubbed the "Painted People" by their enemies, the Romans. The Picts, who conquered the northeast corner of Scotland (including Inverness), were believed to have ruled from the first century A.D. to approximately the ninth century, when they united with the Scots and were lost to written history.

Picts were known for their elaborate full-body tattoos. The local plant they used for their ink, called *woad*, had built-in healing properties, helping to coagulate blood (a property particularly handy in battle). The tattoos gave rise to a truly remarkable fighting technique: going to war naked. The Picts saw their tattoos as a kind of psychological armor, a combination of symbols and magical signs that would protect them more than any metal could. Imagine a Scottish hillside teeming with screaming, head-to-toe dyed-blue warriors, most with complex tattooed designs—and all of them buck naked.

Helpful Hints

Festivals: In mid-June, the city fills up for the **RockNess Music Festival** (www.rockness.co.uk), and there's a **marathon** the first week of October (www.lochnessmarathon.com); book ahead for these times.

Internet Access: You can get online at the **TI** (£1/20 minutes), or for free at the Neoclassical **library** behind the bus station, though you'll be limited to a half-hour session (Mon and Fri 9:00–19:30, Tue and Thu 9:00–18:30, Wed 10:00–17:00, Sat 9:00–17:00, closed Sun, computers shut down 15 minutes before closing, tel. 01463/236-463). **Clanlan** is in the middle of town, between the train station and the river (£1.20/20 minutes, Mon–Fri 10:00–20:00, Sat 11:00–20:00, Sun 12:00–17:00, 22 Baron Taylor Street, tel. 01463/241-223). The launderette listed below also has Internet access (£1/30 minutes).

Baggage Storage: The train station has lockers (£3–5/24 hours, open Mon–Sat 6:30–19:45, Sun 10:45–18:15).

Laundry: New City Launderette is just across the Ness Bridge from the TI (self-service-£8, same-day full-service for £3.50 more, price calculated by weight, Internet access, Mon–Sat 8:00–18:00, until 20:00 Mon–Fri June–Oct, Sun 10:00–16:00, last load one hour before closing, 17 Young Street, tel. 01463/242-507).

INVERNESS

Inverness

1. Melness Guest House
2. Craigside Lodge B&B
3. Dionard Guest House
4. Ardconnel House & Crown Hotel Guest House
5. Ryeford Guest House
6. The Redcliffe Hotel & Rest.
7. Inverness Palace Hotel & Spa
8. To Premier Inn Inverness Centre
9. Inverness Student Hotel & Bazpackers Hostel
10. Café 1
11. Number 27 Restaurant
12. La Tortilla Asesina Rest.
13. Heathmount Hotel & Rest.
14. Hootananny Café/Bar
15. Rocpool Restaurant
16. The Mustard Seed Rest.
17. Rajah Indian Restaurant
18. Girvans Café & Délices de Bretagne Brasserie
19. Leakey's Bookshop & Café
20. Marks & Spencer (Groceries)
21. Co-op Supermarket
22. Library (Internet)
23. Clanlan (Internet)
24. Launderette (Internet)
25. Bus Stop for Culloden & Cawdor

P PARKING

TO A-862

TO A-82 FORT WILLIAM, LOCH NESS (WEST) & OBAN

400 YARDS

400 METERS

Supermarket: The **Co-operative** is handy for picnics (Mon–Sat 7:00–22:00, Sun 9:00–20:00, 59 Church Street).

Tours in Inverness

Walking Tour—Happy Tours offers guided historical walks in spring and summer (£10; April–Sept daily at 11:00, 13:00, and 15:00; one hour, leaves from the steps of the TI, in summer just show up, arrange in advance in winter, tel. 07828/154-683 or

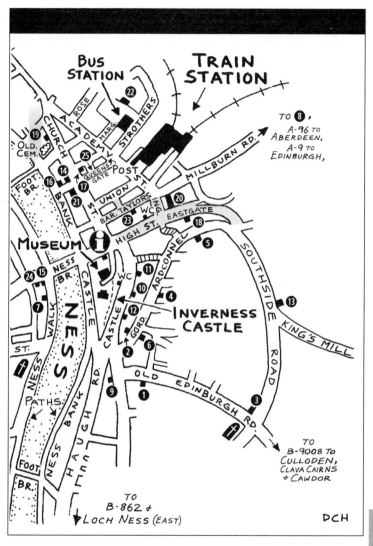

DCH

mobile 0782-815-4683, www.happy-tours.biz). They also do a one-hour "Crime and Punishment" tour nightly at 19:00 and 20:15.

Excursions from Inverness

While thin on sights of its own, Inverness is a great home base for day trips. The biggest attraction is Loch Ness, a 20-minute drive southwest. Tickets are available at the TI, and tours depart from somewhere nearby. It's smart to book ahead, especially in peak season.

Jacobite Tours—This outfit runs a variety of tours, from a one-hour basic boat ride to a 6.5-hour extravaganza (£11–37, most tours run daily April–Sept). Their 3.5-hour "Sensation" tour includes a guided bus tour with live narration, a half-hour cruise of Loch Ness with recorded commentary, and an hour apiece at the Urquhart Castle and the better of the two Loch Ness exhibits (£26, includes admissions to both sights, departs at 10:30 and 13:30 from Bank Street, near the TI, tel. 01463/233-999, www.jacobite.co.uk).

Scottish Tours—Choose from several daylong tours, including one that focuses on the Isle of Skye, with stops along Loch Ness and at scenic Eilean Donan Castle. You'll get a few hours on Skye; unfortunately, it only takes you as far as the Sleat Peninsula at the island's southern end, rather than to the more scenic Trotternish Peninsula (£38, departs from Inverness bus station at 9:30, returns at 19:30; June–Sept runs daily; mid-May and Oct runs several days a week; no tours Nov–mid-May, reservations recommended, tel. 0871-200-0601, www.scottishtours.co.uk). For more on the Isle of Skye, see the previous chapter.

More Options—Several companies host daily excursions to Culloden Battlefield, whisky distilleries, Cawdor Castle, and the nearby bay for dolphin-watching (ask at TI).

Sights in Inverness

"Imaginverness" Museum and Art Gallery—This free, likeable town museum is worth poking around on a rainy day to get a taste of Inverness and the Highlands. The ground-floor exhibits on geology and archaeology peel back the layers of Highland history: Bronze and Iron ages, Picts (including some carved stones), Scots, Vikings, and Normans. Upstairs you'll find the "social history" exhibit (everything from Scottish nationalism to hunting and fishing) and temporary art exhibits (free, Mon–Sat 10:00–17:00, closed Sun, cheap café, in the modern building behind the TI on the way up to the castle, tel. 01463/237-114, http://inverness.highland.museum).

Inverness Castle—Inverness' biggest nonsight has nice views from its front lawn, but the building itself isn't worth visiting. The statue outside depicts Flora MacDonald, who helped Bonnie Prince Charlie escape from the English. The castle is used as a courthouse, and when trials are in session, loutish-looking men hang out here, waiting for their bewigged barristers to arrive.

INVERNESS

Sleeping in Inverness

(area code: 01463)

B&Bs on and near Ardconnel Street and Old Edinburgh Road

These B&Bs are popular; book ahead for June through August (and during the marathon in early October—see "Festivals" under "Helpful Hints," earlier), and be aware that some require a two-night minimum during busy times. The rooms are all a 10-minute walk from the train station and town center. To get to the B&Bs, either catch a taxi (£5) or walk: From the train and bus stations, go left on Academy Street. At the first stoplight (the second if you're coming from the bus station), veer right onto Inglis Street in the pedestrian zone. Go up the Market Brae steps. At the top, turn right onto Ardconnel Street toward the B&Bs and hostels.

$$ Melness Guest House has two country-comfy rooms, a tartan-bedecked lounge, and an adorable West Highland Terrier named Rogie (Db-£70, 2-night minimum in summer, free Wi-Fi, 8 Old Edinburgh Road, tel. 01463/220-963, www.melnessie.co.uk, joy@melnessie.co.uk, welcoming Joy Joyce).

$$ Craigside Lodge B&B has five large, comfortable, cheery rooms remodeled with a tasteful modern flair. Guests share an inviting sunroom and a cozy lounge with a great city view (Sb-£35–40, Db-£65–70, prices depend on season, free Wi-Fi, just above Castle Street at 4 Gordon Terrace, tel. 01463/231-576,

---

Sleep Code

(£1 = about $1.60, country code: 44, area code: 01463)
S = Single, **D** = Double/Twin, **T** = Triple, **Q** = Quad, **b** = bathroom, **s** = shower only. Unless otherwise noted, you can assume credit cards are accepted at hotels and hostels—but not B&Bs—and breakfast is included.

To help you sort easily through these listings, I've divided the rooms into three categories based on the price for a standard double room with bath (during high season):

$$$ **Higher Priced**—Most rooms £75 or more.
$$ **Moderately Priced**—Most rooms between £30-75.
$ **Lower Priced**—Most rooms £30 or less.

Prices can change without notice; verify the hotel's current rates online or by email. For other updates, see www.ricksteves.com/update.

www.craigsideguesthouse.co.uk, enquiries@craigsideguesthouse
.co.uk, Ewan and Amy).

$$ Dionard Guest House, just up Old Edinburgh Road from
Ardconnel Street, has cheerful blue-toned common spaces and six
pleasant rooms, with two on the ground floor (Sb-£40, Db-£65–75
depending on size, 2-night minimum, no single-occupancy rate
during high season, free Wi-Fi, in-room fridges, laundry ser-
vice-£6-12, 39 Old Edinburgh Road, tel. 01463/233-557, www
.dionardguesthouse.co.uk, enquiries@dionardguesthouse.co.uk,
welcoming Val and John).

$$ Ardconnel House has six spacious and relaxing pas-
tel rooms with lots of extra touches (Sb-£42, Db-£72, family
room-£95, family deals but no children under 10, slightly cheaper
off-season or for 2 or more nights, free Wi-Fi, nice lounge, 21
Ardconnel Street, tel. 01463/240-455, www.ardconnel-inverness
.co.uk, ardconnel@gmail.com, John and Elizabeth).

$$ Crown Hotel Guest House has six clean, bright rooms
and an enjoyable breakfast room (Sb-£35, Db-£60, family room-
£80–100, lounge, 19 Ardconnel Street, tel. 01463/231-135, www
.crownhotel-inverness.co.uk, reservations@crownhotel-inverness
.co.uk, friendly Catriona—pronounced "Katrina"—Barbour).

$$ Ryeford Guest House is a great value, with six flowery
rooms and plenty of teddy bears (Sb-£38, Db-£60, Tb-£90, fam-
ily deals, free Wi-Fi, vegetarian breakfast available, small twin
room #1 in back has fine garden view, above Market Brae steps,
go left on Ardconnel Terrace to #21, tel. 01463/242-871, www
.scotland-inverness.co.uk/ryeford, joananderson@uwclub.net, Joan
and George Anderson).

Hotels

The following hotels may have rooms when my recommended
B&Bs are full.

$$$ The Redcliffe Hotel, which is actually in the midst of
all the B&Bs described above, has 12 renovated, contemporary
rooms, some in a six-room townhouse annex across the street.
Though a lesser value than the B&Bs, it's fairly priced for a small
hotel (Sb-£50–60, Db-£80–100, Db suite-£100–130, depends on
season, some castle-view rooms, pay Wi-Fi, 1 Gordon Terrace,
tel. & fax 01463/232-767, www.redcliffe-hotel.co.uk, enquiry
@redcliffe-hotel.co.uk). They also have a good restaurant (listed
later, under "Eating in Inverness").

$$$ Inverness Palace Hotel & Spa, a Best Western, is a
fancy splurge with a pool, a gym, and 88 overpriced rooms. It's
located right on the River Ness, across from the castle (Db-£149,
but you can almost always get a much better rate—even half-
price—if you book a package deal on their website, £70 last-minute

rooms, prices especially soft on weekends, river/castle view rooms about £40 more than rest, breakfast extra, elevator, free Wi-Fi, free parking, 8 Ness Walk, tel. 01463/223-243, fax 01463/236-865, www.bw-invernesspalace.co.uk, palace@miltonhotels.com).

$$ Premier Inn Inverness Centre, a half-mile east of the train station along busy and dreary Millburn Road, offers 55 modern, identical rooms in a converted distillery. While it feels like a freeway rest-stop hotel (nondrivers should skip it), it's fairly affordable, especially for families. The appealing onsite restaurant, Slice, offers steaks, salads, and more (Db for up to 2 adults and 2 kids-about £75, check for specials online, cheaper in winter, continental breakfast-£5.25, full cooked breakfast-£7.75, elevator, Wi-Fi, B865/Millburn Road, just west of the A9 and A96 interchange, tel. 08701-977-141, fax 01463/717-826, www.premierinn.com).

Hostels on Culduthel Road

For inexpensive dorm beds near the center and the recommended Castle Street restaurants, consider these friendly side-by-side hostels, geared toward younger travelers. They're about a 12-minute walk from the train station.

$ Inverness Student Hotel has 57 beds in nine rooms and a cozy, inviting, laid-back lounge with a bay window overlooking the River Ness. The friendly staff welcome any traveler over 18. Dorms come in some interesting shapes, and each bunk has its own playful name (£14 beds in 6- to 10-bed rooms, price depends on season, breakfast-£2, free tea and coffee, cheap Internet access, free Wi-Fi, full-service laundry for £2.50, kitchen, 8 Culduthel Road, tel. 01463/236-556, www.scotlands-top-hostels.com, inverness @scotlands-top-hostels.com).

$ Bazpackers Hostel, a stone's throw from the castle, has a pleasant common room and 34 beds in basic 4- to 6-bed dorms (beds-£14-15, D-£38, cheaper Oct–May, linens provided, reception open 7:30–24:00, no curfew, Internet access, laundry service, 4 Culduthel Road, tel. 01463/717-663, www.bazpackershostel .co.uk).

Eating in Inverness

You'll find a lot of traditional Highland fare—game, fish, lamb, and beef. Reservations are smart at most of these places, especially on summer weekends.

Near the B&Bs, on or near Castle Street

The first three eateries line Castle Street, facing the back of the castle. The last two are right in the middle of the B&B neighborhood.

INVERNESS

Café 1 serves up high-quality modern Scottish and international cuisine with a trendy, elegant bistro flair. This popular place fills up on weekends, so it's smart to call ahead (£9–19 entrées, lunch and early-bird dinner specials 17:30–18:45, Mon–Sat 12:00–14:00 & 17:30–21:30, closed Sun, 75 Castle Street, tel. 01463/226-200).

Number 27 is the Scottish version of T.G.I. Friday's. The straightforward, crowd-pleasing menu offers something for everyone—salads, burgers, seafood, and more (£9–14 entrées, Mon–Fri 12:00–14:45 & 17:00–21:00, Sat 12:00–21:30, Sun 12:30–14:45 & 17:00–21:00, generous portions, noisy bar up front not separated from restaurant in back, 27 Castle Street, tel. 01463/241-999).

La Tortilla Asesina has Spanish tapas, including spicy king prawns (the house specialty). It's an appealing and vivacious dining option (£3–5 cold and hot tapas, a few make a meal, cheap three-course specials; July–Sept daily 12:00–22:00; Oct–June Sun–Thu 12:00–21:00, Fri–Sat until 22:00; 99 Castle Street, tel. 01463/709-809).

The Redcliffe Hotel's restaurant is conveniently located (right on one of the B&B streets) and serves up good food in three areas: a bright and leafy sunroom, a pub, or an outdoor patio (£9–16 dinners, Mon–Sat 12:00–14:30 & 17:00–21:30, Sun 12:30–14:30 & 17:30–21:30, 1 Gordon Terrace, tel. 01463/232-767). Also nearby is the **Heathmount Hotel and Restaurant,** which serves good food in their quiet dining room (£5–9 lunch entrées, £9–17 dinner entrées, Mon–Fri 12:00–14:30 & 17:00–22:00, Sat–Sun 12:30–22:00, Kingsmills Road, tel. 01463/235-877).

In the Town Center

Hootananny is a cross-cultural experience, combining a lively pub atmosphere, nightly live music (Scottish traditional every night, plus rock, blues, and "bar music"), and Thai cuisine. It's got a great join-in-the-fun vibe at night (£6–7 Thai dishes, lunch deals, food served Mon–Sat 12:00–15:00 & 17:00–21:30, music begins every night at 21:30, closed Sun, good for take-away, 67 Church Street, tel. 01463/233-651, www.hootananny.co.uk). Upstairs is the Mad Hatter's nightclub (Thu-Sun only), complete with a "chill-out room."

Rocpool Restaurant is a hit with locals and good for a splurge. Owner/chef Steven Devlin serves creative modern European food in a sleek—and often crowded—chocolate/pistachio dining room (£12 lunch specials Mon–Sat, £14 pre-theater special before 18:45 Sun–Fri, £12–18 dinners, daily 12:00–14:30 & 17:45–22:00, reserve or be sorry, across the Ness Bridge from TI at 1 Ness Walk, tel. 01463/717-274).

The Mustard Seed serves Scottish food with a modern twist and a view of the river in an old church in a lively-at-lunch, mellow-at-dinner atmosphere. It's pricey but worth considering for a nice meal. Ask for a seat on the balcony if the weather is cooperating (£6 lunch specials, £12 early-bird specials before 19:00, £10–15 meals, daily 12:00–15:00 & 17:30–22:00, reservations essential on weekends, on the corner of Bank and Fraser Streets, 16 Fraser Street, tel. 01463/220-220).

Rajah Indian Restaurant provides a tasty break from meat and potatoes, with vegetarian options served in a classy red-velvet, white-linen atmosphere (£9–14 meals, 10 percent less for take-out, Mon–Sat 12:00–22:30, Sun 15:00–22:30, last dine-in order 30 minutes before closing, just off Church Street at 2 Post Office Avenue, tel. 01463/237-190).

Girvans serves sandwiches and tempting pastries in an easygoing atmosphere (£8–14 meals, Mon–Sat 9:00–21:00, Sun 10:00–21:00, 2 Stephens Brae, at the end of the pedestrian zone nearest the train station, tel. 01463/711-900).

Délices de Bretagne, next door to Girvans, is a tiny French brasserie serving £5 croque sandwiches, £3–6 crêpes, and its share of tasty pastries in a lighthearted, Art Nouveau space (Mon–Sat 9:00–17:00, closed Sun, 4A/6 Stephens Brae, tel. 01463/712-422).

Leakey's Bookshop and Café, located in a 1649 converted church, has the best lunch deal in town. Browse through stacks of old books and vintage maps, warm up by the wood-burning stove, and climb the spiral staircase to the loft for hearty home-made soups, sandwiches, and sweets (£3–4 light lunches, Mon–Sat 10:00–16:30, bookstore stays open until 17:30, closed Sun, in Greyfriar's Hall on Church Street, tel. 01463/239-947, Charles Leakey).

Picnic: The **Marks & Spencer** food hall is best (you can't miss it—on the main pedestrian mall, near the Market Brae steps at the corner of the big Eastgate Shopping Centre; Mon–Wed and Fri–Sat 9:00–18:00, Thu 9:00–20:00, Sun 11:00–17:00, tel. 01463/224-844).

Inverness Connections

From Inverness by Train to: Pitlochry (every 1.5-2 hours, 1.5 hours), **Stirling** (every 1.5–2 hours, 2.75–3 hours, some transfer in Perth), **Kyle of Lochalsh** near Isle of Skye (4/day, 2.5 hours), **Edinburgh** (every 2 hours, 3.5–4 hours, more with change in Perth), **Glasgow** (9/day, 3.5 hours, 3 direct, the rest change in Perth). ScotRail does a great sleeper service to **London** (generally £140–190 for first class/private compartment or £100–150 for standard class/shared compartment with breakfast, not available Sat night, www.firstscotrail.com). Consider dropping your car in

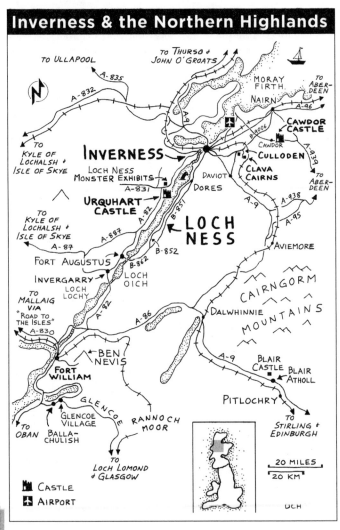

Inverness & the Northern Highlands

INVERNESS

Inverness and riding to London by train. Train info: tel. 0845-748-4950.

By Bus: To reach most destinations in western Scotland, you'll first head for **Fort William** (5/day, 2 hours). For connections onward to **Oban** (figure 4 hours total) or **Glencoe** (3 hours total), see the "Fort William Connections" on page 145. To reach **Portree** on the Isle of Skye, you can either take the direct bus (3/day in summer, 2/day in winter, 3.25 hours direct), or transfer in Fort William. These buses are run by Scottish Citylink; for schedules, see www.citylink.co.uk. You can buy tickets in advance by calling

Citylink at tel. 0871-266-3333 or stopping by the Inverness bus station (Mon–Sat 7:00–18:45, Sun 9:00–17:30, £0.50 extra for credit cards, daily baggage storage-£4–5/bag, 2 blocks from train station on Margaret Street, tel. 01463/233-371). For bus travel to England, check www.nationalexpress.com.

Route Tips for Drivers

Inverness to Edinburgh (150 miles, 3 hours minimum): Leaving Inverness, follow signs to A9 (south, toward Perth). If you haven't seen the Culloden Battlefield yet (described later), it's an easy detour: Just as you leave Inverness, head four miles east off A9 on B9006. Back on A9, it's a wonderfully speedy, scenic highway (A9, M90, A90) all the way to Edinburgh. If you have time, consider stopping en route in Pitlochry (just off A9; see the Between Inverness and Edinburgh chapter).

To Oban, Glencoe, or Isle of Skye: See the "Route Tips for Drivers" at the end of the Oban and the Southern Highlands chapter.

Near Inverness

Inverness puts you in the heart of the Highlands, within easy striking distance of a gaggle of famous and worthwhile sights: Squint across Loch Ness looking for Nessie—or, if you're a skeptic, just appreciate the majesty of Britain's largest body of water by volume. Commune with the Scottish soul at the historic Culloden Battlefield, where Scottish, English, and world history reached a turning point. Ponder three mysterious Neolithic cairns, reminding visitors that Scotland's history goes back even before Braveheart. And enjoy a homey country castle at Cawdor.

Loch Ness

I'll admit it: I had my zoom lens out and my eyes on the water. The local tourist industry thrives on the legend of the Loch Ness Monster. It's a thrilling thought, and there have been several seemingly reliable "sightings" (monks, police officers, and sonar images). But even if you ignore the monster stories, the loch is impressive: 23 miles long, less than a mile wide, the third-deepest in Europe (754 feet), and containing more water than in all the freshwater bodies of England and Wales combined.

Getting There: The Loch Ness sights are a quick drive southwest of Inverness. Various buses go from Inverness to Urquhart

Castle in about a half-hour (8/day, various companies, ask at Inverness bus station or TI).

Sights on Loch Ness

Loch Ness Monster Exhibits—In July of 1933, a couple swore that they saw a giant sea monster shimmy across the road in front

of their car by Loch Ness. Within days, ancient legends about giant monsters in the lake (dating as far back as the sixth century) were revived—and suddenly everyone was spotting "Nessie" poke its head above the waters of Loch Ness. In the last 75 years, further sightings and photographic "evidence" have bolstered the claim that there's something mysterious living in this unthinkably deep and murky lake. (Most sightings take place in the deepest part of the loch, near Urquhart Castle.) Most witnesses describe a waterbound dinosaur (resembling the real, but extinct, plesiosaur). Others cling to the slightly more plausible theory of a gigantic eel. And skeptics figure the sightings can be explained by a combination of reflections, boat wakes, and mass hysteria. The most famous photo of the beast (dubbed the "Surgeon's Photo") was later discredited—the "monster's" head was actually attached to a toy submarine. But that hasn't stopped various cryptozoologists from seeking photographic, sonar, and other proof.

And that suits the thriving local tourist industry just fine. The Nessie commercialization is so tacky that there are two different monster exhibits within 100 yards of each other, both in the town of Drumnadrochit. Each has a tour-bus parking lot and more square footage devoted to their kitschy shop than to the exhibit. The overpriced exhibitions are actually quite interesting—even though they're tourist traps, they'll appease that small part of you that knows the *real* reason you wanted to see Loch Ness.

The better option of the two—worth ▲—is the **Loch Ness Centre & Exhibition,** headed by a marine biologist who has spent more than 15 years researching lake ecology and scientific phenomena. With a 30-minute series of video bits and special effects, this exhibit explains the geological and historical environment that bred the monster story as well as the various searches that have been conducted. Refreshingly, it retains an air of healthy skepticism instead of breathless monster-chasing. It also has some artifacts related to the search, such as a hippo-foot ashtray used to fake monster footprints and the *Viperfish*—a harpoon-equipped

The Caledonian Canal

The Highlands are cut in two by the impressive Caledonian Canal, which connects lakes (lochs) that lie in the huge depression created by the Great Glen Fault (easily visible on any map as the diagonal slash across Scotland). The town of Fort William (described in a previous chapter) is located at the southwest end of the canal, and Inverness sits at its northeast end. The major sights—including the famous Loch Ness—cluster along the scenic 60-mile stretch between these two towns.

Three locks and a series of canals trace the fault. Oich, Loch, and Ness were connected in the early 1800s by the great British engineer Thomas Telford. Traveling between Fort William and Inverness, you'll follow Telford's work—20 miles of canals and locks between 40 miles of lakes, raising ships from sea level to 51 feet (Ness), 93 feet (Lochy), and to 106 feet (Oich).

While "Neptune's Staircase," a series of locks near Fort William, has been cleverly named to sound intriguing,  the best lock stop is midway, at Fort Augustus, where the canal hits the south end of Loch Ness. In Fort Augustus, the **Caledonian Canal Heritage Centre,** three locks above the main road, gives a good rundown on Telford's work (free, April-Oct daily 10:00-13:30 & 14:00-17:30, closed Nov-March, tel. 01320/366-493). Stroll past several shops and eateries to the top of the locks for a fine view.

submarine used in a 1969 Nessie search (£6.50, daily Easter–May 9:30–17:00, June–Oct 9:00–18:00, Nov–Easter 10:00–15:30, in the big stone mansion right on the main road to Inverness, tel. 01456/450-573, www.lochness.com).

The other exhibit, called the **Nessieland Castle Monster Centre** (up a side road closer to the town center, affiliated with a hotel), is less serious. It's basically a tacky high-school-quality photo report and a 30-minute *We Believe in the Loch Ness Monster* movie, which features credible-sounding locals explaining what they saw and a review of modern Nessie searches. (The most convincing reason for locals to believe: Look at the hordes of tourists around you.) It also has small exhibits on local history and on other "monsters" and hoaxes around the world (£5.50, daily May–Sept 9:00–18:00, Oct–April 9:00–17:00, tel. 01456/450-342, www.loch-ness-monster-nessieland.com).

▲**Urquhart Castle**—The ruins at Urquhart (UR-kurt), just up the loch from the Nessie exhibits, are gloriously situated with a view

of virtually the entire lake. Its visitors center has a tiny museum with interesting castle artifacts and a good eight-minute film, but the castle itself is a relatively empty shell. Its previous owners blew it up to keep the Jacobites from taking it. As you walk toward the ruins, take a close look at the trebuchet (a working replica of one of the most destructive weapons of English King Edward I), and ponder how this giant slingshot helped Edward grab almost every castle in the country away from the native Scots (£7, guidebook-£4, daily April–Sept 9:30–18:00, Oct 9:30–17:00, Nov–March 9:30–16:30, last entry 45 minutes before closing, café, tel. 01456/450-551, www.historic-scotland.gov.uk).

Culloden Battlefield

Jacobite troops under Bonnie Prince Charlie were defeated at Culloden (kuh-LAW-dehn) by supporters of the Hanover dynasty in 1746. This last major land battle fought on British soil spelled the end of Jacobite resistance and the beginning of the clan chiefs' fall from power. Wandering the desolate, solemn battlefield, you sense that something terrible occurred here. Locals still bring white roses and speak of "the '45" (as Bonnie Prince Charlie's entire campaign is called) as if it just happened. The battlefield at Culloden and its high-tech Visitors Centre together are worth ▲▲▲.

Orientation to Culloden

Cost and Hours: £10, plus £2 for parking. Daily April–Oct 9:00–18:00, Nov–March 10:00–16:00, closed in Jan.

Information and Services: £5 guidebook, café, tel. 01463/796-090, www.nts.org.uk/culloden.

Tours: Tours with live guides are included with your admission. Check for a schedule—there are generally 3–4/day, focusing on various aspects of the battle.

Audioguide: It's free, with good information tied by GPS to important sites on the battlefield; pick it up at the end of the indoor exhibit.

Getting There: It's a 15-minute drive east of Inverness. Follow signs to *Aberdeen,* then *Culloden Moor,* and B9006 takes you right there (well-signed on the right-hand side). Public buses leave from Inverness' Queensgate street and drop you off in the parking lot (bus #1 or #1A, hourly, 30 minutes, confirm that bus is going all the way to the battlefield).

Length of This Tour: Allow 2 hours.

Background: The Battle of Culloden

The Battle of Culloden (April 16, 1746) marks the end of the power of the Scottish Highland clans and the start of years of repression of Scottish culture by the English. It was the culmination of a year's worth of battles, known collectively as "the '45." At the center of it all was the charismatic, enigmatic Bonnie Prince Charlie (1720–1788).

Charles Edward Stuart, from his first breath, was raised with a single purpose—to restore his family to the British throne. His grandfather was King James II, deposed in 1688 by Parliament for his tyranny and pro-Catholic bias. In 1745, young Charlie crossed the Channel from exile in France to retake the throne for the Stuarts. He landed on the west coast of Scotland and rallied support for the "Jacobite" cause (from the Latin for "James"). Though Charles was not Scottish-born, he was the rightful heir directly down the line from Mary, Queen of Scots—and so many Scots joined the Stuart family's rebellion out of resentment at being ruled by a foreign king (English royalty of German descent).

Bagpipes droned, and "Bonnie" (handsome) Charlie led an army of 2,000 tartan-wearing, Gaelic-speaking Highlanders across Scotland, seizing Edinburgh. They picked up other supporters of the Stuarts from the Lowlands and from England. Now 6,000 strong, they marched south toward London, and King George II made plans to flee the country. But anticipated support for the Jacobites failed to materialize in the numbers they were hoping for (both in England and from France). The Jacobites had so far been victorious in their battles against the Hanoverian government forces, but the odds now turned against them. Charles retreated to the Scottish Highlands, where many of his men knew the terrain and might gain an advantage when outnumbered. The English government troops followed closely on his heels.

Against the advice of his best military strategist, Charles' army faced the Hanoverian forces at Culloden Moor on flat, barren terrain that was unsuited to the Highlanders' guerrilla tactics. The Scots—many of them brandishing only broadswords and spears—were mowed down by English cannons and horsemen. In less than an hour, the government forces routed the Jacobite army, but that was just the start. They spent the next weeks methodically hunting down ringleaders and sympathizers (and many others in the Highlands who had nothing to do with the battle), ruthlessly killing, imprisoning, and banishing thousands.

Charles fled with a £30,000 price on his head. He escaped to the Isle of Skye, hidden by a woman named Flora MacDonald (her grave is on the Isle of Skye, and her statue is outside Inverness Castle). Flora dressed Charles in women's clothes and passed him off as her maid. Later, Flora was arrested and thrown in the Tower of London before being released and treated like a celebrity.

Charles escaped to France. He spent the rest of his life wandering Europe trying to drum up support to retake the throne. He drifted through short-lived romantic affairs and alcohol, and died in obscurity, without an heir, in Rome.

Though usually depicted as a battle of the Scottish versus the English, in truth Culloden was a civil war between two opposing dynasties: Stuart (Charlie) and Hanover (George). In fact, about one-fifth of the government's troops were Scottish, and several redcoat deserters fought along with the Jacobites. However, as the history has faded into lore, the battle has come to be remembered as a Scottish-versus-English standoff—or, in the parlance of the Scots, the Highlanders versus the Strangers.

The Battle of Culloden was the end of 60 years of Jacobite rebellions, the last major battle fought on British soil, and the final stand of the Highlanders. From then on, clan chiefs were deposed; kilts, tartans, and bagpipes became illegal paraphernalia; and farmers were cleared off their ancestral land, replaced by more-profitable sheep. Scottish culture would never recover from the events of the campaign called "the '45."

Self-Guided Tour

Culloden's Visitors Centre, opened in spring 2008, is a state-of-the-art £10 million facility. The ribbon was cut by two young local men, each descended from soldiers who fought in the battle (one from either side). On the way up to the door, look under your feet at the memorial stones for fallen soldiers and clans, mostly purchased by their American and Canadian descendants.

The initial part of the exhibit provides you with some background. As you pass the ticket desk, note the **family tree** of Bonnie Prince Charlie ("Prince Charles Edward") and George II, who were essentially distant cousins. Next you'll come across the first of the exhibit's shadowy-figure **touchscreens,** which connect you with historical figures who give you details from both the Hanoverian and Jacobite perspectives. A **map** here shows the other power struggles happening in and around Europe, putting this fight for political control of Britain in a wider context. This battle was no simple local skirmish, but rather a key part of a larger struggle between Britain and its neighbors, primarily France, for control over trade and colonial power. In the display case are **medals** from the early 1700s, made by both sides as propaganda.

Your path through this building is cleverly designed to echo the course of the Jacobite army. Your short march gets underway as Charlie sails from France to Scotland, then finagles the support of Highland clan chiefs. As he heads south with his army to take London, you, too, are walking south. Along the way, maps show the movement of troops, and wall panels cover the build-up to the attack, as seen from both sides. Note the clever division of information: To the left and in red is the story of the "government" (a.k.a. Hanoverians/Whigs/English, led by the Duke of Cumberland); to right, in blue, is the Jacobites' perspective (Prince Charlie and his Highlander/French supporters).

But you, like Charlie, don't make it to London—in the dark room at the end, you can hear Jacobite commanders arguing over whether to retreat back to Scotland. Pessimistic about their chances of receiving more French support, they decide to U-turn, and so do you. Heading back up north, you'll get some insight into some of the strategizing that went on behind the scenes.

By the time you reach the end of the hall, it's the night before the battle. Round another bend into a dark passage and listen to the voices of the anxious troops. While the English slept soundly in their tents (recovering from celebrating the Duke's 25th birthday), the scrappy and exhausted Jacobite Highlanders struggled through the night to reach the battlefield (abandoning their plan of a surprise attack at Nairn and instead retreating back toward Inverness).

At last the two sides meet. As you wait outside the theater for the next showing, study the chart depicting how the forces were arranged on the battlefield. Once inside the theater, you'll soon be surrounded by the views and sounds of a windswept moor. An impressive four-minute **360° movie** projects the reenacted battle with you right in the center of the action (the violence is realistic; young kids should probably sit this one out). If it hasn't hit you already, the movie drives home how truly outmatched the Jacobites were, and what a hopeless and tragic day it was for them.

Leave the movie, then enter the last room. Here you'll find **period weapons,** including ammunition and artifacts found on the battlefield, as well as **historical depictions** of the battle. You'll also find a section describing the detective work required to piece together the story from historical evidence. On the far end is a huge map, with narration explaining the combat you've just experienced while giving you a bird's-eye view of the field you're about to roam through. Collect your free battlefield **audioguide.** The doors in front of you lead outside.

From the back wall of the Visitors Centre, survey the battlefield. In the foreground is a cottage used as a makeshift hospital during the conflict (it's decorated as it would have been then). To the east (south of the River Nairn) is the site that Lord George Murray originally chose for the action. In the end, he failed to convince Prince Charlie of its superiority, and the battle was held here—with disastrous consequences. Although not far from Culloden, the River Nairn site was miles away tactically, and things might have turned out differently for the Jacobites had the battle taken place there instead.

Head left, down to the **battlefield.** Your GPS guide knows where you are, and the attendant will give you directions on where to start. As you walk along the path, stop each time you hear the "ping" sound (if you keep going, you'll confuse the satellite). The basic audioguide will stop you 10 times on the battlefield—at the Jacobite front line, the Hanoverian front line, and more—taking a minimum of 30 minutes to complete the walking tour. Each stop has additional information on everything from the Brown Bess musket to who was standing on what front line—how long this part of the tour takes depends on how much you want to hear. Notice how uneven and boggy the ground is in parts here, and imagine trying to run across this hummocky terrain with all your gear, toward your almost-certain death.

As you pass by the **mass graves,** marked by small headstones, realize that entire clans fought, died, and were buried together. (The fallen were identified by the clan badge on their caps.) The Mackintosh grave alone was 77 yards long.

When you've finished your walking tour, re-enter the hall where you left, return your audioguide (before 17:50), then catch the last part of the exhibit, which covers the aftermath of the battle. As you leave the building, hang a left to see the wall of **protruding bricks,** each representing a soldier who died. The handful of Hanoverian casualties are on the left (about 50); the rest of the long wall's raised bricks represent the multitude of dead Jacobites (about 1,500).

If you're having trouble grasping the significance of this battle, play a game of "What if?" If Bonnie Prince Charlie had persevered on this campaign and taken the throne, he likely wouldn't have plunged Britain into the Seven Years' War with France (his ally). And increased taxes on either side of that war led directly to the French and American revolutions. So if the Jacobites had won...the American colonies might still be part of the British Empire today.

Clava Cairns

Scotland is littered with reminders of prehistoric peoples—especially along the coast of the Moray Firth—but the Clava Cairns

are among the best-preserved, most interesting, and easiest to reach. You'll find them nestled in the spooky countryside just beyond Culloden Battlefield. These "Balnauran of Clava" are Neolithic burial chambers dating from 3,000 to 4,000 years ago. Although they simply look like giant piles of rocks in a sparsely forested clearing, they warrant a closer look to appreciate the prehistoric logic behind them. (The site is well-explained by informative plaques.) There are three structures: a central "ring cairn" with an open space in the center but no access to it, flanked by two "passage cairns," which were once covered. The entrance shaft in each passage cairn lines up with the setting sun at the winter solstice. Each cairn is surrounded by a stone circle, injecting this site with even more mystery.

Cost and Hours: Free, always open.

Getting There: Just after passing Culloden Battlefield on B9006 (coming from Inverness), signs on the right point to *Clava Cairns*. Follow this twisty road to the free parking lot by the stones. Skip it if you don't have a car.

Cawdor Castle

Homey and intimate, this castle is still the residence of the Dowager (read: widow) Countess of Cawdor, a local aristocratic

branch of the Campbell family. The castle's claim to fame is its connection to Shakespeare's *Macbeth*, in which the three witches correctly predict that the protagonist will be granted the title "Thane of Cawdor." The castle is not used as a setting in the play—which takes place in Inverness, 300 years before this castle was built—but Shakespeare's dozen or so references to "Cawdor" are enough for the marketing machine to kick in. Today, virtually nothing tangibly ties Cawdor to the Bard or to the real-life Macbeth. But even if you ignore the Shakespeare lore, the castle is worth a visit.

INVERNESS

The chatty, friendly docents (including Jean at the front desk, who can say "welcome" and "mind your head" in 60 different languages) give the castle an air of intimacy—most are residents of the neighboring village of Cawdor, and act as though they're old friends with the Dowager Countess (many probably are). Entertaining posted explanations—written by the countess' late husband, the sixth Earl of Cawdor—bring the castle to life, and make you wish you'd known the old chap. While many of today's castles are still residences for the aristocracy, Cawdor feels even more lived-in than the norm—you can imagine the Dowager Countess stretching out in front of the fireplace with a good book. Notice her geraniums in every room.

Stops on the tour include a tapestry-laden bedroom and a "tartan passage" speckled with modern paintings. In another bedroom (just before the stairs back down) is a tiny pencil sketch by Salvador Dalí. Inside the base of the tower, near the end of the tour, is the castle's proud symbol: a holly tree dating from 1372. According to the beloved legend, a donkey leaned against this tree to mark the spot where the castle was to be built—which it was, around the tree. (The tree is no longer alive, but its withered trunk is still propped up in the same position. No word on the donkey.)

The **gardens,** included with the ticket, are also worth exploring, with some 18th-century linden trees, a hedge maze (not open to the public), and several surprising species (including sequoia and redwood). In May and June, the laburnum arbors drip with yellow blossoms.

The nearby remote-feeling **village of Cawdor**—with a few houses, a village shop, and a tavern—is also worth a look if you've got time to kill.

Cost and Hours: £8, good £3 guidebook explains the family and the rooms, May–early Oct daily 10:00–17:30, last entry at 17:00, gardens open until 18:00, closed early Oct–April, tel. 01667/404-401, www.cawdorcastle.com.

Getting There: It's on B9090, just off A96, about 10 miles east of Inverness (six miles beyond Culloden and the Clava Cairns). Without a car, you can either take a guided tour from Inverness (ask at the TI), or hop on public bus #1 or #1A—the same ones that go to Culloden—from central Inverness (hourly, 55 minutes, get on at Queensgate stop, check with driver that bus goes all the way to Cawdor, 15-minute walk from Cawdor Church bus stop to castle, last bus back to Inverness around 18:45).

BETWEEN INVERNESS AND EDINBURGH

Pitlochry and Stirling

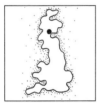

To break up the trip between Inverness and Edinburgh (3 hours by car, 3.5 hours by train), consider stopping over at one of these two worthwhile destinations. The town of Pitlochry, right on the train route, mixes whisky and hillwalking with a dash of countryside charm. Farther south, the historic city of Stirling boasts an impressive castle, a monument to a Scottish hero (William "Braveheart" Wallace), and one of the country's most important battle sites (Bannockburn).

Planning Your Time

Visiting both Pitlochry and Stirling on a one-day drive from Inverness to Edinburgh is doable but busy (especially since part of Pitlochry's allure is slowing down to taste the whisky).

Pleasant Pitlochry is well-located, a quick detour off of the main A9 highway from Inverness to Edinburgh (via Perth) or an easy stop for train travelers. The town deserves an overnight for whisky-lovers, or for those who really want to relax in small-town Scotland. Though many find the town of Pitlochry appealing, it lacks the rugged Highlands scenery and easy access to other major sights found in Oban and Glencoe.

Stirling, off the busy A9/M9 motorway between Perth and Edinburgh, is well worth a sightseeing stop, especially for historians and romantics interested in Scottish history. (If skipping Stirling, notice that you can take M90 due south over the Firth of Forth to connect Perth and Edinburgh.) Stirling also works well as a stop-off between Edinburgh and points west (such as Glasgow or Oban)—just take the northern M9/A80 route instead of more direct M8.

Between Inverness & Edinburgh

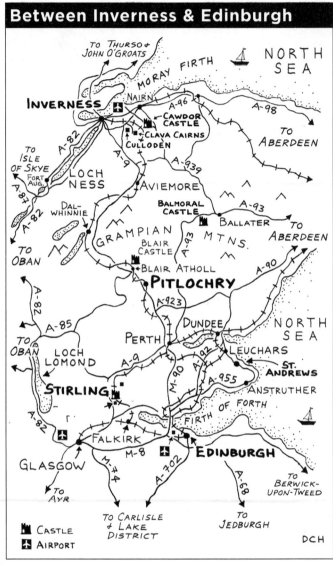

Pitlochry

This likable tourist town, famous for its whisky and its hillwalking (both beloved by Scots), makes an enjoyable overnight stop

on the way between Inverness and Edinburgh. Just outside the craggy Highlands, Pitlochry is set amid pastoral rolling hills that offer plenty of forest hikes (brochures at TI). A salmon ladder climbs alongside the lazy river (free viewing area—best in May and June, 10-minute walk from town).

Orientation to Pitlochry

(area code: 01796)

Plucky little Pitlochry (pop. 2,500) lines up along its tidy, tourist-minded main road, where you'll find the train station, bus stops, the TI, and bike rental. The River Tummel runs parallel to the main road, a few steps away. Most distilleries are a short drive out of town, but you can walk to the two best; see my self-guided hillwalk, below. Navigate easily by following the black directional signs to Pitlochry's handful of sights.

Tourist Information

The helpful TI provides train schedules, books rooms for a £4 fee, and sells good maps for walks and scenic drives (July–mid-Sept Mon–Sat 9:00–19:00, Sun 9:30–17:30; mid-Sept–June Mon–Sat 9:30–17:30, Sun 10:00–16:00; exit from station and follow small road to the right with trains behind you, turn right on Atholl Road, and walk 5 minutes to TI on left, at #22; tel. 01796/472-215, pitlochry@visitscotland.com).

Helpful Hints

Bike Rental: Escape Route Bikes, located across the street and a block from the TI (away from town), rents a variety of bikes for adults and kids (£10/4 hours, £18/24 hours, price varies by type of bike and includes helmets and lock if you ask, Mon–Sat 9:00–17:30, Sun 10:00–17:00, shorter hours in winter, 3 Atholl Road, tel. 01796/473-859, www.escape-route.biz).

Self-Guided Hillwalk

Pitlochry Whisky Walk

If you've ever suspected you were a hobbit in a previous life, spend an afternoon hillwalking from downtown Pitlochry to a pair of top distilleries. The entire loop trip takes two to three hours, depending on how long you linger in the distilleries (at least 45 minutes to an hour of walking each way). It's a good way to see some green rolling hills, especially if you've only experienced urban Scotland. The walk is largely uphill on the way to the Edradour Distillery; wear good shoes, bring a rain jacket just in case, and be happy that you'll stroll easily downhill *after* you've had your whisky samples.

At the TI, pick up the *Pitlochry Walks* brochure (£1). You'll be taking the **Edradour Walk** (marked on directional signs with the yellow hiker icons; on the map it's a series of yellow dots). Leave the TI and head left along busy A924. The walk can be done by going either direction, but I'll describe it counterclockwise.

Within 10 minutes, you'll come to **Bell's Blair Athol Distillery.** If you're a whisky buff, stop in here (described under "Sights in Pitlochry"). Otherwise, hold out for the much more atmospheric Edradour. After passing a few B&Bs and suburban homes, you'll see a sign (marked *Edradour Walk*) on the left side of the road, leading you up and off the highway. You'll come to a clearing, and as the road gets steeper, you'll see signs directing you 50 yards off the main path to see the "Black Spout"—a wonderful waterfall well worth a few extra steps.

At the top of the hill, you'll arrive in another clearing, where a narrow path leads along a field. Low rolling hills surround you in all directions. It seems like there's not another person around for miles, with just thistles to keep you company. It's an easy 20 minutes to the distillery from here.

Stop into the **Edradour Distillery** (also described later). After the tour, leave the distillery, heading right, following the paved road (Old North Road). In about five minutes, there's a sign that seems to point right into the field. Take the small footpath that runs along the left side of the road. (If you see the driveway with stone lions on both sides, you've gone a few steps too far.) You'll walk parallel to the route you took getting to the distillery, and then you'll head back into the forest. Cross the footbridge and make a left (as the map indicates), staying on the wide road. You'll pass a B&B, and hear traffic noises as you emerge out of the forest. The trail leads back to the highway, with the TI a few blocks ahead on the right.

Sights in Pitlochry

Distillery Tours—The cute **Edradour Distillery** (ED-rah-dower), the smallest in Scotland, takes pride in making its whisky with a minimum of machinery. Small white-and-red buildings are nestled in an impossibly green Scottish hillside. Wander through the buildings and take the £5 guided tour (3/hour in summer, 2/hour in winter, 50 minutes). They offer a 10-minute A/V show and, of course, a free sample dram. Unlike the bigger distilleries, they allow you to take photos of the equipment. If you like the whisky, buy some here and support the local economy—this is one of the few independently owned distilleries left in Scotland (May–Oct Mon–Sat 10:00–17:00, Sun 12:00–17:00; June–Sept Mon–Sat opens at 9:30, Nov–April Mon–Sat 10:00–16:00, Sun 12:00–16:00, Jan–Feb closed Sun; last tour departs one hour before closing, tel. 01796/472-095, www.edradour.co.uk). Most come to the distillery by car (follow signs from the main road, 2.5 miles into the countryside), but you can also get there on a peaceful hiking trail that you'll have all to yourself (follow my "Pitlochry Whisky Walk," earlier).

The big, ivy-covered **Bell's Blair Athol Distillery** is more conveniently located (about a half-mile from the town center) and more corporate-feeling, offering £5 45-minute tours with a wee taste at the end (Easter–Oct tours depart 2/hour Mon–Sat 9:30–17:00, July-Aug until 17:30, June–Oct also Sun 12:00–17:00, last tour departs one hour before closing; Nov–Easter tours depart Mon–Fri at 11:00, 13:00, and 15:00, closed Sat–Sun; tel. 01796/482-003, www.discovering-distilleries.com/blairathol).

Pitlochry Power Station—The station, adjacent to the salmon ladder, offers a mildly entertaining exhibit about hydroelectric power in the region (free, April–Oct Mon–Fri 10:00–17:00, closed Sat–Sun, July–Aug also open weekends, closed Nov–March, tel. 01796/473-152). Although walkers can reach this easily by crossing the footbridge from the town center (about a 15-minute walk), drivers will head east out of town (toward Bell's Blair Athol Distillery), then turn right on Bridge Road, cross the river, and backtrack to the power station.

Theater—From May through October, the **Pitlochry Festival Theatre** presents a different play every night and concerts on some

Sundays (both £17–27 Sun–Thu, £18–28 Fri–Sat, purchase tickets online, at TI, or theater—same price, box office open daily 10:00–17:00, tel. 01796/484-626, www.pitlochryfestivaltheatre.com).

Garden—The **Explorers Garden,** adjacent to the theater, has a six-acre woodland garden with plants and wildflowers from around the world (£3, April–Oct daily 10:00–17:00, last entry at 16:15, tel. 01796/484-626, www.explorersgarden.com).

Near Pitlochry

Balmoral Castle—The Queen spends each August and September here on her 50,000-acre private estate, located within Cairngorms National Park. The grounds and the ballroom are open to visitors part of the year (except when the Queen's in residence), but they're overpriced (£8.70, audioguide requires £5 deposit, April–July 10:00–17:00, closed Aug–March, tel. 013397/42534, www.balmoral castle.com).

For a free peek at another royal landmark, stop at **Crathie Kirk,** the small but charming parish church where the royal family worships when they are at Balmoral, and where Queen Victoria's beloved servant John Brown is buried. The church is just across the highway from the Balmoral parking lot.

Getting There: Balmoral is on A93, midway between Ballater and Braemar, about 50 miles northeast of Pitlochry and about 75 miles southeast of Inverness.

Sleeping in Pitlochry

$$ Craigroyston House is a quaint, large Victorian country house with eight Laura Ashley–style bedrooms run by charming Gretta and Douglas Maxwell (Db-£70–90, less off-season, family

---

Sleep Code

(£1 = about $1.60, country code: 44, area code: 01796)
S = Single, **D** = Double/Twin, **T** = Triple, **Q** = Quad, **b** = bathroom, **s** = shower only.

To help you sort easily through these listings, I've divided the rooms into two categories based on the price for a standard double room with bath (during high season):

$$ Higher Priced—Most rooms £50 or more.
$ Lower Priced—Most rooms less than £50.

Prices can change without notice; verify the hotel's current rates online or by email. For other updates, see www .ricksteves.com/update.

room, cash only, above and behind the TI—small gate at back of parking lot—and next to the church at 2 Lower Oakfield, tel. & fax 01796/472-053, www.craigroyston.co.uk, reservations@craig royston.co.uk).

$ Pitlochry's fine **hostel** has 62 beds in 12 rooms, including some private and family rooms. It's on Knockard Road, well-signed from the town center, about a five-minute walk above the main drag and offering nice views (£18 bunks in 3- to 8-bed rooms, Db-£60; £2 more for non-members, breakfast-£4.25, packed lunch-£5, Internet access and Wi-Fi, self-service laundry, kitchen, office open 7:00–10:00 & 17:00–23:00, tel. 01796/472-308, www .syha.org.uk, pitlochry@syha.org.uk).

Eating in Pitlochry

Plenty of options line the main drag, including several bakeries selling picnic supplies. For a heartier meal, try **Victoria's** restaurant and coffee shop, located midway between the train station and the TI (£5–9 sandwiches, £9 pizzas, £8–12 lunch entrées, £11–20 dinners, daily 10:00–21:00, patio seating, at corner of memorial garden at 45 Atholl Road, tel. 01796/472-670) or **Fern Cottage,** just behind Victoria's (pre-theater £18–22 dinner specials 17:30–18:45, tel. 01796/473-840). **Port-na-Craig Inn** is a fancy option across from the theater (tel. 01796/472-777).

Pitlochry Connections

The train station is open daily 8:00–18:00 (maybe less in winter).

From Pitlochry by Train to: Inverness (every 1.5–2 hours, 1.5–1.75 hours), **Stirling** (every 1.5–2 hours, 1.25 hours, some transfer in Perth), **Edinburgh** (6/day direct, 2 hours), **Glasgow** (9/day, 1.5–1.75 hours, most transfer in Perth). Train info: tel. 08457-484-950, www.nationalrail.co.uk.

Stirling

Once the Scottish capital, the quaint city of Stirling (pop. 41,000) is a mini-Edinburgh with lots of character and a trio of attractions: a dramatic castle, dripping with history and boasting sweeping views; the William Wallace Monument, honoring the real-life Braveheart; and the Bannockburn Heritage Centre, marking the site of Robert the Bruce's victorious battle.

Orientation to Stirling

(area code: 01786)
Stirling's old town is situated along a long, narrow, steep hill, with the castle at its apex. The **TI** is near the base of the old town (daily 10:00–17:00, 41 Dumbarton Road, tel. 01786/475-019, stirling @visitscotland.com).

Getting Around Stirling
Stirling's three main sights (Stirling Castle, the Wallace Monument, and the Bannockburn Heritage Centre) are difficult to reach by foot from the center of town, but are easily accessible by frequent public bus (the bus station is a short walk from the train station) or by taxi (£4–5).

Sights in Stirling

▲Stirling Castle
"He who holds Stirling, holds Scotland." These fateful words have proven, more often than not, to be true. Stirling Castle's strategic position—perched on a volcanic crag overlooking a bridge over the River Forth, the primary passage between the Lowlands and the Highlands—has long been the key to Scotland. This castle of the Stuart kings is one of Scotland's most historic and popular. Offering spectacular views over a gentle countryside, and a mildly interesting but steadily improving exhibit inside, Stirling is worth a look.

Cost and Hours: £9, daily April–Sept 9:30–18:00, Oct–March 9:30–17:00, palace apartments reopen in spring 2011 after renovation, last entry 45 minutes before closing, tel. 01786/450-000, www.stirlingcastle.gov.uk.

Getting There: Similar to Edinburgh's castle, Stirling Castle sits at the very tip of a steep old town. If you enter Stirling by car, follow the *Stirling Castle* signs, twist up the mazelike roads to the esplanade, and park at the £2 lot just outside the castle gate. Without a car, it's a bit more complicated: From the train or bus station, you can either hike the 20-minute uphill route to the castle, or you can take a taxi (about £4 to castle).

Tours: Posted information is skimpy, so a tour or audioguide is important for bringing the site to life. You can take the included 45-minute guided tour (generally hourly April–June, 2/hour July–Sept, 4/day Oct–March, depart from the Castle Close just inside the entry, includes a tour of Argyll's Lodging, a 17th-century townhouse) or rent the very good £2 audioguide from the kiosk near the ticket window. Knowledgeable docents posted throughout can tell you more.

Background: Stirling marks the site of two epic medieval battles where famous Scotsmen defeated huge English armies despite impossible odds: In 1297, William Wallace (a.k.a. "Braveheart") fended off an invading English army at the Battle of Stirling Bridge. And in 1314, Robert the Bruce won the battle of nearby Bannockburn. Soon after, the castle became the primary residence of the Stuart monarchs, who turned it into a showpiece of Scotland (and a symbol of one-upmanship against England). But when the Crown moved to London, Stirling's prominence waned. The military, which took over the castle during the Jacobite Wars of the 18th century, bulked it up and converted it into a garrison—damaging much of its delicate beauty. Since 1966, the fortress has been undergoing an extensive and costly restoration to bring it back to its glory days and make it, once again, one of Britain's premier castles.

❍ Self-Guided Tour: From the parking lot at the esplanade, go through the gate to buy your ticket (ask about tour times, and consider renting the audioguide), then head up into the castle through another gate. If you have time to kill before your tour, dip into the grassy courtyard on the left to reach an introductory **castle exhibition** about the history of the town and its fortress. Historians at Stirling are proud of the work they've done to rebuild the castle—and they're not shy about saying so.

Then head up through the main gateway into the **Outer Close.** Tours depart from just to your right, near the Grand Battery, which boasts cannon-and-rampart views. Down the hill along this wall is the Great Kitchens exhibit (where mannequin cooks oversee medieval recipes); below that the North Gate leads to the Nether Bailey (dating from the castle's later days as a military base). Back in the Outer Close, at the top of the courtyard (to your left as you enter), is a narrow passageway lined with exhibits about Stirling's medieval craftspeople.

Hike up into the **Inner Close,** where you're surrounded by Scottish history. Each of the very different buildings in this complex was built by a different monarch. Facing downhill, you'll see the Great Hall straight ahead. This grand structure—Scotland's biggest medieval banqueting hall—was built by the great Renaissance king James IV. Step inside the grand, empty-feeling space to appreciate its fine flourishes. The Chapel Royal, where Mary, Queen of Scots was crowned in 1543, is to your left and also worth a visit. To your right is the Palace, which reopens in spring 2011 after the restoration of six ground-floor apartments, done up as they might have looked in the mid-16th century. Costumed performers play the role of palace attendants, happy to chat with you about palace life. Behind you is the King's Old Building, with a regimental (military) museum (closes 45 minutes before the castle).

▲William Wallace Monument

Commemorating the Scottish hero better known to Americans as "Braveheart," this sandstone tower—built during a wave of Scottish nationalism in the mid-19th century—marks the Abbey Craig hill on the outskirts of Stirling. This is where Wallace gathered forces for his largest-scale victory against England's King Edward I, in 1297.

From the base of the monument, you can see the Stirling Bridge—a stone version that replaced the original wooden one. Looking out from the same vantage point as Wallace, imagine how the famous battle played out, and consider why the location was so important in the battle (explained in more detail inside the monument).

After entering the monument, pick up the worthwhile £1 audioguide. You'll first encounter a passionate talking Wallace replica, explaining his defiant stand against Edward I. As you listen, ogle Wallace's five-and-a-half-foot-long broadsword (and try to imagine drawing it from a scabbard on your back at a dead run). Then take a spin through a hall of other Scottish heroes. Finally, climb the 246 narrow steps inside the tower for grand views. The stairways are extremely tight and require some maneuvering—claustrophobes be warned.

Cost and Hours: £7.50, £1 audioguide, daily July–Aug 10:00–18:00, April–June and Sept–Oct 10:00–17:00, Nov–March 10:30–16:00, last entry 45 minutes before closing, café and gift shop, tel. 01786/472-140, www.nationalwallacemonument.com.

Getting There: It's two miles northeast of Stirling on A8, signposted from the city center. You can catch a public bus from the Stirling bus station (a short walk south of the train station) to the the Monument's parking lot (10/hour on a number of different bus lines, 15 minutes). Taxis cost about £5. From the parking lot's Visitors Pavilion, you'll need to hike (a very steep 10 minutes) or take a shuttle bus up the hill to the monument itself.

▲Bannockburn Heritage Centre

Just to the south of Stirling proper is the Bannockburn Heritage Centre, commemorating what many Scots view as their nation's most significant military victory over the invading English: the Battle of Bannockburn, won by a Scottish army led by Robert the Bruce against England's King Edward II in 1314.

In simple terms, Robert—who was first and foremost a politician—found himself out of political options after years of failed diplomatic attempts to make peace with the strong-arming English. Wallace's execution left a vacuum in military leadership, and eventually Robert stepped in, waging a successful guerrilla campaign that came to a head as young Edward's army marched to Stirling. Although the Scots were greatly outnumbered, their strategy and use of terrain at Bannockburn allowed them to soundly beat the English and drive Edward out of Scotland for good.

This victory is so legendary among the Scots that the country's unofficial national anthem, "Flower of Scotland"—written 600 years after the battle—focuses on this one event. (CDs with a version of this song performed by The Corries can be purchased at the Heritage Centre. Buy one and learn the song, and you might soon find yourself singing along at a pub.)

The Heritage Centre, though small, has excellent exhibits and a worthwhile film about the battle and events leading up to it. You can even try on a real chainmail shirt and helmet.

Cost and Hours: £5.50, March–Oct daily 10:00–17:00, April–Sept until 17:30, last entry 45 minutes before closing, closed Nov–Feb, tel. 0844/493-2139, www.nts.org.uk/Property/95.

Getting There: It's two miles south of Stirling on A872, off M80/M9. For non-drivers, it's an easy bus ride from the Stirling bus station (a short walk south from the train station; several bus lines run on this route, 6/hour, 9–15 minutes).

Stirling Connections

From Stirling by Train to: Edinburgh (2/hour, 50 minutes), **Glasgow** (3/hour, 30–45 minutes), **Pitlochry** (every 1.5–2 hours, 1.25 hours, most transfer in Perth), **Inverness** (every 1.5–2 hours, 2.75–3 hours, most transfer in Perth). Train info: tel. 08457-484-950, www.nationalrail.co.uk.

PRACTICALITIES

This section covers just the basics on traveling in Scotland (for much more information, see the latest edition of *Rick Steves' Great Britain*). You can find free advice on specific topics at www.ricksteves.com/tips.

Money

For currency, Scotland uses the British pound (£), also called a "quid": 1 British pound (£1) = about $1.60. One pound is broken into 100 pence (p). To convert prices in pounds to dollars, add about 60 percent: £20 = about $32, £50 = about $80. (Check www.oanda.com for the latest exchange rates.)

The standard way for travelers to get pounds is to withdraw money from a cash machine using a debit or credit card, ideally with a Visa or MasterCard logo. Before departing, call your bank or credit-card company: Confirm that your card will work overseas, ask about international transaction fees, and alert them that you'll be making withdrawals in Europe.

Your US credit card might not work at some stores or at automated machines (e.g., train and subway ticket machines, luggage lockers, toll booths, parking garages, and self-serve gas pumps), because they're designed to accept European credit cards with a PIN code. If your card doesn't work, you have several options: Pay with pounds, try your PIN code (ask your credit-card company in advance or use a debit card), or find a nearby cashier who should be able to process the transaction.

To keep your valuables safe, wear a money belt. But if you do lose your credit or debit card, report the loss immediately to the respective global customer-assistance centers. Call these

24-hour US numbers collect: Visa (410/581-9994), MasterCard (636/722-7111), and American Express (623/492-8427).

Phoning

Smart travelers use the telephone to reserve or reconfirm rooms, reserve restaurants, get directions, research transportation connections, confirm tour times, phone home, and lots more.

To call Scotland from the US or Canada: Dial 011-44 and then the area code (minus its initial zero) and local number. (The 011 is our international access code, and 44 is Great Britain's country code.)

To call Scotland from a European country: Dial 00-44 followed by the area code (minus its initial zero) and local number. (The 00 is Europe's international access code.)

To call within Scotland (or Great Britain): If you're dialing within an area code, just dial the local number; but if you're calling outside your area code, you have to dial both the area code (which starts with a 0) and the local number.

To call from Scotland to another country: Dial 00 followed by the country code (for example, 1 for the US or Canada), then the area code and number. If you're calling European countries whose phone numbers begin with 0, you'll usually have to omit that 0 when you dial.

Tips on Phoning: To make calls in Scotland, you can insert coins or your credit card into a public pay phone; or you can buy international phone cards, which work with a scratch-to-reveal PIN code at any phone, allowing you to call home to the US for about a dime a minute (and also work for domestic calls within Great Britain). However, since you'll pay a big surcharge to use these cards from pay phones, they're cost-effective only if used from a fixed phone (such as one at your B&B) or a mobile phone. A mobile phone—whether an American one that works in Britain, or a European one you buy when you arrive—is handy, but can be pricey. For more on phoning, see www.ricksteves.com/phoning.

Emergency Telephone Numbers in Great Britain: To summon the **police** or an **ambulance**, call 999. For passport problems, call the **US Embassy** (in London, tel. 020/7499-9000, passport info tel. 020/7894-0563) or the **Canadian High Commission** (in London, tel. 020/7258-6600). For other concerns, get advice from your hotel.

Making Hotel and B&B Reservations

To ensure the best value, I recommend reserving rooms in advance, particularly during peak season. Email the hotelier or B&B host with the following key pieces of information: number and type of rooms; number of nights; date of arrival; date of departure; and any special requests. (For a sample form, see www.ricksteves.com/reservation.) Use the European style for writing dates: day/month/year. For example, for a two-night stay in July, you could request: "1 double room for 2 nights, arrive 16/07/11, depart 18/07/11." Hoteliers typically ask for your credit-card number as a deposit.

Know the terminology: An "en suite" room has a bathroom (toilet and shower/tub) actually inside the room; a room with a "private bathroom" can mean that the bathroom is all yours, but it's across the hall; and a "standard" room has access to a bathroom that's shared with other rooms and down the hall.

In these times of economic uncertainty, some hotels are willing to deal to attract guests—try emailing several to ask their best rate. In general, hotel prices can soften if you do any of the following: stay in a "standard" room, offer to pay cash, stay at least three nights, or travel off-season.

Eating

The traditional "Scottish Fry" breakfast, which is usually included at your B&B or hotel, consists of juice, tea or coffee, cereal, eggs, bacon, sausage, toast, a grilled tomato, sautéed mushrooms, and sometimes haggis or black pudding. If it's too much for you, only order the items you want.

To dine affordably at classier restaurants, look for "early-bird specials" (offered about 17:30–19:00, last order by 19:00). At a sit-down place with table service, tip about 10 percent—unless the service charge is already listed on the bill.

Smart travelers use pubs (short for "public houses") to eat, drink, and make new friends. Pub grub is Scotland's best eating value. For about $15–20, you'll get a basic hot lunch or dinner. The menu is hearty and traditional: stews, soups, fish-and-chips, meat, cabbage, and potatoes, plus often a few Italian or Indian-style dishes. Meals are usually served from 12:00 to 14:00 and from 18:00 to 20:00, not throughout the day. Order drinks and meals at the bar; they might bring it to you when it's ready, or you'll pick it up at the bar. Pay as you order, and don't tip unless there's full table service.

Most pubs have lagers (cold, refreshing, American-style beer), ales (amber-colored, cellar-temperature beer), bitters (hop-flavored ale, perhaps the most typical British beer), and stouts (dark and somewhat bitter, like Guinness).

Transportation

By Train and Bus: Great Britain's 100-mph train system is one of Europe's best...and most expensive. To see if a railpass could save you money—as it often does in Britain—check www.ricksteves .com/rail. If buying tickets as you go, you'll get the best deals if you book in advance, leave after rush hour (after 9:30), or ride the bus. Train reservations are free and recommended for long journeys or any trip on Sundays (reserve at any train station before 18:00 on the day before you travel). For train schedules, see www .nationalrail.co.uk; for bus and train routes, visit www.traveline. co.uk. Long-distance buses (called "coaches") are about a third slower than trains, but they're also much cheaper.

By Car: A car is useful for scouring the remote rural sights of the Scottish Highlands. It's cheaper to arrange most car rentals from the US. For tips on your insurance options, see www .ricksteves.com/cdw. Bring your driver's license. For route planning, try www.viamichelin.com. Speedy motorways (similar to our freeways) let you cover long distances in a snap. Remember that the Scottish drive on the left side of the road (and the driver sits on the right side of the car). You'll quickly master Scotland's many roundabouts: Traffic moves clockwise, cars inside the roundabout have the right-of-way, and entering traffic yields (look to your right as you merge). Be warned that "camera cops" strictly enforce speed limits by automatically snapping photos of speeders' license plates, then mailing them a ticket.

Helpful Hints

Time: Scotland uses the 24-hour clock. It's the same through 12:00 noon, then keep going: 13:00, 14:00, and so on. Scotland, like the rest of Great Britain, is five/eight hours ahead of the East/West Coasts of the US (and one hour earlier than most of continental Europe).

Holidays and Festivals: Scotland celebrates many holidays, which can close sights and attract crowds (book hotel rooms ahead). For information on holidays and festivals, check Scotland's website: www.visitscotland.com. For a simple list showing major—though not all—events, see www.ricksteves.com/festivals.

Numbers and Stumblers: What Americans call the second floor of a building is the first floor in Europe. Europeans write dates as day/month/year, so Christmas is 25/12/11. For most measurements, Great Britain uses the metric system: A kilogram is 2.2 pounds, and a liter is about a quart. For driving distances, they use miles.

PRACTICALITIES

Resources from Rick Steves

This Snapshot guide is excerpted from the latest edition of *Rick Steves' Great Britain,* which is one of more than 30 titles in my series of guidebooks on European travel. I also produce a public television series, *Rick Steves' Europe,* and a public radio show, *Travel with Rick Steves.* My website, www.ricksteves.com, offers free travel information, free vodcasts and podcasts of my shows, free audio tours of major sights in Europe (for you to download onto an iPod or other MP3 player), a Graffiti Wall for travelers' comments, guidebook updates, my travel blog, an online travel store, and information on European railpasses and our tours of Europe.

Additional Resources

Tourist Information: www.visitscotland.com
Passports and Red Tape: www.travel.state.gov
Packing List: www.ricksteves.com/packlist
Cheap Flights: www.skyscanner.net
Airplane Carry-on Restrictions: www.tsa.gov/travelers
Updates for This Book: www.ricksteves.com/update

How Was Your Trip?

If you'd like to share your tips, concerns, and discoveries after using this book, please fill out the survey at www.ricksteves.com/feedback. Thanks in advance—it helps a lot.

INDEX

INDEX

INDEX

Audio Europe

Free mobile app (and podcast)

With the **Rick Steves Audio Europe** app, your iPhone or smartphone becomes a powerful travel tool.

This exciting app organizes Rick's entire audio library by country—giving you a playlist of all his audio walking tours, radio interviews, and travel tips for wherever you're going in Europe.

Let the experts Rick interviews enrich your understanding. Let Rick's self-guided tours amplify your guidebook. With Rick in your ear, Europe gets even better.

Thanks Facebook fans for submitting photos while on location! From top: John Kuijper in Florence, Brenda Mamer with her mother in Rome, Angel Capobianco in London, and Alyssa Passey with her friend in Paris.

Find out more at ricksteves.com/audioeurope

Join a Rick
Steves tour

Enjoy Europe's warmest welcome...

with the flexibility and friendship of a small group

getting to know Rick's favorite places and people.

It all starts with our free tour catalog and DVD.

Great guides, small groups, no grumps.

tours.ricksteves.com

Start your trip at

Free information and great gear to

▶ Plan Your Trip

Browse thousands of articles and a wealth of money-saving tips for planning your dream trip. You'll find up-to-date information on Europe's best destinations, packing smart, getting around, finding rooms, staying healthy, avoiding scams and more.

▶ Eurail Passes

Find out, step-by-step, if a railpass makes sense for your trip—and how to avoid buying more than you need. Get a bunch of free extras!

▶ Graffiti Wall & Travelers' Helpline

Learn, ask, share—our online community of savvy travelers is a great resource for first-time travelers to Europe, as well as seasoned pros.

Rick Steves' Europe Through the Back Door, Inc.

ricksteves.com

turn your travel dreams into affordable reality

▶ Free Audio Tours & Travel Newsletter

Get your nose out of this guide book and focus on what you'll be seeing with Rick's free audio tours of the greatest sights in Paris, London, Rome, Florence and Venice.

Subscribe to our free Travel News e-newsletter, and get monthly articles from Rick on what's happening in Europe.

▶ Great Gear from Rick's Travel Store

Pack light and right—on a budget—with Rick's custom-designed carry-on bags, roll-aboards, day packs, travel accessories, guidebooks, journals, maps and DVDs of his TV shows.

130 Fourth Avenue North, PO Box 2009 • Edmonds, WA 98020 USA
Phone: (425) 771-8303 • Fax: (425) 771-0833 • www.ricksteves.com

NOW AVAILABLE: eBOOKS, APPS, DVDS, & BLU-RAY

eBOOKS

Most guides available as eBooks from Amazon, Barnes & Noble, Borders, Apple iBook and Sony eReader, beginning January 2011

RICK STEVES' EUROPE DVDs

Austria & the Alps
Eastern Europe, Israel & Egypt
England & Wales
European Travel Skills & Specials
France
Germany, Benelux & More
Greece & Turkey
Iran
Ireland & Scotland
Italy's Cities
Italy's Countryside
Rick Steves' European Christmas
Scandinavia
Spain & Portugal

BLU-RAY

Celtic Charms
Eastern Europe Favorites
European Christmas
Italy Through the Back Door
Surprising Cities of Europe

PHRASE BOOKS & DICTIONARIES

French
French, Italian & German
German
Italian
Portuguese
Spanish

JOURNALS

Rick Steves' Pocket Travel Journal
Rick Steves' Travel Journal

APPS

Rick Steves' Ancient Rome Tour
Rick Steves' Historic Paris Walk
Rick Steves' Louvre Tour
Rick Steves' Orsay Museum Tour
Rick Steves' St. Peter's Basilica Tour
Rick Steves' Versailles

PLANNING MAPS

Britain, Ireland & London
Europe
France & Paris
Germany, Austria & Switzerland
Ireland
Italy
Spain & Portugal

Avalon Travel
a member of the Perseus Books Group
1700 Fourth Street
Berkeley, CA 94710

Printed in the USA by Worzalla
First printing February 2011

ISBN 978-1-59880-495-9

For the latest on Rick's lectures, guidebooks, tours, public radio show, and public television series, contact Europe Through the Back Door, Box 2009, Edmonds, WA 98020, 425/771-8303, fax 425/771-0833, www.ricksteves.com, rick@ricksteves.com.

Europe Through the Back Door Reviewing Editors: Cameron Hewitt, Risa Laib
ETBD Editors: Sarah McCormic, Gretchen Strauch, Tom Griffin, Cathy McDonald, Jennifer Madison Davis, Cathy Lu
Research Assistance: Cathy McDonald, Cameron Hewitt, Lauren Mills
Avalon Travel Senior Editor and Series Manager: Madhu Prasher
Avalon Travel Project Editor: Kelly Lydick
Copy Editor: Naomi Adler-Dancis
Proofreader: Jennifer Malnick
Production and Layout: McGuire Barber Design
Cover Design: Kimberly Glyder Design
Graphic Content Director: Laura VanDeventer
Maps and Graphics: David C. Hoerlein, Laura VanDeventer, Brice Ticen, Lauren Mills, Barb Geisler, Pat O'Connor, Mike Morgenfeld
Front Matter Color Photos: Cameron Hewitt, Sarah Murdoch, Rick Steves, Dominic Bonuccelli
Front Cover Photo: Neist Point © Cameron Hewitt
Additional Photography: Rick Steves, Cameron Hewitt, Gene Openshaw, Bruce VanDeventer, Lauren Mills, David C. Hoerlein, Jennifer Hauseman, Jennifer Schutte, Ken Hanley, Sarah Murdoch, Darbi Macy, Dominic Bonuccelli

ABOUT THE AUTHOR

RICK STEVES

 Since 1973, Rick Steves has spent 100 days every year exploring Europe. Rick produces a public television series (*Rick Steves' Europe*), a public radio show (*Travel with Rick Steves*), and a podcast (*Rick Steves Audio Europe*); writes a bestselling series of guidebooks and a nationally syndicated newspaper column; organizes guided tours that take thousands of travelers to Europe annually; and offers an information-packed website (www.ricksteves.com). With the help of his hardworking staff of 70 at Europe Through the Back Door—in Edmonds, Washington, just north of Seattle—Rick's mission is to make European travel fun, affordable, and culturally enlightening for Americans.